The Islands o ORKNEY

Liv Kjørsvik Schei

with photographs by

Gunnie Moberg

Colin Baxter Photography, Grantown-on-Spey, Scotland

For Lenore and Connie

First published in Great Britain in 2000 by
Colin Baxter Photography Ltd
Grantown-on-Spey,
Moray PH26 3NA
Scotland

Paperback edition first published in 2007

Text Copyright © Liv Kjørsvik Schei 2000, 2007
Photographs Copyright © Gunnie Moberg 2000, 2007
Map © Wendy Price 2000
Illustration p1 'Visiting Houses at Hogmanay' © Ian Scott

ISBN 978-1-84107-359-0

Front Cover Photograph: Hoy Sound from Warbeth Beach
Back Cover Photograph: Stones of Stenness
p3: The seaward wall is continuous and surrounds the whole island of North Ronaldsay
p4: Some 20 km of hilly road circles the island of Rousay
p8: Black Craig, near Stromness, is a walker's paradise
Printed in China

The Islands of
ORKNEY

Contents

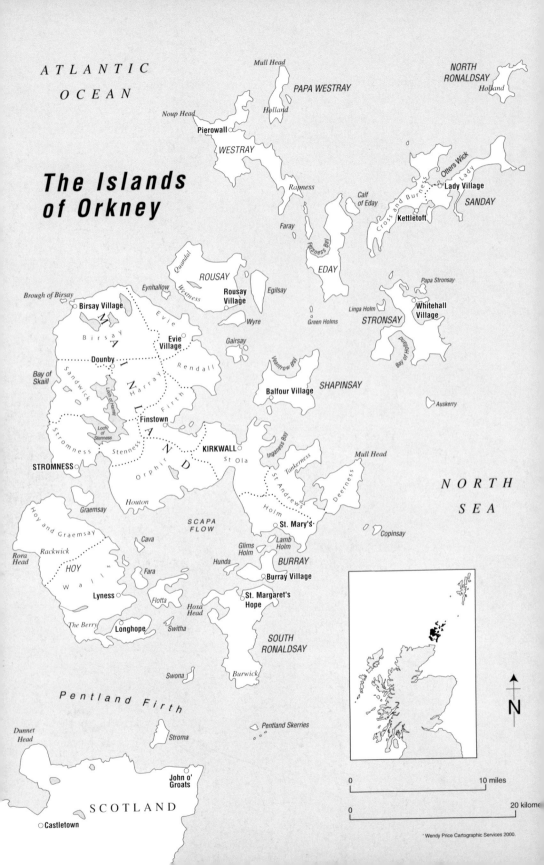

Preface

In this work we focus on place. Each inhabited island is presented in a separate chapter; in Mainland we go by the old parish borders, and we try to show the special images of each place. 'Little things are the last to be found', says an old Icelandic proverb, and we were impressed by much of what we saw when we focused directly on the small community. What follows is mostly the main aspects of local history, but directly or indirectly many of these also affect Orkney's general history. Not so much is said about the status of the islands today, as even as we write the picture changes!

So many people have helped us in our work on this book, in so many different ways, and we would like to thank them all. We are particularly grateful to: Andy Alsop, Robert M Baikie, Sidney Bichan, Lenore Brown, Elaine Bullard, Dee and Michael Cockram, Eileen and Leslie Cooper, Karl Cooper, Ann S Corrigall, Katie Costie, Richard Cotterill, Rowena Cotterill, Dr Barbara E Crawford, Jean and Bill Crichton, Sheila Dass, P Dennison, Mabel Eunson, Margaret and I M Flaws, Mary Anne Fotheringham, Arnie and Leslie Foubister, Julie Gibson, Betty and Peter Grant, Connie and Alan Grieve, Mary Anne Harvey, Ena Hewison, Kirstin and Willie Hourie, Robin Irving-Lewis, Rosemary Jenkins, Dr Sigrid Kaland, Nora Kennedy, Alastair Laing, Dr Raymond Lamb, Peter Leith, Robert Leslie, J W Linklater, Alison MacKenzie, William and Sandy McEwen, Valerie and David McGill, Christopher Macrae, Malcolm R S Macrae, William Mowatt, Christine and Thomas Muir, Tom Muir, Paul Newman, Graham Nicholson, M J Park, Claude Peace, Revd Ria Plate, Emma Popplewell, Marguerite Reardon, Jocelyn Rendall, Duncan Robertson, Ian Scott, Doris and Ingram Shearer, Ronald Simison, Renée Simm, David Sinclair, Elisabeth Elstad Slevolden, Beverley Ballin Smith, Sheila and Albert Spence, M S Stevenson, Malcolm Stout, Frans-Arne Stylegar, Pat and Richard Sullivan, Alison Sutherland, Mary-Ann Thomson, W P L Thomson, William and David Towrie, James A Troup, Jean Wallace, Dr K F Woodbridge, and Alfie Work. We would like to thank the staff of Kirkwall Library, Kristiansand Folkebibliotek and Stromness Library for their interest and zeal in finding the right books.

Our heartfelt thanks also go to Archie Bevan, Gerry Meyer, and Anders Schei for their untiring efforts in reading the chapters as soon as they were written. The fact that they gave their opinions from completely different backgrounds was a help and a bonus that we greatly appreciate.

Gunnie Moberg   *Liv Kjørsvik Schei*

Introduction

Orkney was always a place apart, geographically and culturally. In Norse times the islands 'west over sea' were often referred to as *Eyjar*, the islands, as if that said it all. After centuries of Norse, Scottish and British rule the islands are still very much a world of their own, perhaps so formed by being left to themselves much of the time. 'At one time it possessed its own language and political institutions and, on that basis, Orkney may be regarded as one of the forgotten sub-nations of Europe.' (Thomson, 1987.) Today the islands have their own flag, the St Magnus Cross. A red cross on a yellow background, the flag incorporates the colours of the Norwegian Royal Lion and the Scottish Royal Standard.

Orkney's position between the Atlantic and the North Sea, separated from Britain by the tidal race of the Pentland Firth, can perhaps explain the self-reliance that makes Orcadians jokingly refer to Britain as an adjacent island. And yet, the future is not assured for a population of some 20,000 people, with the number living in the outer isles falling steeply, and the economy depending almost solely on one product. But then, the future never was assured, and people's ability to take most things in their stride in a laid-back way is part of the unique character and charm of Orkney.

There is a different rhythm to island life, another concept of time, and the stresses and problems of modern life seem far away. There is freedom to roam at will, along the shore and on the hill, unless a farmer's barbed wire stops you, but when faced by 20 curious bulls on the other side of the fence, you may decide to feel grateful to him, after all. There is also the unlocked door, and people's helpfulness and care when you ask the way.

Orkney people are generally gentle and courteous to visitors who are 'eens fae aff', literally 'ones from off'. They are also efficient and independent, as they have to be in today's industrialised farming community. Orcadians may be reluctant to push themselves forward or behave emotionally, and they are sceptical of too much enthusiasm, 'no' bad' being a safe opinion on most things. The writer Eric Linklater described his fellow Orkneymen, whom he loved 'more than any people on earth', as 'honest and kind, shrewd and strong to endure.'

Perhaps the most striking element of the Orkney world is the special light that sometimes gives the landscape an almost spiritual quality. It comes suddenly and changes everything, making the most ordinary stone house look sculpted, like a piece of art. Nobody has described this phenomenon with such awe as Eric Linklater, who would have seen it from his home on the Loch of Harray, time and again. 'Light is the dominating factor...beneath a changing sky Orkney can change from ugliness and bleakness to a radiant panorama of lakes more brightly blue than the Mediterranean, a dazzling chequer-board of grass and ploughland, the shadow-and-claret of hills that flow in sweet unbroken lines. It can put on beauty like a song or a dance, so light and airy it is, so brisk, and tender, and gay. And then, in less time than it takes to count the colours, the colours will change again, and the land looks grave and peaceful.' (1935)

The combination of scenery, birds and seals, and an illustrated cavalcade of history makes the islands into a walker's paradise. An incredible 800 km of coastline offers a choice of high cliffs, sudden geos and gloups, low rocky shores and beaches dressed with golden sand. The sea is everywhere close, battering against the western cliffs and slowly wearing them down. In the kennings, the Norse metaphors, the sea became 'the swan's path' and 'the whale road', but also the sombre 'widowmaker'. The sea and the sun meet in memorable sunsets.

There is a variety of breeding habitats for birds, and some 90 species make regular use of them. From the low holms come the atonal calls of the seals, about 3000 grey seal calves being born in Orkney every year. The Orkney vole (*Microtus arvalis orcadensis*), the only sub-species unique to Orkney, is not found on every island, but the otter seems to be almost everywhere, and just outside Kirkwall a sign tells us 'Otters crossing. 100 yards.'

In spring and early summer the grass is lush and green, and wild flowers grow profusely. Sea-pinks hug the cliffs and along the roadsides are wild orchids and red campions. The large areas of sandy pastures known as links have hardy plants not commonly found elsewhere, but Orkney remains treeless because brine-laden winds stunt any growing trees.

The climate is considered fairly equitable on the whole, but the daily weather still comes in many variations. It is aptly described by George Mackay Brown, the Orkney writer: 'In the course of a single day you can see, in that immensity of sky, the dance of sun, cloud, sea-mist, thunder, rain.' We can see the rain clouds coming and learn to calculate the time it will take before we get drenched. The weather is so much a part of people's lives, and is always commented on. Even Tacitus, the Roman historian who wrote the first description of Orkney, took an interest in the weather. According to him, the sky is foul with frequent rain and showers, but 'harshness of cold there is not'. And Tacitus is right, there is rarely freezing weather, but often a bitter wind – 'he's blowan hard the day!' An old Orkney joke points out that people are so accustomed to walking sideways to the wind that if it were suddenly to stop, everybody would just keel over.

We must take the weather as it comes, as an exhilarating challenge, for if we wait for the right day or hour we will never get anywhere. But the fury of sky and sea is worth seeing, and hopefully at the end of the day there will be the welcome sight of a peat fire blazing in an open hearth! And then there may be the sudden wonder of a summer's night when the sea is hazed in mist – the summer haar.

The spring months are the time when Orkney weather is at its best. In the olden days it was a time of joy after the long winter months that were sometimes difficult to get through. Still, early spring could be capricious, so 'Ne'er cast a cloot – Till May be oot' was sensible advice. Midsummer was feasting time, with Johnsmas night being celebrated with all-night fires on hilltops all over the islands. And midsummer, when the nights are nearly non-existent, is festival time even today, the St Magnus Festival having been a regular event for more than 20 years, followed by others later in the summer.

A walk in Orkney takes us through an ancient landscape where the links with the past are often strikingly visible. Prehistoric villages, burial chambers and stone circles illustrate aspects of the life of people once living in the islands, and are evidence of a now vanished culture. The Orkney landscape that makes amateur historians of us all, takes us on an enthusiastic journey through time. And then the next major archaeological find is made, upsetting all our theories and making it necessary to start again. In all there are some 3000 known archaeological sites in Orkney, and more will surely be discovered in the future. In spite of meagre resources, excavation is always going on somewhere in the islands, although many sites are taken by the sea without even being recorded.

The rich soil in Orkney provides almost ideal conditions for pastoral farming, making the beef cattle and dairy herds justly famous. When transport systems for trade outlets to the south were opened, Orkney became the most prosperous and progressive agricultural county in Scotland. The European Union ban on British beef was a hard blow to the islands, as Orkney remains first and foremost a farming community. In the new Scottish Parliament part of the standing orders states that all legislation has to be vetted from an island point of view, and islanders are hopeful that their voice will be listened to from now on.

Orkney farmers are eager to find new methods and ways of doing things. Currently they are trying out peas as a new and very nutritious fodder for cattle. This go-ahead attitude may of course be the result of a century of progressive farming, but it is not confined to agriculture alone. We are told by Captain Fresson, who pioneered flights to Orkney in the 1930s, that 'the Orcadians took to flying as ducks to water'.

'Faill not to keep your sone diligent reading', instructs the Revd William Baikie, of Holland in Stronsay, who in 1683 left his collection of 160 books to 'the Ministers of Kirkwall for a Publick Library to be kept within the Toune'. This became the Biblioteck of Kirkwall, the first public library in Scotland and still much frequented today. Orkney is also a land of story-telling and vivid folklore. The writer Edwin Muir says of his childhood in the islands that 'The Orkney I was born into was a place where there was no great distinction between the ordinary and the fabulous; the lives of living men turned into legend'.

A group of Orkney's best-known prehistoric monuments was in the 1990s Britain's only nomination for the prestigious World Heritage List, which includes sites of special historical interest all over the world. Just before the turn of the millennium the news came that the area known as The Heart of Neolithic Orkney had been added to the list of World Heritage Sites that 'deserve protection for the benefit of humanity.' This part of West Mainland is a key area in Orkney archaeology, including such outstanding monuments as the Ring of Brodgar and the Stones of Stenness, the village of Skara Brae and the chambered tomb of Maeshowe.

Prehistory (c.3600 BC – c.AD 800)

Orkney has been called an archaeologist's paradise. The number of visible monuments must always have been large, but archaeological effort over the last 100 years and more has greatly increased it. The islands now have the highest concentration of prehistoric monuments in northern Europe, and it is possible within a short distance to walk among buildings and cultural remains representing a time span of more than five millennia. The fierce erosion of the western coastline has prompted rescue excavations that have been a race against time. Probably archaeologists will have work to do in Orkney for some time yet, as the gently rolling landscape gradually gives up its secrets.

The Old Red Sandstone that is found almost everywhere in Orkney splits easily into flags, and has proved an excellent and popular building material through the ages. Certainly Neolithic, or Stone Age, people, who had only stone tools to work with, found it so. The soil was easily cultivated as there were no dense forests: only birch, hazel and willow trees, and the climate was maritime and equable and warmer than today.

Early hunter-gatherers were probably the first people in Orkney but their presence is difficult to prove as they built no lasting houses. At some point sheep, pigs and cattle were brought to the islands. The earliest settlement site on record so far in Orkney, as indeed in north-west Europe, is the pair of Neolithic houses at Knap of Howar in Papa Westray. Radiocarbon dating shows that the houses were occupied c.3600-3100 BC, but as they are in many ways rather sophisticated, there may have been earlier farms that have yet to be found. The people who lived at Knap of Howar had adopted a new way of life and were both farmers and hunter-gatherers, as finds show that they grew wheat and barley but also caught birds, fish and whales, and gathered sea molluscs.

The Neolithic Age in Orkney, which according to present knowledge began in the early fourth millennium BC and lasted for some 2000 years, was a golden age for the islands. Such a wealth of buildings, monuments and artefacts was produced that Orkney has become a veritable museum of the period. Although Orkney may geographically have been on the periphery of the known world, it was no isolated backwater in Neolithic times, and trends seem to have found their way easily to and from the islands.

Knap of Howar appears to have been a solitary farm but during the third millennium BC the lifestyle may have changed, as people appear to have gathered in villages. So far five villages have been found. Of these the cluster of houses known as Skara Brae is the best preserved as well as perhaps the most interesting example.

The move into villages may have made the organisation of communal work easier. And only by a common effort over generations could the extraordinary monuments left by Neolithic builders have been realised. Much labour was spent on building tombs for the dead. As these were often placed on the edge of cultivated land and therefore mostly undisturbed, as many as some 80 chambered cairns have survived, but there may have been many more. The building technique was similar to that used for the villages, but if anything, the houses built for the dead were more elaborate than those built for the living.

There are two distinct types of tombs. The more numerous kind is the stalled cairn where the main chamber is divided into burial compartments by upright slabs. Midhowe chambered tomb in Rousay is an impressive example. An unusual variety of pottery bowls known as Unston Ware has been found in some of the stalled cairns as well as at the Knap of Howar farm; it is named after the tomb of Onston in Stenness where it was first found.

Of the later and scarcer tomb known as the Maeshowe type, only some ten sites have so far been identified, and it is not found outside Orkney; the largest is on Papa Westray, but the inventive art of the ancient Orcadians culminates in Maeshowe in Stenness, which stands out as the finest Neolithic chambered tomb in Europe. The Maeshowe type of tomb consists of a rectangular or square chamber with side cells, and access is gained through a long and low tunnel opening. These tombs may have some adornment, such as decorated stones; the pottery particular to the Maeshowe type is known as Grooved Ware and is found in many parts of Britain.

Most of these tombs are located on promontories and headlands or on rough hill land close to the fertile land, on sites that are visible from far away. There seems to be a correlation between cultivated land and tomb, which indicates that these tombs were also territorial markers. No grave-goods for the dead have been found in them, further evidence that the tombs may have represented a declaration of territorial rights for the living as much as a stage on the way to an afterlife for the dead.

Generations of ancestors may have given an extended family the right to the land, in the same way that later Norse settlers obtained an odal right to the land they farmed. The venerated *haugbúi* – the farmer in the mound – that in Orkney later became the folklore figure known as the 'hogboon', was the first settler on the family farm, and *haugóðal* was the right to the land around it obtained from a grave mound.

The Maeshowe tomb may have been part of a large ceremonial area connected with the isthmus between the two large lochs of Stenness and Harray. Two henge monuments are found in this striking setting: the Ring of Brodgar and the Standing Stones of Stenness. The area may have been a meeting place for people from all over the islands, but the purpose of the henges can only be guessed at.

A change came around 2000 BC with the beginning of the Bronze Age. Whereas Orkney enjoyed the privilege of having a perfect raw material in the Stone Age, the new alloy of copper and tin, called bronze, put Orkney at a disadvantage, as the only tin mine in Britain was in Cornwall. Although some bronze artefacts have been found in Orkney, there is not much evidence of metal work. Bronze swords and daggers would perhaps have been more for decoration and ceremony than for daily use, as bronze is not a strong material, and probably the old tools of stone and flint were used as they had been through most of the second millennium.

Some of the concepts of the new age were adopted in Orkney, although much of the old innovative energy seems to have gone. A distinctive kind of pottery consisting mostly of bell-shaped beakers seems to have become popular. It was decorated in horizontal lines with finely stamped markings. A quantity of shards but only one complete beaker have been found in Orkney.

The old tombs were deliberately filled with rubble and closed, as a new burial practice found its way to Orkney in the Bronze Age, and the use of modest single cists under earthen mounds became common instead of communal graves. One of the mounds in a group known as the Knowes of Trotty was found to contain a burial cist with grave-goods described by the archaeologist Dr V Gordon Childe as 'wealth worthy of a Wessex princess – four gold sun disks and an amber necklace'. He saw Orkney as a participant in 'the far-flung network of largely maritime trade which linked Denmark, Ireland and Cornwall and of which some vital threads were in the hands of the lords of Wessex, although it was ultimately supported by the reliable market of rich Mycenae.' But in spite

Midhowe Broch, Rousay.

of the unique variety of short burial cists of this period, just the one has contained treasure, and we can only guess at the way a mound in the wilds of Harray came to contain such exotic wealth.

Where did the Bronze Age people live? Settlement sites and remains from the Bronze Age in Europe are generally few and far between, but in Orkney farmstead sites and clear traces of land use from this period can be seen, frozen in time, under blanket peat in the islands of Eday and Calf of Eday. Funerary landscapes can be found at Els Ness, Tres Ness and Tafts Ness in Sanday. Significant climatic changes took place after 1500 BC, with increased rainfall and declining temperatures. Peat formed and land became scarce and precious.

The Iron Age in Orkney is generally dated to between 800 BC and AD 715, and was a period when great changes took place. An innovation from the first millennium BC was the substantial roundhouse with internal stone fittings, which may later have developed into the broch. At Quanterness in St Ola the archaeologist Dr Colin Renfrew excavated the earliest roundhouse so far found; it was occupied from *c.* 700-200 BC. At the multi-period site of Howe, near Stromness, a roundhouse was found, defended by walls and ditches; two brochs were built over it. At the nearby site of Bu, the roundhouse had a 5 m thick outer wall and must therefore be regarded as a defended structure. Promontory forts, such as the Castle of Burwick in South Ronaldsay, may also belong to the same period as the roundhouses, but they have not so far been excavated, and their date of origin is therefore not known.

The Iron Age in Orkney is first and foremost the age of the brochs. Most of them were probably constructed sometime around the end of the first millennium BC. The name derives from the Norse word *borg*, for fortification, and is used about the striking, circular towers that are scattered around Orkney, but also found in Shetland, Caithness and the Hebrides, a location pattern that made some nineteenth-century scholars believe they might be of Norse origin.

Brochs are found mainly in coastal positions close to good land and thus to some extent serve the same purpose as Neolithic tombs, as markers of land rights. It seems difficult to doubt that the brochs were serious fortifications, but many different ideas about their purpose have been presented. They have been seen as defence structures built against possible invaders in times of unrest, as well as a kind of miniature medieval castle, the stronghold of a conquering aristocracy securing itself against the native population whom it had enslaved. Today the brochs are mostly thought to be the defended houses of local chieftains skirmishing against their neighbours.

The building of the brochs is an amazing achievement that must not only have cost much in the way of labour but must also have required quite sophisticated technical knowledge. 'To construct stable walls of such height, in unmortared masonry of undressed stones shaped only by splitting, called for an engineer's understanding of force and stress; how that understanding was developed remains one of the more controversial questions of European prehistory.' (Lamb, 1980.) The key principle of broch building seems to be the hollow or double wall. The two parallel walls built about a metre apart and secured by lintel slabs at regular intervals prop each other up, so that in effect two narrow walls are stronger and more stable than one solid wall.

The need for defence or protection seems to have disappeared relatively quickly; at any rate, later houses and slab-built structures were constructed within the outworks of some brochs, and many of them were probably robbed of stone at an early stage. People in the post-broch period seem mostly to have lived at individual farmsteads, but some of the broch villages may have been inhabited into Norse times.

In AD 297 a Roman writer referred to the inhabitants of the north of Britain as *Picti*, the painted ones. Pictland, or the kingdom of the Picts, stretched northwards along the eastern coast from the Firth of Forth to the

Pentland Firth. The Picts spoke a Celtic language that was closer to Welsh than Gaelic, and left behind a heritage of beautifully carved memorial stones and crosses. Some of these have been found in the Northern Isles. As the stones often portray warriors with swords, shields, spears and crossbows, the Picts have been thought of as a warlike people, but no Pictish weapons have been found.

At some point Orkney and Shetland were made part of Pictland. The historical Picts of Orkney were probably direct descendants of the local broch-builders. The historical sources are meagre, but now and then the islands are mentioned. In *c*.561 St Columba of Iona visited the Pictish King Bridei mac Maelchon at his court near Inverness, and there met the King of Orkney. The saint persuaded Bridei to help protect his Christian missionaries in Orkney waters:

> Some of our people have gone forth seeking a remote place
> across the unsailed seas; should they, after long travel,
> reach the islands of Orkney, command this *regulus* [sub-
> king] whose hostages you hold, that no evil befall them
> within his territory.

St Columba's words conjure up a picture of a vassal king kept obedient through hostage-taking. He is the first individual to appear from Orkney, but he is still without a name.

Irish annals record that *c*.682 Orkney was devastated by Bridei mac Bile, King of Pictland, and a major expedition is implied. Further warfare is recorded in 709. Along with Pictland itself, Orkney was christianised from Northumbria in the period after 715. An early eighth-century network of eight churches dedicated to St Peter was established throughout Orkney, with each church standing on top of a mound containing a substantial broch site. The St Boniface complex in Papa Westray was the site of the early bishopric.

The name *papar* was used about the men of the early church and is found in several placenames, such as Papa Westray and Papa Stronsay. These places probably came to belong entirely to the Church, along with Papley in South Ronaldsay and Paplay in Holm. These were all areas consisting of very good farmland. Some kind of mutual benefit system seems to have existed between the Church and the King of Picts. The names were given by the Norsemen and reflect the status of the Church when they arrived. In 843 the Pictish kingdom fell to the Scots of Dalriada, and the reign of the Picts was over.

Norse Times (c.800–1468)

The Norse period in Orkney lasted from 780 till around 1500, with the so-called Viking Age coming to an end around 1100, and the latter part usually known simply as late Norse. The date 780 does not refer to any special event, but few if any archaeological finds go further back. The first known Viking raids in the north-west came in the following decade, beginning with the attack on the monastery at Lindisfarne in 793. According to the *Annals of Ulster* for 794, this raid was soon followed by the 'devastation of all the islands of Britain by the gentiles'. Not even the island of Iona was spared.

The Norse expansion in the Viking Age depended on the advances in maritime technology, represented by the Viking ships. The strength of the Vikings rested heavily on their skill in constructing and navigating ships, both on the open sea and in shallow rivers. The ships were light and could be beached almost anywhere. The art of iron making had also been perfected, and the quality of the weapons they produced may have given their users an edge over their foes.

The first Norse grave finds in Orkney go back to about 800, and it is therefore possible that the raiders used the islands as a base. Some of them may possibly have settled there, charmed by what they found. During most of the eighth century Pictish Orkney seems to have been a stable, rather complacent province of Pictland, until lightning struck with the sudden appearance of Vikings and their superior maritime technology. The mainland Picts seem to have been more interested in horses than in ships, and in the changed circumstances the Orkney Picts may have felt under threat.

In old Russia the Slavs invited Swedes, known as the Rus, to help them through a critical period. The same thing may have happened in Orkney; it is possible to imagine Norse sailors being invited as mercenaries for general protection and then staying on to become the new military aristocracy. They may have married local women. This might explain the story told by recent excavation sites: a blending of Norse and native culture, with the architecture mostly Norse and the domestic artefacts representing normal native Pictish types.

The trading post of Dublin was founded by Norsemen in 841. Two years later came the union of Pictland and Dalriada under Kenneth mac Alpin, after which the Picts mysteriously ceased to exist as a national entity, a development that would have made the position of the Roman Church in Orkney difficult.

King Harald Fairhair's unification of Norway in the second part of the ninth century made many people leave the country. Not all of them went to Iceland – many of them might also have gone to Orkney. 'It is said that the Orkney Islands were colonised in the days of Harald the Fairhaired, but previously they were a station for Vikings.' (Anderson, 1873.) The original expression used in the *Orkneyinga Saga* is *víkinga-bæli*, and there is no mention of Picts or Church, only Vikings, who might have been aristocratic exiles from Harald's politics, and still trying to wage war against the King. There has been much heated discussion about when and how the Norse takeover of power in Orkney happened; perhaps we should trust the saga more. To the mind of the saga-writer the Norse history of the islands begins at the end of the ninth century with the establishment of the earldom.

We are told in the saga that King Harald went to Orkney to settle with the Vikings there once and for all. These Vikings would raid in Norway during the summer and have Shetland and Orkney as their winter base. King Harald was accompanied by his friend Rognvald, Earl of Møre in western Norway and father of Hrolf, first Duke of Normandy, and an ancestor of William the Conqueror. Rognvald lost another son in battle during their campaign, and King Harald presented him with Shetland and Orkney as compensation, but Rognvald gave the islands to his brother Sigurd who was forecastleman on the King's ship. Thus the earldom was established, and Sigurd, so we are told, became a great ruler.

Some remarkably richly furnished Viking graves and treasure hoards dating back to the early tenth century have been found, the most impressive perhaps being the boat burial at Scar in Sanday. The use of grave-goods was a pagan custom. A revival of paganism at the top level of society is indicated also by the placename patterns sometimes found close to the early Christian centres, as power and insight into Norse mythology would have been required to introduce them. According to the saga, Christianity was not officially accepted until relatively late, and at the Battle of Clontarf in Ireland in 1014 Earl Sigurd II Hlodvisson the Stout fought and fell for the old faith, carrying his raven banner for Odin. His death meant the end of Norse expansion westwards.

The Church estates would have been taken over gradually by the earl

Brough of Birsay with remains of some fine Norse hall houses.

or his men. There seems to have been some continuity in the land system. The earls had a considerable estate, divided into a well-planned system of administrative sites known as veizla farms where the earl or his men would stay when visiting the islands. Probably these veizla farms were called Holland or the Bu and were run by regional administrators. The earl also had two main residences, in Birsay and Orphir respectively. At some point the language and the placenames, as well as the physical culture, became completely Norse. This development is difficult to explain, and has been used as an argument for armed conquest. There is no evidence to support the idea that all the Picts were killed or driven out, probably they would have become gradually absorbed into the Norse population but perhaps have remained for some time at the bottom of the social ladder.

The *Orkneyinga Saga* covers 300 years of Orkney history, from roughly 900-1200 – the golden years of the earldom. Although the saga is mostly concerned with the earls and Orkney's political history, we do catch glimpses of the common people now and then. The saga lists Sigurd Eysteinsson, the first earl, Thorfinn the Mighty (*c.*1009-65) and rather surprisingly Harald Maddadarson (*c.*1133-1206) as the three most powerful earls of Orkney.

The first Norse church built in Orkney may have been St Olaf's Church in Kirkwall, perhaps on an old chapel site. It was built by Earl Rognvald Brusason, who was killed by Earl Thorfinn the Mighty in 1046. Earl Thorfinn went on a pilgrimage to Rome to atone for his sins, and later built 'a splendid minster' near his residence in Birsay, and called it Christ Church. The remains of some very fine Norse hall houses on the Brough of Birsay may date from this period.

The title of earl was at times given to brothers and cousins, so that the earldom was sometimes shared between two earls, at other times divided into three parts. The kings of Norway seem to have supported such a crippling *divide et impera* or divide and rule system, and were quick to acknowledge new contenders as earls, perhaps out of fear that a strong earl would mean a threat to royal power. In 1117 Hakon Paulsson and Magnus Erlendsson, grandsons of Thorfinn the Mighty and both Earls of Orkney, met at Egilsay to settle their differences. The tryst ended in the death of Magnus, who was later canonised.

The connection between king and earl became closer when Kali Kolsson, a young nobleman from Agder in southern Norway and on his mother's side a nephew of St Magnus, became Earl of Orkney in 1136. He took the name of Rognvald after Earl Rognvald Brusason, whom he admired. Although in many ways no less ruthless than other earls before him, he held the earldom with greater distinction, and ruled Orkney through its second golden age. This is how he described himself when he was still quite a young man:

> At nine skills I challenge –
> a champion at chess:
> runes I rarely spoil,
> I read books and write:
> I'm skilled at skiing
> and shooting and sculling
> and more! – I've mastered
> music and verse.

The driving force behind Rognvald was his father Kol, a man shrewd enough to realise that his son's way to the earldom did not go through the Norse king but through his being the nephew of the martyred St Magnus. 'I want you to make a vow to him, that should he grant you your family inheritance and his own legacy, and should you come to power, then you'll build a stone minster at Kirkwall more magnificent than any in Orkney, that you'll have it dedicated to your uncle the holy Earl Magnus and provide it with all the funds it will need to flourish.' Kol was principal supervisor of the construction and had the most say in it.

The first recorded bishop of Orkney is William the Old, who served for 66 years, from 1102 to 1168. In 1152 the bishopric became part of the see of Nidaros in Norway. In that same year Bishop William accompanied Earl Rognvald and many of his friends on a crusade to the Holy Land, leaving the 19-year-old Harald Maddadarson to look after the earldom in their absence. Among the Orkneymen who took part were the Earl's poets Thorgeir Safakoll and Thorbjorn the Black, as well as Oddi Glumsson the Little and Armod, who were Icelanders. The story of their two-year visit to the Mediterranean is the highlight of the *Orkneyinga Saga*, an exuberant tale of friendship and high adventure, with five poets composing their verses and vying for the attention of the fair Queen Ermingerd of Narbonne.

Harald Maddadarson ruled as earl for 48 years after the death of Earl Rognvald II in 1158, the last wholly Norse earl of Orkney. Civil war raged in Norway, leading to the death of King Magnus Erlingsson in 1184. A group of islanders known as the *Eyjarskeggjar*, or Island Beardies, objected to the rule of King Sverrir, his successor. Supported by Earl Harald, they collected forces in Orkney and went to Norway, to the Oslo area, where they had King Magnus's son proclaimed King. They seized Bergen and held it for some months until they were defeated and nearly all slain by King Sverrir in the bloody Battle of Florvåg, near Bergen, in 1194.

Earl Harald made his peace with a furious King Sverrir, but had to accept that Shetland was forfeited to the crown of Norway, along with all the land belonging to the rebels. This gave the King large estates in Orkney, especially in the North Isles, and more genuine authority. Earl Harald also had trouble with King William the Lion of Scotland who invaded Caithness in 1202, and took the Earl's eldest son hostage, mutilating him until he died. Jon Haraldsson succeeded his father, but was killed in Thurso in 1230.

The Norse line of earls had really died out with Rognvald II, but Harald Maddadarson and his sons lived in Orkney and identified with the earldom, although the difficult position of owing allegiance to the monarchs of two countries begins with them. Later earls were wholly Scots, beginning with the Earls of Angus who held the earldom from

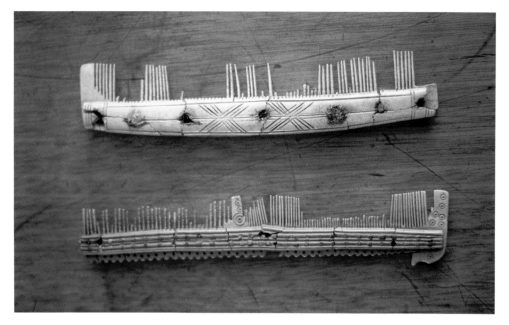

Norse combs found at Pool, Sanday and Skaill, Deerness.

1231 until it was taken over by the Earls of Stratherne around 1320. They were shadowy characters who had only a nominal connection with Orkney. Earl Magnus III is the only earl of the Angus line who has been prominent enough to come under the scrutiny of history. When King Hakon Hakonsson went on his expedition to the Western Isles of Scotland, Earl Magnus sailed with the fleet from Bergen to Orkney, but left it there, as his divided loyalty to the two kings left him no choice.

The records of the thirteenth and fourteenth centuries are few and scanty, but the death of King Hakon Hakonsson in Kirkwall in 1263 represented the end of an era, as from this year the Orkney earldom was administered directly from Norway by royal representatives known as sysselmen. When the 19-year-old Princess Margaret of Scotland married the child-king Eirik Magnusson of Norway in 1281 a strange marriage contract was signed. If Eirik did not consummate the marriage on becoming 14 years old 'the whole land of Orkney, with all rights due to Norway's king' would be ceded to Scotland. If, on the other hand, it was Margaret who was unwilling, the King of Scotland was to 'cede to king Eirik the whole island of Man with all royal rights, and the king of Norway's letter ceding this island is to be rendered null and void'.

As it turned out, neither alternative had to be considered further, as by the time Eirik was 15 he was already the father of a little girl named Margrete. He was also a widower, as Margaret had died in childbirth in 1283. Little Margrete became Queen of Scotland by the time she was three years old, as her maternal grandfather, King Alexander III, died in 1286. The Scots negotiated a marriage with the future Edward II of England and demanded that the princess come to Scotland before 1 November 1290. Margrete and her companions were to meet the Scottish and English ambassadors in Kirkwall, on Norwegian territory. But King Eirik could hardly bear to part with his daughter, and the voyage was delayed so long that the autumn storms had begun. Margrete became ill during a terrible crossing and died in the arms of Bishop Narfi of Bergen, on arrival in Orkney.

When Henry Sinclair was chosen by King Hakon VI Magnusson to become Earl of Orkney in 1379, he was also given Shetland back as part of the earldom. King Hakon must evidently have thought highly of him and his qualities as a future earl and faithful vassal. His mother was the daughter of Earl Malise of Stratherne and Orkney, and had married into the Sinclair, or St Clair, family. They came originally from Normandy, but had roots in Scotland going back to the eleventh century.

Henry broke the series of shadowy, absentee earls, and seems to have become an Orkneyman. One of the terms of Henry Sinclair's installation in 1379 was, 'The earl shall not build castles or other fortifications in the islands without the king's consent'. But King Hakon died within a year, and Earl Henry appears to have ignored this clause, as he built the formidable Kirkwall Castle in *c.*1380. His son and successor bore the same name, but spent little or no time in the islands.

Just before he died in 1420, Henry II Sinclair appointed his brother-in-law Sir David Menzies of Weem as his representative in the islands. Sir David became hated for his harsh regime, and after only four years a long list of complaints was sent to the King. It accused Menzies, among other things, of taking the seal of the country from the Lawman and using it as he pleased, and of having brought in a lot of foreigners who 'were a veritable pest to the people and did much harm and great injury in the country'. The last of the Sinclair earls was William, who was installed as earl in 1434.

Norway ceased to exist as a separate kingdom in the fourteenth century when the royal line died out on the male side; in accordance with the Kalmar Union of 1397 the Danish, Swedish and Norwegian crowns were united under Queen Margrete. Sweden left the union in 1523, but Norway did not prove strong enough to do so, and remained in the union until 1814.

By 1468 a transfer of Orkney to Scotland was probably inevitable. Much of the time Orkney was rented out to tacksmen, those who held a lease and sublet, who could do more or less as they pleased. Both earls and bishops were Scots who would have found the rights of the Danish-Norwegian King an encumbrance. King Christian I was always in debt, and looking for a way out. An open and final transfer would probably not have been considered politically practical as confrontation with the Norwegian *riksråd* – the state council – would then have been difficult to avoid.

When Princess Margrete of Denmark, the only daughter of King Christian I, married King James III in 1468, she received a dowry of 60,000 florins of the Rhine. King Christian raised the money by pledging the crown rents from Orkney and Shetland. In a clever move King James III forced Earl William Sinclair to exchange his earldom estates for land in central Scotland; in 1471 both island groups were annexed to the Scottish Crown. In 1472 the bishopric was transferred from the see of Nidaros to that of St Andrews. There was to be no possible way back. Some scholars believe a secret agreement for permanence may have been entered into and that King Christian never intended to pay the sum. But there were those who did not give up hope, and even at its last meeting in 1533 the Norwegian state council had the question of Orkney and Shetland on its agenda.

In Scotland (1468–1707)

The King of Scotland acquired all rights to the Orkney earldom in 1471, and immediately had it annexed to the Crown by an Act of Parliament, stipulating that the islands were not to be given away 'excep alenarily to ane of ye Kingis sonis of lauchful bed', that is, a royal prince. This did not happen; almost immediately the practice began of leasing, feuing or mortgaging the islands to various tacksmen for an annual rent, until they were finally given as an irredeemable grant to the Earl of Morton in the middle of the eighteenth century.

Still, the appointment of the first tacksman was met with approval. Lord Henry Sinclair first came to Orkney in 1480 to manage the conquest land that was privately owned by his grandfather, but stayed on as the king's tacksman. He tried to ease the changes that came with the reorganisation of the land, and was responsible for compiling the invaluable land rentals of 1492 and 1500. When Lord Henry was killed at the Battle of Flodden in 1513, the tack was given to his widow, Lady Margaret Sinclair, as their son was still a minor.

The rebellion that broke out in the islands in 1528 seems rather to have been a feud between the various branches of the Sinclair family, but no less violent for that. One of the reasons may have been that Lady Margaret was an absentee holder of the tack; another may have been infighting over the conquest land. The rebels were led by James Sinclair, who became governor of Kirkwall Castle, and was a descendant of the earlier Sinclair earls.

The Earl of Caithness set sail for Orkney with soldiers on board, ostensibly to keep law and order, as he had received a royal mandate, but perhaps with vicarious motives, as he was a Sinclair too, and there were those who believed he coveted the former family estates. The attackers were defeated in a regular pitched battle at Summerdale in the Stenness hills. There are many unexplained factors in the battle, but still the resounding victory of the Orcadians served to give them back some of their old independent spirit.

James Sinclair was later knighted by King James V and installed as tacksman. Seemingly eager to placate his new subjects, and perhaps wishing to avoid any political complications, the King visited Orkney in 1540 with a fleet of 16 ships and some 3000-4000 men. He declared that the Orkney islands 'be the chief nourishers and storers of all the southland with corne, victell and oil'.

The visit probably made the King realise the economic potential of Orkney. He therefore changed the terms for the tack and gave it to Oliver Sinclair of Pitcairns, despite Lady Margaret's protests. The office of Lawman was replaced by that of Sheriff, and the roithmen (members of head court) of old became 'suitors of court'. Oliver Sinclair was appointed Sheriff, Justice, Admiral and Baillie, and had to hold courts for all of these four functions.

Adam Bothwell was appointed Bishop of Orkney in 1559 when he was still a very young man. He was the last Vatican-appointed Bishop of Orkney, and became the first Protestant bishop as well. As he was thus the only bishop who stood in apostolic succession from the pre-Reformation to the post-Reformation church, he was in 1568 asked to crown the infant James VI.

It is to Adam Bothwell's credit that the Cathedral did not share the fate of churches and abbeys in mainland Scotland, but survived the Reformation intact. But he was surrounded by greedy clergy and predatory relatives, and proved unable to withstand their pressure. Bishopric lands were feued to family and friends. Bothwell's sister Margaret and her husband Gilbert Balfour were endowed with the bishopric land in Westray. The castle of Noltland seems to have been built by Balfour with more or less forced labour.

Within a short time many of the old farms had been taken over by incomers, tradesmen had settled in Kirkwall, and Scottish names had spread through the islands. Local customs and speech appear, however, to have been adopted by the newcomers. In 1567, under Mary Queen of Scots, the old Norse laws were ratified by the Scottish Parliament, but in spite of promises to maintain the independence of the laws of Orkney, Scots law and land tenure gradually crept in. The Sinclair family were dethroned as leaders of Orkney society by incoming families such as the Balfours and Bellendens. Bishop Bothwell was suspended for some time, and never returned to the islands.

In 1564 Lord Robert Stewart (1533-93), King James V's illegitimate son, received the crown lands of Orkney and Shetland as a gift from his half sister, Mary Queen of Scots. He soon became Sheriff Principal in the islands, and by exchanging his property in Scotland for the estates of the bishopric, he acquired almost absolute power in Orkney. His negotiations and dealings with the King of Denmark were suspected of being treasonable and led to his arrest. He was imprisoned in Linlithgow

The Earl's Palace, Birsay.

for a couple of years, but was never brought to trial. He seems to have charmed his young nephew, King James VI, so much that in 1581 he was made 'Earl of Orkney, Lord of Shetland, and Knight of Birsay'.

Above the door of Robert Stewart's palace in Birsay were his arms and the inscription *Sic fuit, est, et erit* – 'As it was, is and will be'. He obviously had ambitions for his rule in the islands, and was not scrupulous about the means he used. The year 1584 is described by the Orkney historian J Storer Clouston as Robert Stewart's 'vintage year' of oppression in the islands, when land was confiscated on the flimsiest of pretexts.

Robert Stewart was succeeded by his son, Earl Patrick (*c.*1569-1615) in the early 1590s. He earned the nickname of 'Black Patie' and seems to have lacked his father's ability to charm his way out of trouble. But like his father he had an eye for architecture, and in the New Palace of the Yards, now known simply as the Earl's Palace, in Kirkwall, he left a legacy of unexpected beauty.

Earl Patrick's outrageous behaviour and many alleged crimes in Orkney made Bishop James Law in 1608 write the following to King James VI, 'Alas, dear and dreaded Sovereign, truly it is to be pitied that so many of your Majesty's subjects are so manifoldly and grievously oppressed; some by ejection and banishment from their homes and native soil, others by contorting the laws and extorting their goods, the most part being so impoverished that some of them neither dare nor may complain, but in silent and forced patience groan under their grievance.'

On the death of Queen Elizabeth I in 1603, King James VI of Scotland had succeeded to the English throne as well, and was therefore perhaps inclined to take a more serious view of such complaints. Earl Patrick was arrested in 1609 and accused among other things of having forced people to work for him at 'all manner of work and labour by sea and land', but in the end he was indicted only on seven charges of treason. Even so, he would probably have been allowed to return to Orkney, were it not for his utter folly in sending his young illegitimate son Robert to the islands with instructions to win back what had been lost. Young Robert mustered some 200 men and recaptured Kirkwall castle, which then held out for five weeks against the invasion of the Earl of Caithness and his men. Robert was taken to Edinburgh and hanged at the Mercat Cross, on 1 January 1615. Five weeks later his father, Earl Patrick, was beheaded at the same place.

The Stewart rule of Orkney had come to an end. Although they seem to have been thoroughly unattractive characters, nothing was ever proved against the Stewart earls. Like the Vikings before them, they had their history written by their worst enemies.

'With the heading of Pate Stewart and the hanging of the son', writes J Storer Clouston in his *A History of Orkney*, 'the history of the "country of Orkney" ends, and the annals of a remote Scottish county begin.' A few years earlier, in 1611, the 'Lordis of Secret Council' had abolished the old Norse laws. Although the laws were poorly understood and often ignored, their abrogation and the forfeited earldom still meant a stepping-up of feudalism in the Northern Isles, thus bringing them into line with the rest of Scotland.

'The real tragedy was not the downfall of Patrick Stewart, for whom execution was at least rough justice, but that he brought down with him all that remained of the structure of semi-autonomous government. Had these institutions remained intact, Orkney could have emerged into modern times with the home-rule status which is found in other islands with a Norse past such as the Isle of Man and Faroe.' (Thomson, 1987.)

There was not much change for the better after the political changeover in 1615. King James and his successor King Charles I were always short of means and treated the islands simply as a source of income. A confusing number of their absentee tacksmen in effect ruled Orkney in the following years. Bishop Law was succeeded by Bishop Graham who started another round of feuing church land, mostly to his own sons, who became notable landowners.

Nothing much is heard from the Orkney people in the seventeenth century, but they are known to have suffered greatly during a run of poor seasons that caused periods of famine. A climatic deterioration known as the 'little Ice Age' may have decreased the mean temperature by as much as 5°C. The king's tacksmen gave the islanders no reprieve, and in 1627 a minister writes, 'in respect of the great duty paid to His Majesty out of this udal land, and the augmentation of it so oft, and of the great number of people sustained upon this land, these mean udal people are not able to live.' During the famine years of 1631 and 1633, 3000-4000 people are believed to have perished.

Orkney's long association with the earls of Morton began in 1643, during the Civil War. William Douglas, the seventh earl, had lent large sums to King Charles I, and was in return granted the earldom lands of Orkney and Shetland by Royal Charter; the King retaining the right to redeem the land for the sum of £30,000. During the Civil War, Cromwellian soldiers were for some time quartered in Orkney. After the Restoration of the Stuarts in 1660 the ninth Earl of Morton again took over control of the earldom lands, but not before King Charles II had extracted some £182,000 from the islands.

In 1664 an unexpected and dramatic incident made King Charles annex the lands to the Crown. In December of that year the Dutch East Indiaman *Kennermerland* was wrecked on Out Skerries in Shetland, while sailing 'north about' to Batavia with a rich cargo on board. According to island lore some 60 barrels of wine and spirits were washed ashore, and the Skerries people had one long feast. When more than three weeks had passed and they had not come to Whalsay to collect their Christmas supplies, the fate of the East Indiaman at last became known. The *Kennermerland* was thought to have carried a fortune in gold. The Earl of Morton fell into disgrace, as the King believed that he had taken the bullion for himself. In actual fact the gold had been sent by another ship.

Orkney people were not much affected by the religious strife that tore Scotland apart during parts of the seventeenth century, although the wreck of the *Crown* that was washed up in a storm at Scarvataing in Deerness would have brought it home to them. The Covenanters on board were the losers from the Battle of Bothwell Bridge in 1679, who were being banished to the American colonies. The cartographer, Murdoch Mackenzie, who at one time taught at Kirkwall Grammar School, obviously observed a lack of religious fervour in the Orcadians:

> The Religion is Presbyterian, as established in Scotland,
> without Bigotry, Enthusiasm or Zeal; and without any
> Dissenters except a very few of the Episcopal Persuasion.
> The Mirth, Diversions and reciprocal Entertainmants of the
> Christmas and other Holy-days are still continued, tho' the
> Devotion of them is quite forgot. *Orcades, or geographical
> and hydrographical Survey of Orkney and Lewis, 1750.*

The seventeenth century was the nadir of Orkney history. Most of the population had become tenants; at the end of the century only some three per cent of the farmers were proprietors who did not rent any land. The comparatively few big land-owners were either incomers who felt little closeness or loyalty to the local people, or they were absentee landlords who ran their estates as purely commercial ventures.

Famine returned in the last decade of the century, with the harvest of 1696 being less than a twentieth of the normal crop. There was not a ship left in the islands. The period was later remembered as 'Brand's Years' after the tacksman Sir Alexander Brand who became notorious for trying to obtain rent and tax from starving tenants. Much of the land had no tenants at all and remained fallow for many years to come.

In 1707 the Earl of Morton was restored as tacksman on the same terms as before; later these were converted into an irredeemable grant. In the same year Scotland accepted the Act of Union with England.

In Britain from 1707

Although the eighteenth century in many ways represented a period of transition to a more diversified society, Orkney still remained first and foremost a farming community. The farming was badly in need of reform, as the land had gradually become split up into a complicated system of narrow, impractical strips known as run-rig. A cultivated area made up a unit known as a tunship. A tunship was surrounded by a turf dyke, and the uncultivated land outside it was a common. Oats and bere, a special kind of barley, were grown. The land never lay fallow, and drainage and crop rotation were unknown.

However, times were changing and new possibilities were opening up. At the beginning of the century the connection with the Hudson's Bay Company begins. As the passage through the English Channel was not always considered safe in wartime and the North Sea swarmed with privateers, traffic at sea often went 'north about'. Stromness, with its good harbour, was strategically placed for direct access to the open Atlantic Ocean, and to the New World. This was the last port of call in Europe for the Hudson's Bay Company, where they recruited men for work in their fur trade enterprises in Canada. Many young men went to work for some time in the 'Nor Wast', because adventure called and the pay was better than at home. Towards the end of the century the majority of the Company's labour force were Orcadians, and according to an old report this was because of 'their prudent demeanour among the Indians, notwithstanding they have annually exposed themselves to all the dangers incident to the trade for 15 years past, they have not sustained the loss of a man.'

The Davis Strait whaling fleet also called at Stromness in the eighteenth century, to take on water and provisions, as well as an Orkney crew. Whaling paid well when the voyage was successful, but the life on a whaler was often exposed and hard, with provisions running low and the crew suffering from scurvy, as in 1830, when 19 ships were crushed in the ice. By the 1870s whaling was no longer important and fewer ships called at Stromness.

The Revd George Low, minister of the united parishes of Birsay and Harray, describes in the *Statistical Account of Orkney, 1795-1798* the work possibilities in his district. Many young men feel the call of the sea. 'Most of the people of the barony and Marwick are bred fishermen; and multitudes of our young men go to sea, both in merchant and in his Majesty's service; few in proportion of whom ever return to settle here.' There is also inshore fishing, from small boats. 'In this parish, 18 fishing boats run from 4 different summer stations, besides 2 small ones used occasionally.' But there are no large boats, nor any proper harbours.

The women 'spin a great deal of lint for so much a hank, or buy bags of lint, at about a guinea, which they work up into linen.' The linen industry began in the middle of the eighteenth century, and reached its peak in the early nineteenth century, with a production of 57,320 yards of linen material in 1801. Much of the flax was imported from the Baltic countries, and during the Napoleonic Wars it was difficult to get enough of it. The linen industry died out by the 1830s.

Although the Jacobite Rebellion of 1745 did not really concern Orkney in any direct way, the romance of 'the Forty-five' was the stuff that dreams are made of, and the dour lairds are said to have raised their glasses in tribute to 'the king over the sea'. A long-standing feud between two lairds, Captain Moody of Melsetter in Walls and Sir James Steuart of Burray, became even more embittered when mixed up with Jacobite politics. This feud had far-reaching and bitter consequences, affecting not only the families concerned but also drawing others into the fray. When the Act of Indemnity was passed in 1747 the lairds in hiding were free again, but the rifts in the social weave took time to heal.

The same Steuart laird alleged that the earls of Morton as Superiors of the earldom had over the years manipulated the old weights and measures so that the lairds had paid more in dues to the earldom than they should have. Sir James therefore urged other landowners to withhold superior duties. The lairds supported him in the ensuing legal action, known as the Pundlar Process, which proved to be a long and acrimonious legal battle, dragging on for 26 years.

The Pundlar Process finally ended in victory for the Earl of Morton, who was also unscathed by the political upheavals following the Rebellion. But all the disputes may have disillusioned him, and he seems to have grown increasingly interested in affairs outside Orkney. As time went on he became more and more of an absentee landlord, and in 1766 the Morton estates were sold to Sir Lawrence Dundas of Kerse for £63,000. Although Sir Lawrence's younger brother represented Orkney and Shetland in Parliament for a period of time, the Dundas family never became integrated in Orkney life, but remained absentees.

The production of kelp began in Stronsay in the 1720s, and for a century it was a very important industry. In many ways it was ideally suited to the Orkney topography of beaches and low shores. The seaweed was collected and dried, then burnt in shallow pits above the high tide mark. The process was labour-intensive, but no expensive equipment was necessary. The alkaline extract thus obtained was used in the glass and soap-making industries.

The great kelp boom began in the 1770s. Due to unrest in Europe the demand for kelp from Orkney rose, so that at its peak the industry employed some 3000 men, women and children. A number of local ships transported the product south. The highest price achieved was £20 per ton, and as the lairds at times could keep up to 75 per cent of the selling price as personal profit, some of them grew very rich.

To invest their profit as well as look after their interests, many of them turned into merchant lairds. For that reason they built town houses in Kirkwall, the capital and centre of major commercial enterprise, as well as the social centre for the landowners, where they spent the winter when little was happening in their island estates. Again in the *Statistical Account*, the minister of St Andrews and Deerness complains that there 'are five gentlemen proprietors in St Andrews, and five in Deerness, none of whom reside in the parish, which is manifestly against the improvement of the land, and general advantage and comfort of the people.' Some of the improved island economy did, however, filter back to the kelp workers, at least enough to shelter them from the worst effects of the harvest failure in the years 1782-5.

The lairds seem to have been more interested in buying more land to enlarge their estates than in improving the land they already owned. Sir Lawrence Dundas abolished the run-rig system in many of the tunships belonging to his estates, and for some time there was a flurry of interest in land improvement among the landowners. The potato was adopted in the middle of the eighteenth century, along with kale which is a rich source of vitamin C, and therefore was important in the fight against the all too prevalent scurvy. Enclosed areas known as 'kail-yards' became common. Geese were popular because of their feathers, used in bedding materials, and even became an export commodity.

The practice of forcing seamen to man the Royal Navy was not new, but during the wars with France at the close of the eighteenth and the beginning of the nineteenth centuries the press-gang became particularly oppressive in Orkney and Shetland. As the war dragged on for more than 20 years, and not enough men enlisted voluntarily, new men had to be found by scouring the country. Each district had to make up a certain quota, and £40 had to be paid for every man not found.

In Orkney the method of choosing the men for the war was questionable, to say the least. A group of lairds met in private and made up a list of the young men they could do without. The young able-bodied men therefore always felt at risk, as they did not know whether their names were on the list, and the press-gang did not pay too much attention to the lists in any case, but grabbed whomever they thought suitable. Many men therefore went underground, and so-called press-gang stories abound, telling of imaginative ways of eluding the search through the islands. And yet the islands played a vital role in the Napoleonic Wars, with some 2000 Orkney men serving in the Royal Navy. Such a figure represented a twelfth of the total population. The losses were great; many of the men never returned.

By 1830 the price of kelp had fallen to a fifth of what it had once been, with serious consequences for islands like North Ronaldsay where life had become geared to kelp production at the expense of work on the land. Bankruptcies among the lairds were not uncommon. But the collapse of the kelp industry led to a renewed interest in farming. As there was nothing left but the land, the lairds had to improve their estates or give them up. The work of planking or dividing the land into fields began, making the holdings more compact. The common grazing was divided among the tenants.

A lot had to be done in order to make the agricultural pattern a viable one, but the lairds and farmers went to the task with determination, and for some years the land hummed with activity. Old tools were replaced and new breeds of cattle were brought in. A rapid rise in prosperity followed, and Orkney began to be noticed as a go-ahead agricultural county. More people stayed in Orkney, and in 1861 a peak population of 32,395 inhabitants was reached; by comparison the number 100 years later, in 1961, was down to 18,747 people.

The radical change in farming was the most important happening in the nineteenth century. The change was so far-reaching that it has come to be called the Agricultural Revolution. The losers in the new deal were the tenants. They still had short leases, lived in hovels and were completely at the mercy of the proprietors. In 1883 the Napier Commission began

Scrimshaw on sperm-whale teeth, by a Birsay whaleman.

enquiring into the conditions of the farming population in the north of Scotland. A crofter in Rousay explained that he had to leave the farm he used to rent when planking of the land was carried out.

> I then got permission to build a dwelling on the hillside where I now live, where there was no cultivation of any kind, nor houses. I began to build, and got up with much trouble a humble cottage and outhouses suitable. I ditched and drained more than I was able and got a little of the heather surface broken up. At this time I paid twelve shillings; but again, as I improved, more and more rent was laid on until I am now rented at a sum which is five times the rent I paid at first for a house I built myself. At the same time the common was taken away from me, as from all others... Lord Napier: *Royal Commission of Enquiry into the conditions of crofters and cottars in the Highlands and Islands,* 1884.

The Crofters' Act was passed in 1886. The tenants could remain secure on their farms with a reasonable rent, and the right of tenure was hereditary. The pendulum had swung so far in the other direction that in many ways the tenant was better off than the freeholder. Even today a landowner is wary of renting out farm-land, for fear that it will be difficult to terminate the lease.

Increased taxation, death duties and general economic conditions after the First World War caused almost all the landowners to sell their estates. The land was mostly bought at 25 years' purchase by the tenants, who became owner-occupiers, like the odallers of old. Agriculture became mechanised, and Orcadians took to the machines eagerly, as if they had been waiting for them; they have always been interested in finding out how things work. Machines have made it possible to increase acreage by cultivation of moor and hill land.

Most Orkney farms are family owned and run. The rearing of beef cattle is the primary activity, but during the Second World War a dairy industry grew up in order to meet the needs of troops stationed in the islands. Several million litres of milk are now processed into butter and cheese in Orkney annually. An egg export industry sprang up, but the environment is not really suitable for hens. The wind can discourage disease, but can also blow a whole egg industry away, as happened during the stormy night of 15 January 1952, when wind speeds topped 125 mph. Seven thousand chicken-coops and 86,000 hens disappeared.

In two world wars the strategically placed anchorage of Scapa Flow was the base of the British Royal Navy. The anchorage is deep and safe from storms, but its many entrances make it vulnerable to submarine attacks. During the First World War the entrances were filled up with blockships, but failure to maintain these defences left the way open for the German submarine *U-47* to enter the Flow and sink the battleship *Royal Oak* in October 1939.

Life in Orkney changed dramatically in times of war. The number of soldiers stationed there could be as many as four times the native population. All kinds of defence structures were built in a hurry; many of these remain today, either as historical monuments or as eyesores, depending on who is looking at them. In June 1919, German crews scuttled the surrendered ships of their High Seas Fleet in the Flow, and for the Stromness school children out for the day on board the *Flying Kestrel*, the sight of the overturning ships was one they would always remember.

In the 1970s oil was discovered in the North Sea, and in 1974 work started on the Piper oil field. Rumours were rife about possible developments in Orkney, but the Orkney Islands Council took matters firmly in hand. It had won the status of Island Authority in 1975 and negotiations with the oil company were a baptism of fire. By the time the oil started flowing in 1976, it was settled that the Orkney involvement in the exploitation of North Sea oil was restricted to the building and maintaining of a large landfall terminal at Flotta, for oil from the Piper and Claymore fields. The only other oil-related activities in Orkney have been some offshore servicing and the operation of helicopter services.

The Flotta terminal has, with changing ownership, offered welcome employment over many years. Oil revenues have enabled the Orkney Islands Council to build up substantial cash reserves, which have been put aside for a rainy day or used to fund a wide range of social and economic development in the islands. The whole Flotta complex was constructed and landscaped in such a way as to minimise the visual impact on the Scapa Flow scenery.

Orkney came to terms with North Sea oil, but saw the prospect of uranium mining as the ultimate disaster, to be resisted at all costs. In 1976 the South of Scotland Electricity Board had acquired from local landowners what the landowners believed was the right to carry out test bores, when in actual fact they had signed away extraction rights for a period of seven years. The area in question lay directly north of Stromness. The Electricity Board hoped to dig up an estimated 2000 tons of uranium from the 11 km stretch of land, which became known as 'The Uranium Corridor'.

The unequal battle began between central government on the one side, and the Orkney Islands Council, supported by the Orkney Heritage Society and an unusually united population, on the other. The 'No Uranium' campaign began, with posters appearing in every shop window. A large protest march was staged in Kirkwall, with some 1500 people taking part. The spontaneous exclamation of 'they're no' comin' and they're no' diggin', became the motto of the campaign. After what has been likened to a David and Goliath confrontation, the Orcadians were cautiously optimistic for the future, as no further move was made to prospect for uranium.

The main concern in Orkney today is to stem the depopulation of the outer islands. Orkney will be the poorer for a concentration of people in the central areas only. The amalgamation of farms into larger units has made it difficult for young people to break into farming unless they have inherited a property. Today the 'one man and a tractor' idea is possible; a large farm can be run with machines and very little manpower. Socially, however, this has a negative effect. Hopefully, it is not too late to turn the tide.

North Ronaldsay

Rough seas and lack of a sheltered harbour make North Ronaldsay the most difficult to reach of the Orkney islands even today. It is the most northerly of the group, as well as the furthest east, so close to Norway that when the city of Bergen burned in 1902 a red glow was seen on the horizon. It was also the last island in Orkney to receive electricity from the national grid.

The Norse name for the island was *Rinansey*, believed to be the same as 'Ringan's Isle', Ringan being another name for St Ninian. Until recently the name was pronounced Rinnalsay, but as early as the fourteenth century it had become hopelessly confused with the name of the southern island of Rognvaldsey. To distinguish one from the other they became North and South Ronaldsay.

The island is nowhere higher than 20 m, with a gently rolling landscape. The soil varies in quality, the best is very dark, and known as 'black mould'. The seashore has geos and flat rocks, seals, shags and sheep, and the beautiful white sandy beaches of Linklet Bay and Nouster Bay, making a walk around the island an exciting experience.

There is a feeling of closeness to nature in North Ronaldsay. More perhaps than in any other Orkney island the tides and the changing weather influence the way of life. In winter, gales are frequent, and the 'sea-gust' is sprayed over the farmland by strong winds. Winters are on the whole windy and wet, but snow and really cold weather are rare. On clear nights The Northern Lights, or the Aurora Borealis, known in Orkney as 'The Merry Dancers', shimmer and whirr across the sky. The Norsemen believed that The Northern Lights were the shields of the Valkyries and a bridge to Asgard, home of the gods.

The seasons bring changes, but these are not always welcome. Even May and June can be made bleak by south-easterly winds with their accompanying 'black frosts'. But there are days of magic, when the wind is invigorating, the skylark flies high above pouring out his song, and the colour of everything is clear and vibrant.

Birds are everywhere in North Ronaldsay, both seen and heard; it is an exciting place for birdwatchers, and many come in spring and autumn to see their migratory flights. In 1987 a bird observatory was established on the old croft at Twinyes; the wardens also operate a bird-ringing station among the trees in the grounds of Holland House.

The native sheep who live on seaweed.

The native short-tailed sheep is one of the most attractive and interesting features of North Ronaldsay. The ability of this breed to live on seaweed is unique. In the spring the ewes with lamb are let inside the dyke; otherwise they are confined to a narrow strip of foreshore. 'They are little dark-coated sheep, very wild and charming to look at, and they make the sweetest mutton in the world, if you are hard-hearted enough to kill them', says the Orkney writer Eric Linklater. In 1974 The Rare Breed Survival Trust moved some of the sheep to Linga Holm off Stronsay. They were left to cope on their own for three years, and their number rose three times over.

In a field on Holland is the Stan Stane, the only standing stone on the island. As it is more than 4 m high and can be observed from some distance, it may have been an out-marker for a stone circle, which is believed to have stood at Tor Ness. It is pierced by a hole 2 m up, but this is too small to have been used by hand-clasping courting couples, in the way the sadly missed Odin stone of Stenness was. Instead, couples danced around it, as the Revd William Clouston tells us in his report for the *Statistical Account of Orkney, 1795-1798*: 'The writer of this has seen 50 of the inhabitants assembled there on the first day of the year, and dancing with moon light, with no other music than their own singing'.

The look of the land and the wealth of fish and shellfish in the surrounding sea may have attracted the first settlers. A number of slight mounds, filled with shells and other settlement deposits, can be seen around the island and these have also been found below many of the farms, as well as at The Brae of Stenabreck, a large prehistoric house with a cluster of rooms. In South Bay, excavation at Howmae Brae revealed the remains of a settlement, laid out on a very irregular plan and believed to belong to the period immediately before the brochs.

Probably both sites date roughly from the second half of the first millennium BC. They were excavated in the 1880s by Dr William Traill, the laird of Holland. Earlier, during the summers of 1870 and 1871, he had worked on the Broch of Burrian; his excavations being considered of a higher standard than was common at the time. He found that it was possible to distinguish between two distinct levels of occupation inside the broch, and that the objects found on the upper and lower floors were different. On the upper or secondary level the finds included spindle whorls and gaming pieces, a small ecclesiastical bell, as well as a stone inscribed with the popular and well-known Burrian cross. Alongside the cross is an ogam inscription.

The Broch of Burrian, or the Castle of Burrian, as it is known locally, was probably built towards the end of the first millennium BC as a purely defensive structure. For a middle period of some 200 years it does not seem to have been used; at least, no finds have been made. Most of the finds suggest that the tower, and the settlement on the landward side, were re-used from about the fifth century until well into Norse times. The broch was strategically sited on the most southerly headland, but it is in a very exposed position, and parts of the broch have been eroded by the sea. According to local tradition, there existed at one time traces of another broch at the extreme north end, by Trolla Vatn.

In Linklet Bay is a fishing-mark known as Knockan, found in Gaelic as *cnocan*. In Twinyes, the name of the south-western promontory, the two syllables both mean 'ness', as the Norse *nes* must have been added on to the Pictish name.

North Ronaldsay may have attracted the spearhead of Norse colonisation, and been one of the first places in which settlements occurred. The *Orkneyinga Saga* tells of how the island played an important part in Norse times. Turf-Einar, the one-eyed son of Rognvald, legendary earl of Møre, here killed Halfdan Hálegg, one of the many sons of King Harald Fairhair. He captured Halfdan on Rinar's Hill, and 'gave' him to Odin by killing him in a ritualistic way. Then he had a cairn raised over Halfdan. The whereabouts of the cairn is not known, nor where Rinar's Hill is, but it seems probable that it would be on the highest point, which is Holland. Before he turned up in Orkney, the rebellious Halfdan had surprised Earl Rognvald at his home in western Norway, and burnt him to death along with many of his followers. By killing Halfdan, Turf-Einar was protecting his earldom from usurpers as well as avenging his father.

Some 200 years later, North Ronaldsay again became the stage in a play for the earldom, when the young Kali Kolsson, the nephew of Earl Magnus Erlendsson assumed his part of both hero and knave in trying to wrest power from Earl Paul Hakonsson by fair means or foul. Probably fearing an invading force, Earl Paul had the beacon system of Orkney reinforced.

The beacons had to be lit when as many as five warships could be seen. Beacons, known in Norse as *varða* or *viti*, were built in strategic places in most islands. But once alerted, the chain-reactive beacon system could not be halted, so raising a false alarm was looked upon as a serious offence.

The *Orkneyinga Saga* relates how Kol, Kali's ingenious father, succeeded in sabotaging the system so that no warning beacon was lit at Ward Hill in Fair Isle, when their invading fleet was passing, thus enabling Kali to go on to become the second Earl Rognvald. There is no sign of a beacon in North Ronaldsay today, but according to tradition it was sited at Holland. This makes sense, as the Holland farms were probably the earl's administrative seats and therefore necessarily close to local beacons.

The man in charge of the beacon in North Ronaldsay was Thorstein, 'a man of great strength'. This places him at Holland, or perhaps at Busta, which, judging by the name, must have been a primary Norse farm. We are told that Thorstein lived with his mother Ragna, and on one occasion, when he was weather-bound on the island, Earl Paul spent three nights with them. An outspoken woman, Ragna then tried to advise the Earl on his affairs, but was told off in no uncertain terms: 'You are a wise woman, Ragna, but you have not yet been made Earl of Orkney, and you shall not rule the land here'.

Another storm-stayed guest at their house was the Icelandic poet Hall

The old lighthouse at Kirk Taing.

Thorarinsson. Through Ragna's efforts he became friendly with Earl Rognvald, and they later worked together on a rhyming dictionary called *Háttalykill enn forni*, or *The old metre-key*. Every two stanzas show one *háttr* or verse metre.

The Norse language was preserved longer in North Ronaldsay than anywhere else and even today a large number of Norse words are in daily use. The island has a long tradition of story-telling. In the notes to his novel *The Pirate*, published in 1829, Sir Walter Scott uses the following story which he knew on good authority, to show that the old Norse language was long remembered by the fishermen of Orkney and Shetland.

> A clergyman, who was not long deceased, remembered well when some remnants of the Norse were still spoken in the island called North Ronaldshaw. When Gray's Ode, entitled the "Fatal Sisters", was first published, or at least first reached that remote island, the reverend gentleman had the well-judged curiosity to read it to some of the old persons of the isle, as a poem which regarded the history of their own country. They listened with great attention to the preliminary stanzas:

> *Now the storm begins to lour,*
> *Haste the doom of hell prepare,*
> *Iron sleet of arrowy shower*
> *Hurtles in the darken'd air.*

But when they had heard a verse or two more, they interrupted the reader, telling him they knew the song well in the Norse language, and had often sung it to him when he asked them for an old song. They called it the Magicians, or the Enchantresses.

It was really the *Darraðarljóð* the clergyman had heard, a visionary poem in the heroic style of the Edda. On Good Friday morning a man in Caithness had a vision of 12 women weaving a terrible web. The weaving was magical, they were shaping the battle which must follow their will – thus foretelling the fate of the men just then fighting in battle. They were Odin's maidens, the Valkyries, who chose those who were to die. They sang the song while they worked, repeating to themselves the line that has probably given it the name:

Vindum, vindum, vef darraðar – Wind we, wind we, the web of war. The battle in question was fought at Clontarf between Brian Boru, High King of Ireland, and Sigtrygg, the Norse King of Dublin, on Good Friday in 1014. Sigurd the Stout, Earl of Orkney, fell in the battle. *Vef darraðar* may have been a kenning for banner, and the well-known story, that Sigurd falls in the battle because he carries his raven banner, may well have inspired the song, which is believed to have originated in Orkney. The Battle of Clontarf shocked the Norse world. It is described in *The Saga of Burnt Njál*, perhaps the greatest of the Icelandic sagas, and the song enhances the story of the battle.

The story shows how at one time the sea joined the lives of people in such widely scattered areas as Iceland, Ireland, Caithness and Orkney. In a similar way the sea around North Ronaldsay has been a highway to the whole world, used by all the countries around the North Sea, as the island's wreck list will show. In stormy weather the low-lying island would be all but invisible, and for ocean-going vessels there is no natural harbour.

The four offshore shoals, with the romantic names of The Altars of Linnay in the north-west, and the Seal Skerry in the north-east, the Reefdyke off Bride's Ness and Twinyes Point in the south-west, are dangerous traps, easily hidden by spray in the winter and fog in the summer.

Driving spindrift is caused by strong tides surging through the North Ronaldsay Firth on the south side of the island and the wide channel that separates Orkney and Shetland to the north. During ebbtide the current is north-westerly, only to turn the opposite way during floodtide, causing strong and widespread rösts.

The sea is never far away in North Ronaldsay. To the people of today the roaring, white-topped breakers of winter, the 'white horses', are beautiful to watch and to listen to. To the earlier inhabitants of Orkney the winter storms might mean the imminent danger of shipwreck, which would always involve the islanders, as stranded crews must stay until better weather and be given board and shelter.

The most dramatic wreck of all was perhaps the *Svecia*, of Gothenburg in Sweden, which struck the Reefdyke on 18 November 1740. The ship belonged to the Swedish East India Company and was homeward bound from a voyage to Bengal. It carried a valuable cargo of dyewood and saltpetre, as well as silk and cotton materials. The ship had run into all kinds of trouble and was several weeks late. In Orkney waters it ran into a storm, and was driven helplessly on to the Reefdyke where it stuck for three days.

The ship's carpenter and 12 seamen managed to get to shore on a piece of the quarterdeck. The 31 men who got away in the longboat made it safely to Fair Isle, but the other 60 men on board drowned. Much of the valuable cargo, valued by some as high as £500,000, was lost. Among the goods saved were 18,969 handkerchiefs. Tales of the shipwreck have been part of North Ronaldsay lore for generations. The *Svecia* was found in 1975, and for some summers a team of divers looked for the remains of the cargo, but no treasure was found.

Some four years later, another Indiaman, the Danish *Kronprinsen* with 160 men and 30 chests of 'treasure' on board, grounded at Save Geo in the north-western part of the island, without loss of men or cargo. The shipwrecked crew stayed for nine months, and in addition no fewer than four Danish ships came to transport everything back home. The place in Linklet Bay used for this rescue operation is still known as Denmark Geo.

On 20 December 1782, the *Grevinde Schemelman* from Copenhagen making for St Croix in the West Indies ran ashore in Linklet Bay, without loss of life. But the boat from Kirkwall with customs officials and crew on board – 14 men in all – fared differently.

They set out from Kirkwall on 28th December, 1782, but a
violent storm breaking out before they could reach the
island drove them out to sea and they have not been heard
of since, which makes them almost despaired of as it was
thought scarce possible that they could live in the open sea.
There were nine of the fourteen married, who amongst
them leave eighteen children and two of their wives are
with child. (*From a private letter*).

In the eighteenth century the political situation in France made the
English Channel less attractive to traffic, so northern sea routes became
more used. The number of shipwrecks occurring in the north of Scotland
made the building of lighthouses vital. The lighthouse that still rises to
some 20 m close to high-water mark at Kirk Taing, was the second to be
built in Scotland and was constructed in 1789. Made of local stone and
lime, it stood the test of time, but its position soon proved unsatisfactory
and in 1854 a new lighthouse was erected, by one of the famous
Stevenson lighthouse engineers, on the knoll of Versabreck at Dennis
Head. A popular and impressive landmark, the Dennis Head lighthouse
was one of the highest and best equipped in Scotland. On 30 March
1998, when the northern lighthouse flag was lowered for the last time, it
meant the end of the long tradition of manned light-keeping in Scotland,
with automation taking over.

Hopefully, it will always be possible to climb to the top of the lighthouse,
for the bird's-eye-view it gives of North Ronaldsay and the surrounding
islands. It shows how the island is divided by dykes, the sheep dyke going
all around the shore, and the two shallow, prehistoric turf dykes, or treb
dykes, cutting right across the island. The Muckle Gersty and the
Matches Dyke divide the island into three parts, known as South Yard
and North Yard, with Linklet in the middle. There is a certain similarity
to the Papa Westray land division in particular, but remains of dykes
have been found on other islands as well, and the system probably goes
back a long way.

The whole island was originally skatted as four urislands. North Yard
comprised the two tunships of Ancum and Easting. Linklet made up a
urisland tunship by itself, and South Yard consisted of Busta, Holland
and Ness. Traditionally each tunship had a measure of self-government.

North Ronaldsay does not figure in the older rentals, but it seems to
have consisted mostly of old kingsland, so called because it belonged to the

Norwegian Crown. This suggests a forfeited estate, and brings to mind what happened to the Island Beardies after the Battle of Florvåg in 1194.

In 1595, most of North Ronaldsay belonged to the earl, but there were still nine small odal properties, amounting to about one-twelfth of the island. By 1727 they had disappeared, and James Traill had become sole proprietor. Until quite recently North Ronaldsay has remained an estate island, belonging to descendants of the same family. Although often absentee landlords, some of them proved shrewd and forward-looking.

The old run-rig system of agriculture long prevailed, with a lot of time spent on going from field to field. In the eighteenth century this was not so important, as more attention was paid to the production of kelp; North Ronaldsay yielded about a tenth of the Orkney production, averaging 150 tons a year.

A lot of people were needed for the kelp production, which was very labour-intensive. Both farming and fishing suffered. The many kilometres of beaches were allocated to the crofters, and kelp production became a condition for keeping the croft. The population grew, and some crofts housed more than one family. From 1801 to 1831 the population rose from 411 to 522 and when the price of kelp fell disastrously after the Napoleonic Wars, and a prolonged slump set in, starvation threatened the overcrowded island. The laird, who also held a medical post in India, set about introducing a revolutionary way of working the land. His factor, or land-grieve, at the time of the land-squaring, was popularly known as 'Ald Art' and as 'a mesterfu' man'.

By 1832 the run-rig system was replaced by land-squaring; crops were rotated, water-logged fields were drained, the enclosure dykes were strengthened and the sheep confined to the foreshore to live on seaweed. In just over five years the population fell by some 80 people, because of emigration overseas, and to the neighbouring island of Eday, which found room for 32 North Ronaldsay people on its west side. By 1881, the population there was higher than ever, reaching a total of 547 people.

The men returning from the First World War were no longer so interested in an island croft, and within a decade or two the population almost halved; this downward trend has continued ever since. Although tractors and other mechanical tools have changed agriculture drastically, a lot of land remains uncultivated. The larger farm units give a higher standard of living, but carry fewer people – a complete reversal of earlier problems. This also makes the communal work of looking after the substantial stone dyke, which keeps sheep from the infield, difficult to keep up. But the old Sheep Court, the last remnant of the old Orcadian system of communal agriculture, has been revitalised and is firmly under island control.

Culturally, North Ronaldsay more than holds its own. One who has elected to stay on his island in spite of all the honours heaped on him, is the sculptor and painter Ian Scott. He returned to the family farm of Antabreck after specialising in sculpture

Dennis Head lighthouse.

at Gray's School of Art in Aberdeen. His best-known work is his bronze statue in Longhope cemetery in Hoy, in honour and memory of the lifeboat crew that was lost on 17 March 1969. But he has also captured the onslaught of the sea at Rysageo; through his paintings the North Ronaldsay landscape is depicted in all its moods.

Several books have been written by islanders, both on the history and life of the people and on the lore and legend that abound. A stream of books goes from the Orkney County Library to the island. The North Ronaldsay children do well at Kirkwall Grammar School – too well, perhaps, because today the children are educated away from the island.

Sanday

As the island's name points out, there is sand in Sanday, the sandy soil areas being hardy enough for cattle to be outwintered even in a wet season, without running the risk of ruining next summer's grass. The shape of the island is habitually compared to that of a lobster; a shape that makes for distances and variations. The south-western peninsula is a ridge of Eday sandstones, with hill land extending southwards from the Bay of Brough. The highest point is The Wart, at 65 m. In old times this was the *varða*, or beacon, to be lit at a time of crisis. The rest of the island is very low, barely reaching 15 m above the sea, and, in the words of an early writer, 'flatness is the characteristic of its whole surface'.

There is no doubt that in early times Sanday was considered the richest of the Orkney islands, as it was taxed very heavily. Whereas Stronsay and Westray, about the same size as Sanday, both had a skat value of around 13 urislands, the value of Sanday was set as 36.5 urislands. Sanday's high taxation status was based on its suitability for growing bere, the old kind of barley. The island was known as the 'granary of Orkney' and for centuries exported grain to Norway.

Because of its light sandy soil Sanday has been exposed to brutal land erosion, both from the sea and the wind. In the early rentals the expression 'blawin' land' is often used about land that is no longer under cultivation. The Revd William Clouston, a Sanday minister of the late eighteenth century, tells us that 'In many places the sea gains upon the land; and, in a few places, the land gains on the sea, by throwing up banks of stones and sand, which serve as ramparts or dykes against its future attacks.' Such ridges of dunes can be seen along Newark Bay.

In many bays the tide ebbs far out, leaving immense stretches of sand. After a storm in the 1840s, fossilised trees lying on a bed of moss were reportedly found at low ebb in the Bay of Otters Wick. In *A Description of the Isles of Orkney*, published posthumously in 1693, the Revd James Wallace includes an Orkney map he had made himself. This map shows a comparatively large island off Burness. Tradition has it that this island was the 'ba' green' or shoal ground known as Runnabrake. In the same way, the rocky shoal now known as the Riv was not so long ago the green Holms of Riv, where horses might be taken for pasture.

The Sanday writer and folklorist Walter Traill Dennison recounts another tradition bearing on the subject:

Some time, long ago, a Sanday woman in her youth went to live in Norway, and continued long in that country. When an old woman, she returned to her native island; and after looking around her, she put this question to the Sanday people, 'What has become of the rabbit links of Kattasand, the woods of Otterswick, and the ba'green of Runnabrake?'

All three had disappeared during her residence in Norway.

The Sanday coastline is mostly very low, with few landmarks high enough to be seen from a distance, so that in the old days it was difficult to navigate safely around it, as the numerous shipwrecks show. In difficult years, such as the period of appalling weather and failed crops in the early 1780s, a shipwreck would sometimes be a heaven-sent aid to the island. This is expressed in the prayer which tradition has it was made by a Sanday minister, 'Nevertheless, if it please Thee to cause helpless ships to be cast on the shore, oh! dinna forget the poor island of Sanda!' Another minister speaks up for the islanders by pointing out that Sanday people do not actively cause shipwrecks, and that nowhere have people 'had less reason of complaints against the inhabitants'.

The shipwrecks made good stories that were handed down from one generation to another, and told in the darkness of winter around the warming fires. The story of the *Utrecht* is perhaps the most dramatic of the Sanday shipwrecks, and one that in many ways gave the islanders more than they had bargained for. It took place in February 1807, during the Napoleonic Wars when Britain and the Netherlands were in conflict. The *Utrecht* was a Dutch frigate on its way to defend the island of Curaçao in the West Indies from the British Navy. The ship was armed with 32 guns, and must have been quite large, as there were some 450 men on board. Of these 200 were trained gunners.

Bad weather drove the ship inexorably off course and on to the Holms of Ire. The *Utrecht* was wrecked, the craft capsized with the loss of a large number of the crew, and it was freezing cold. The captain surrendered with his 366 remaining men to the laird of Scar. According to his diary the captain actually did consider taking the island by force – 'we could have become masters of the island' – but on doing a quiet reconnaissance he found only two ships 'which the same storm had thrown up on the coast and which were completely useless to me'. And so the island of Curaçao fell to the British.

In all probability the *Utrecht* would have negotiated the recently built lighthouse in Sanday on its way north, before choosing to head west along the passage between Fair Isle and North Ronaldsay. After the first Orkney lighthouse had been built in North Ronaldsay, it was found that ships tended to make for the light; this brought them so dangerously close to Sanday that it was considered necessary to build another lighthouse there. In 1802 an unlit beacon was therefore erected at Start Point, the most easterly point of Orkney. Today Start is a small tidal island, but at the time it may still have been joined to Sanday. In 1806 the beacon was fitted with a revolving light, the first in Scotland.

In the summer of 1814 Sir Walter Scott joined the lighthouse yacht on a voyage around the north of Scotland, in the company of the famous lighthouse builder, Robert Stevenson. He visited the Start lighthouse and was so impressed with the establishment of the keepers he compared it to his own 'baronial mansion of Abbotsford'. To the visitor his advice was 'Go to the top of the tower and survey the island which, as the name implies, is level, flat and sandy, quite the reverse of those in Zetland: it is intersected by creeks and small lakes and, though it abounds with shell marle, seems barren'. In 1870 the old tower was replaced by a striking, vertically striped, 50 m high lighthouse.

The easily cultivated soil of Sanday attracted settlers as early as the fourth millennium BC. Many of the prehistoric remains are now gone, because of marine encroachment or due to the tolls of intensive agriculture. But there is still much to be found, as the sand yields its secrets. The farm mounds that are characteristic of North Ronaldsay are also found in Sanday, as well as in the Harstad area of North Norway. Some of the mounds turn out to be just farm middens built up over a long continuous occupation, but others hide old buildings as well. Buildings went out of use, and new houses were built on top, so that some of the mounds stand 3 to 4 m high. Many early farms, such as How and Beafield, are built on such mounds.

On the eastern side of the long and flat promontory of Els Ness we find the spectacular chambered cairn of Quoyness. It is the largest of the Orkney tombs, with a very high central chamber and six irregularly shaped side-cells. It was initially excavated in 1868 by James Farrer, who left a lot of the human remains just as he had found them. The tomb was re-excavated by Dr V Gordon Childe during the summers of 1951 and 1952. Radiocarbon dating of the bones found in the cells dates them to *c*.2900 BC.

The Chambered Cairn of Quoyness.

Just south of the Quoyness tomb is what is probably a chambered cairn, known as Augmund Howe, much of which has been taken by the sea. Around it, 11 mounds form a half circle; one of them was found on excavation to contain two cists with human bones. Over the southernmost part of the ness at least 26 cairns are scattered. It has been suggested that this was once a sacrificial site, which burned continuously.

The name Tafts Ness, which also occurs as Tofts Ness, at once suggests early settlement and use, as the original word *toptir* is used in conjunction with building remains. It is an extensive and well-preserved complex, consisting of large mounds and a great number of cairns. Whether there are brochs and settlements here or whether this is mostly a funerary site, cannot be ascertained without excavation. Several very large artificial mounds at Tafts Ness are surrounded by long dykes, with cairns at regular 10 m intervals. Some of the dykes surround the mound in a large semi-circle, rather similar to the site at Augmund Howe. Selective excavation has identified remains from the Neolithic as well as the Bronze Age.

Some of the more important recent archaeological excavations in Orkney have been made at Pool and Scar, on the western and northern sides of Sanday, and have been in the nature of rescue operations because of acute coastal erosion. The name Pool derives from the Norse *pollr*, which means a small rounded bay. Here the sea and the wind had torn away part of a mound, some 4 m high and 70 m wide, exposing several layers of settlement. The lower zone has a complex of small stone houses, and the tip deposits show the orange-red colour that has come to be seen as typical of the Neolithic period. Pottery of the Grooved Ware variety was found in this zone. The upper, darker zone belongs to the later Iron Age and the Norse period.

The site was continuously occupied from some time in the fourth millennium BC until it was abandoned around the end of the third millennium. Then in the fourth to sixth centuries AD a thriving farming community seems to have worked there, living in small, cell-like houses with a common, flagged exterior. A rectangular courtyard may have been used as a meeting place. A symbol stone, with an ogam inscription, was found in a central, probably ceremonious, position. Then in the seventh century a gradual abandonment of the settlement seems to have begun.

Carbon dating shows the Norse impact on the site began early, perhaps even in the seventh century, but its nature is not easily interpreted. The artefacts were not culturally one or the other, but a mixture of native and Scandinavian types. It may therefore have been more a question of Norse cultural impact than of actual settlement, in a period defined by the archaeologists as a phase of cultural interface. Thus a roundhouse, the pride of the old community, survived in its original form until the eleventh century. But the new houses built in this period were rectangular, with a central hearth, and steatite became common. Norse burials of a man and a woman have been found at nearby Lambaness. The brooches found in the woman's grave belonged to a type of craft work found in Norway around AD 800.

The boat-burial at Scar in Burness surpasses earlier Norse finds made in Sanday, and perhaps even in Orkney. The boat was discovered just before the sea took it, and the excavations in November and December 1991 turned into an exciting race against time and weather. Tool-marks still survived in the clay where the Viking grave-diggers had made a large pit for the boat, a millennium ago and more. The wood of the boat had rotted away, but it was clinker-built, and the nails and rivets were still there. The boat had been 7 m long, and was made in the Norse boat-building tradition.

A simple burial chamber, some 3.5 m long, had been made inside one end of the boat; the rest was filled up with stones. There were three bodies inside the chamber: those of a child, a woman and a man. The man was probably in his thirties, and had been about 181 cm tall, whereas the woman was in her seventies, and the child was around 10 years old. Parts of the skeletons as well as perhaps half of the grave-goods had been washed away before excavation started, but there are still a great number of objects, and they are of an impressive quality. The man was equipped with, among other things, a sword in a sheepskin-lined scabbard, a quiver of eight arrows and 22 gaming-pieces, made of whalebone.

Apart from a gilded bronze brooch and a comb, the woman's goods were practical working utensils, thus she had both a pair of shears and a small sickle. But given pride of place in the grave, propped up against the wall, was a whalebone plaque, probably to be used as a board for smoothing linen. Stylised horse heads are carved on to it, and it is perhaps the finest of its kind ever to be discovered, a plaque found at Trondenes in Troms, North Norway, being its only rival. The gilded brooch is of the so-called Troms type, and gives another connecting link to this part of Norway. The find has been carbon dated to the middle of the tenth century.

At some point the placenames became almost completely Norse, the only exception being the word *treb*, or *trave*, used about the broad, prehistoric linear earthworks that ran across Sanday and North Ronaldsay. In Burness, the remnants of such a dyke run from the farm of West Thrave into the large mound known as the Braes of Gorn, a probable settlement site, only to emerge again on the other side of it.

The Norse land-taking in Sanday probably took place long before the earldom was established around 900. Significantly, many of the nesses belonged to the earl from an early date; thus there were earldom estates known as Bus at the long nesses of Tafts, Lopness, Tresness, and Hacksness. The fifth earldom estate was the Bu of Walls in the district now known as Nortwa. All these private earldom farms extended to one urisland and were unskatted bordland. One theory is that these farms date back to an early 'ness-taking' by Viking settlers, and were used by them as strongholds for their piratical summer activities in Norway. According to the saga sources, King Harald Finehair at one point came to Orkney to settle with them, and probably took their farms. At the same time he made his friend Rognvald of Møre the first Earl of Orkney,

Farm of Taft, an old earldom estate.

as a gesture when his son Ivar was killed in the islands. According to tradition Ivar lies buried in Ivar's Knowe on the east shore of Otters Wick. Later, the revenues of three of these old Sanday Bus belonged to the Sang School attached to St Magnus Cathedral in Kirkwall.

The name of Bea, which occurs today as the name of a promontory and a loch near Backaskaill Bay, is a primary, high-status type of name and probably points to an important settlement farm in this area. The large, early farm of Backaskaill used to be known as Southerbie, meaning the southern part of Bea. The now derelict, sixteenth-century church of Cross is built on a broad, raised site close to the sandy bay. This may possibly cover the centre of an important settlement complex, as the situation would be close to ideal.

The island had no fewer than three parishes, all bearing the same name as the parish church: Cross or Sancta Crucis in the south-western part, Sancta Mariae or Our Lady in the east, and Sancti Columbi in the north-west. The last parish has mostly been known as Burness, and it included North Ronaldsay at one time. Remains of as many as 29 early chapels have been found in Sanday. Going by the tradition in Iceland in early Christian times, this would mean that there were many odal farms, as any farmer of noteworthy status would build a chapel on his land. The chapel of Cleat seems to have had special importance, and was much frequented. As late as 1601 there were as many as 70 small odallers in Sanday, but by the early eighteenth century this number had been reduced to about ten.

In later Norse times there was a royal Huseby farm in the Pool area. Much of the neighbouring land was the property of the earldom, and after the pledging of Orkney to Scotland, much of this land became the odal estate of Warsetter, belonging to a branch of the Sinclair family. Sir William Sinclair, First of Warsetter, was Justice of Orkney after his elder brother fell in the Battle of Flodden in 1513, and was one of the most distinguished men in Orkney. His two illegitimate sons, James and Edward Sinclair, led the Orkneymen to victory in the Battle of Summerdale in 1529.

Gradually the odal land became absorbed into feudal estates. In the 1745 rebellion some of the Sanday lairds may have sided with the Jacobites, but of these only John Traill of Elsness was careless enough to have signed a letter to that effect. He was one of the four lairds from the North Isles to have done so. All four went underground in a Westray cave, and were never found by the Hanoverian troops, led by the revengeful Captain William Moodie of Melsetter, who looked for them everywhere, but had to be content with plundering and burning their houses. In his humorous dialect story 'Why the Hoose o' Hellsnes wus Brunt', written more than a century afterwards, Walter Traill Dennison describes the destruction of Elsness in June 1746.

This was by no means the last time the Traills of Elsness entered politics, with disastrous results. John Traill's grandson, John Traill Urquhart, was a friend of George Traill of Hobbister, who won the Orkney and Shetland seat in the controversial parliamentary election of 1833. When the result became known, a riot broke out in Broad Street in Kirkwall, and John Traill Urquhart died from a blow he received in the fray. In Sanday he is perhaps best remembered for building the beautiful, but now derelict, mansion house of Geramount. According to tradition it was built on an old odal property that once belonged to a man called Geirmund.

In Lady parish much of the land was the property of the Traills of Hobbister and Rattar, a Caithness family. Their estate home was the house of East Brough, which they renamed Newark. In the early nineteenth century the Elsness estate also became part of this property. In

1880 the whole Hobbister estate went bankrupt. It proved impossible to sell as it was, and had to be split up and sold to tenants. The final sale was not settled until the 1930s.

In the parish of Burness we find another Traill property, known as the Westove estate. The laird's home was Savil House, until a new house was built at Scar. This necessitated the moving of the Savil stone to the new and large walled garden. This is a famous boulder of gneiss, weighing over 20 tons, which was popularly imagined to have been flung there by a witch in Eday, but in actual fact it was carried on an ice sheet all the way from Norway, sometime in the Ice Age. Moving the stone took a whole summer and wore out three horses.

No other island had so many Traill estates. In Kirkwall the number of town houses along the main street belonging to members of the Traill family inspired this ditty:

> Traills up the toon,
> Traills doon the toon,
> Traills in the middle.
> De'il take the Traills' guts
> For strings to his fiddle.

The early nineteenth century was on the whole a good time for the lairds, as well as for the crofters and cottars. Kelp paid dividends during the boom period 1780–1830, when Sanday with its long coast produced some 550 tons a year. Agricultural improvements were carried out by some of the more enterprising lairds; among them Samuel Laing of Stove. It took time before these changes paid off; then the sudden fall in the price of kelp hit many and ruined some of the lairds, Laing among them.

The common people also saw another side to the picture. During the Napoleonic Wars the press-gang scoured the island for men for the Navy, and would grab anybody in sight. Sir Walter Scott perhaps did not see the islanders' point of view, and was shocked to find during his visit to Sanday in 1814 that one man's cattle had been stabbed to death, probably because he was taking up names for the militia, and thus was considered an informer.

How did the crofters and cottars live? In his diary for a day in March 1847 Walter Traill Dennison wrote:

> Took a very long walk in search of specimens. Attacked by
> a monstrously uncivil storm of wind and rain. Sought
> refuge in the house of T.R., weatherbound there for three

hours. Gave T.R. a piece of tobacco and chatted with him
on affairs of Church and State. His is a miserable house
some 14 by 12 feet. Seeing only one bed in house, asked
him how he and his wife and six children put up all night.
'Weel', said he, 'jeust look i' the inside o' the bed, an' ye'll
say it's weel planned tae haud eight o' us.' ...Struck with
his ingenuity in packing human beings, I took the following
measurements of the family packing-box: - length of bed 5
feet 8 inches, breadth 3 feet 10 inches, height from bottom
boards to roof, 4 feet 8 inches.

Walter Traill Dennison (1825-94) leased the farm of West Brough with
his brother. Together with some other likeminded Sanday people they
broke with the Free Church in 1860 and set up a 'Preaching Station' of
their own, also known as the Dennison Kirk. Today this is a garage. At
the same time he was an enthusiastic collector of island lore, both
stories and artefacts, among these was the telescope of the pirate Gow.
His most popular work is probably *The Orcadian Sketch-Book*, with the
subtitle *Traits of Old Orkney Life*. It was written partly in the Sanday
dialect and published by William Peace & Son in Kirkwall in 1880. It
should have been reissued long ago; now it has become the gem of a
collector's library.

The stories and lore he used for his writing were collected among the
islanders, and he saw clearly that this source was in danger of drying up.
'– they possess – (alas! I should rather say, at one time possessed) – a very
interesting and most abundant store of what may be called oral lore.'
And he goes on to praise his informants: 'The Orcadian peasantry are
surpassed by none of their class in Europe for general intelligence, and
are equalled by none in gentleness of manner and natural politeness.
They had – I speak of the last by-gone generation – a keen fondness for
and lively appreciation of any mental enjoyment suited to their
uncultivated capacities. In the absence of books this taste was gratified,
and abundantly cultivated, by hearing and reciting their own traditions,
by the fireside, in the long winter nights of their northern clime.'

According to Ernest Marwick, another Orkney folklorist, Dennison
'saved from extinction, almost single-handed, a whole corpus of myth
legend and historical tradition which educated Orcadians of his time
ignored, even deplored.' Others knew how to appreciate his work, even
in his own lifetime; he became an honorary member of the

distinguished Viking Club of London, and lectured to them shortly before his death.

In the nineteenth century more than 2000 people lived in the three parishes, with six churches and four schools. The growth in population figures was caused by extensive agricultural improvements, fishing and kelp production, which gradually also changed much of the social picture. For the first time a crofter had some spare coins: 'The kelp pays the rent, and buys the coal, and there's a pound or twa over.' When the market was favourable, then kelp was king, and kelp excuses for the children's absence from school were the despair of the teachers.

Today there are around 500 inhabitants of Sanday. The main income comes from farming, mainly beef cattle, and this is greatly helped by the improved transport facilities.

A knitting firm, Orkney Angora, was established in 1982, as a family enterprise. They started off making white socks, but now produce a wide range of thermal clothing. The white Angora rabbits are on view at their Burness premises.

Bringing rabbits to Sanday would seem to be superfluous, as for centuries they have been considered a pest. The Revd Brand wrote in 1700, '– I never saw a greater number of Conies running in any place than I did here. Hence the Heretors kill several hundreds of them yearly for their use.'

The wide beaches of Sanday are sanctuaries for many birds, especially wintering waders, and also for seals and otters. An area in Nortwa has been designated a Site of Special Scientific Interest (SSSI), as it is a home for many different kinds of birds. Plants thrive there also in the wet machair. In Newark Bay, sheltered by the sand dunes, marram and lyme grass abound. In the eighteenth century the nearby Plain of Fidge used to be Orkney's favourite golfing links. Some years ago golf was given a new lease of life when a new nine-hole course was developed in the same area.

Sand of Rothiesholm in the Bay of Holland.

Stronsay and Papa Stronsay

Large bays with wide white beaches are the most striking feature of
Stronsay. The many nesses give the island a feeling of size and distance.
The sandy bays have been a haunt of seals, and the Bay of Holland was
considered the best whale-trap in Orkney in the days when the droves of
pilot whales, also known as caa'ing whales, were a major source of
lighting and income as well as a welcome diversion. A whole fleet of
small craft would chase them on to the Sand of Rothiesholm. Pilot
whales have been washed up and stranded by exceptionally high tides in
recent times as well, but today the problem is not how to chase them on
to the beach, but off it. Stronsay waters are rough, and tides run fiercely
in places. At Rothiesholm Head the tides run counter to each other, and
form a boiling röst.

'Hawks and Falcons have their Nests in several places of these Islands,
as ...at Rousum-head and Lambhead in Stronsa', wrote James Wallace in
1693. This is doubtful today, but the south-east and south-west cliffs of
Stronsay are still good places in which to watch birds, and with luck both
the great and Arctic skua can be observed. In the old days a lot of young

cormorants, known in Orkney as 'scarfs', used to be taken on these cliffs in the wintertime, buried for a day or two to become tender, and then eaten as a delicacy. Twice a year migrant birds find a haven on Stronsay, while on their long flights north or south. On the east shore is the Stronsay Bird Reserve, run by a bird artist and his wife. Many rare and interesting birds have been found there, the most interesting observation being that of a yellow-breasted bunting, found feeding in the ripening oats.

The small Holm of Huip shelters the northern part of Stronsay, where the airfield is. The island is mostly inhabited by birds and seals, and is an important breeding site for the Atlantic grey seal in particular. The uninhabited island of Linga Holm was for 25 years the home of a colony of North Ronaldsay sheep. This was part of a conservation project run by The Rare Breeds Survival Trust. In the summer of 1999 the island was bought by the Scottish Wildlife Trust in order to protect the colony of grey seals breeding there, one of the largest single island colonies of these seals in the world. More than 2000 grey seal pups have been counted there.

Stronsay is low-lying, yet the island gives an impression of varied scenery, making walking around very pleasant. Until the common was divided up, the central ridge of Stronsay was uncultivated hill pasture. Today we find uncultivated land mostly in the Rothiesholm peninsula, which through the centuries provided the island with peat, and in the area around Burgh Hill which, at 46 m, is the highest point in the island. Here heath and moorland plants grow willingly.

The origin of the name Stronsay is obscure. The Norse form is *Strjónsey*; the first element *strjón* being found only in placenames. Its meaning is unknown. Many fanciful interpretations have been suggested over the years, but none of them rings true, and so far the name remains an enigma.

In many ways Stronsay's history is as obscure as its name. The *Orkneyinga Saga* describes a meeting of reconciliation between Earl Erlend Haraldsson and Svein Asleifarson off the north coast, but the island as such is not important in this context. Otherwise Stronsay is hardly mentioned in early sources, Stronsay farms being inexplicably missing in the early rental and not actually mentioned until 1595. The Orkney scholar, Dr Hugh Marwick, puts it this way: 'To the student of history and archaeology, Stronsay is in the highest degree baffling and tantalising … at the same time one constantly meets isolated names or facts that, elusive though they may be, seem to illumine the darkness for a moment, and give one a glimpse of the island's unlit past.' (1926-7.)

A fertile island, Stronsay must have attracted settlers from a very early age. The many prehistoric remains point to this, but as in so many of Orkney's more fertile areas, farming has been the enemy of historic remains, which are found mainly where the tractor cannot reach, and Stronsay is no exception in this respect. Also, there has so far been surprisingly little scientific interest in the island's plentiful archaeological remains, so that these have been allowed to retain an aura of mystery.

A broch site at Hunton was explored by the Orkney amateur archaeologist George Petrie in 1863, but it is not visible today. The cliffs of Odin Bay have not only the finest natural arch in Orkney, The Vat of Kirbister, but also hermitage stacks and the remains of an Iron-Age fort. On the promontory of Lamb Head, in a very dramatic place, are a broch-mound and two side-chambers which were partially explored by Thomas and Petrie around the middle of the nineteenth century. The Hillock of Baywest in Rothiesholm conceals perhaps both a broch and a village.

Close to Lamb Ness is the mysterious, L-shaped Danes Pier, which according to tradition was an artificial jetty and was used as a harbour by the Norsemen. It is quite long, and one story is that the ubiquitous Cubbie Roo built it as a bridge to Shapinsay; its similarity to other structures, such as the pier at Rerwick Point in St Andrews, is strange. The same giant was also busy carrying stone to Strainie Water in Rothiesholm where we find Cubbie Roo's Lade. A natural marvel is the Mermaid's Chair in Mill Bay where the mermaid would sit at night, calming the waves with her strange atonal songs. It is quite true, according to island tradition; boatmen have seen and heard her. Later the storm witch Scota Bess would sit in the Chair and pronounce her spells.

Placename patterns also have a tale to tell, although it may not always be simple. On the east side of Stronsay we find the large open Mill Bay with the Norwegian oil capital of Stavanger as the nearest landfall to the east. It takes no great flight of the imagination to see the wooden ships of the Norsemen come this way 1000 years ago and more. Always beautiful, in a storm the bay is magical: underwater barriers extending from each ness make only the middle third of the bay passable, the rest of the horizon shows the water in furious spray. The visual impression is striking.

Old kiln on the farm of Odiness.

Mill Bay is named after the old mill on the shore. Probably the original name was derived from the Norse word *melr*, for sand, so that the transition from one name to another would have been easy. On the beach, close to the large farm of Hunton, lies the sacred Well of Kildinguie. According to all the old travel descriptions this was the main attraction of Stronsay. The water should be drunk with the reddish-brown seaweed dulse (*Rhodymenia palmata*) from the nearby geo known as Guiyidn, or Geo Odin. 'The water of Kildinguie, and the dulse of Guiyidn, can cure all maladies except black death', quoted the Revd John Anderson in his description of Stronsay life in the *Statistical Account of Orkney, 1795-1798*. Through the centuries people came from afar to try this cure; today only the Hunton cattle enjoy the water from this sacred spring.

On the grassy edge above the well, some scattered stones are all that remains of an old chapel. It is not known what name or dedication this chapel had, but it is an established fact that the first Christian churches were, as often as not, built close to pagan cult places. In that way the sacral effect was channelled into the new faith. It is therefore probable that the cult of the well is older than the chapel, and that it goes back to pagan times. The chapel may even have replaced a pagan temple.

If we look at the map of Mill Bay we see a litany of pagan names, a veritable pantheon. The southern ness is called Odness, but is also known as Odin Ness. The large bay to the south-east is called Odin Bay, and a little further west we find Tor Ness. On the south side of Odin Ness we find two adjoining geos known as North and South Ramna Geo, the geos of the raven. Odin, the Allfather, was the god of war, but also of wisdom, and every day he learnt the news of the world from his two ravens, Hugin and Munin, or Thought and Memory. On the north side of the ness lies the farm of Hescombe. This name may derive from *hestr*, a horse, and *kambr*, meaning kame or ridge, and a horse's neck. The horse was, of course, Odin's special animal, and his magical horse, Sleipnir, had eight feet and would take him across the sky on nightly rides.

The northern ness of Mill Bay is called Grice Ness, meaning the ness of the pig, an animal symbolising both Odin and another important god, Yngvi-Freyr. According to the historian Snorri Sturluson, Yngvi-Freyr was the god of rain and sunshine and the fertility of the earth, and good harvests depended on his bounty. The first element of Kildinguie means spring or well, and a natural interpretation of the name is therefore the Well of Yngvi-Freyr, also known as Ing. The local pronunciation of the name – 'kildin·gi' – meaning literally the well of Ing, bears out this interpretation.

Why were the incoming Norsemen so eager to demonstrate their pagan faith? The Stronsay placenames seem to differ from the usual pattern of down-to-earth topographical descriptions. It is possible that the settlers in Stronsay at one time felt under pressure from Christianity. The Picts of Orkney were, it seems, mostly Christian when the Norsemen came, and the church of St Peter in Papa Sound may have been there already. It was built on top of a broch, like so many of the first Pictish churches. Strangely, close to the church site we find the Bay of Franks; does the name perhaps refer to an old trading connection?

Across the sheltered anchorage of Papa Sound lies the small fertile island of Papa Stronsay, known in Norse times as *Papey in litla*. The remains of two early chapels can still be seen, dedicated to St Nicholas and to St Bride respectively. In 1998 a team of archaeologists began excavating the site of the St Nicholas Chapel, which was demolished in 1782. Foundations of a Norse chapel, believed to date back to the early thirteenth century were discovered. Later excavations revealed that this medieval chapel was built on top of an earlier building that may date back to the eighth or ninth century and therefore be contemporaneous with the church of St Peter in Papa Sound.

The *Orkneyinga Saga* recounts the dramatic story that took place on Papa just before Christmas in 1046. The two earls that ruled together, Thorfinn the Mighty and Rognvald Brusason, had long fought each other bitterly. Arnor Thordarson, the Icelandic skald, loved them both and wrote:

> I saw both my benefactors
> battering the other's men
> – fierce was my grief –
> fighting on the Firth.

Believing Thorfinn to be dead, Rognvald feels safe enough to go to Papa Stronsay to fetch malt for the Christmas ale. Thorfinn and his men follow but Earl Rognvald manages to escape. 'Suddenly they heard a dog bark among the rocks down by the sea. Rognvald was carrying his lap-dog with him and it was this that betrayed him. They killed him on the spot among the rocks.' About halfway between the two old chapels the rising ground is known as Earl's Knowe.

Earl Rognvald must have gone to Papa Stronsay because the best malt was there, probably made by the monks. Otherwise little is known about them. After all these centuries there are again monks in Papa Stronsay. The island has been purchased by the order known as the Transalpine Redemptorists, which was founded in 1988. They do not accept all the modern practices of the mainstream Roman Catholic Church, and therefore use Latin in mass. Papa Stronsay was chosen for its solitude and religious history.

The Stronsay soil is rich and makes good farming land, yet Stronsay was skatted in early times considerably less than neighbouring Sanday; along with Papa Stronsay it was valued as around 13 urislands. Of course, much of the land was earmarked for administrative purposes and exempt from taxes: Houseby, considered the best farm in Orkney by some, was a military area in Norse times, and Holland was the earl's bordland. According to the 1595 rental there were practically no farmer-owners in the island at that time, as about 73 per cent of the cultivated area was earl's land, 26 per cent was church land, and just under one per cent was odal land. Stronsay odal families may have sided with the Island Beardies and thus lost their land to King Sverrir after the Battle of

Florvåg near Bergen in 1194. This would explain the almost total absence of odal land.

Like Sanday, Stronsay was divided into three parishes, St Peter in the north, St Mary in the west and St Nicholas in the east part of the island. The church land was concentrated in two areas. Thus all of Rothiesholm was church property, along with many farms in the Everby tunship, such as Airy, Hescombe, Odiness and Kirbuster. By 1727 there was not a single farmer-owner living on his farm. In 1794 there were 14 owners, or 'heritors' as they were called, and the only farm to be owner-occupied then was Kirbuster, as the former owner had left his property divided equally among his three unmarried daughters. But the heritors had able men to run their farms, and the Stronsay lairds were among the first to regularise the field pattern from the running strips known as run-rig, to squares, which make a very striking pattern.

Today Stronsay has some of the largest farms in the county, and much of local history and lore is connected with them. The northernmost farm of Huip, an old urisland farm, is named for the long, shallow oyce leading up to it, from the Norse *hóp*, a narrow bay. Even the Icelanders evidently got it wrong, as the *Orkneyinga Saga* refers to Hofsnes, the ness of the *hof* or pagan temple, instead of Hopsnes, as the place of the aforementioned meeting of reconciliation. But with all the other pagan names in Stronsay, this was a natural mistake for the saga writer to make! And for all we know, there might have been a *hof* there.

King and earl possessed almost all the land in the northern parish of St Peter. The name of Whitehall is fairly recent, and today's farm represents only a part of the original estate, which was skatted as two urislands and stretched right across the island, including Clestrain and Hunton. This estate was known as Strenzie or Strynie, and may possibly have been the same as the Brekkur of the *Orkneyinga Saga*, and later a seat of the Sinclair earls, as an old document has the earl mention his 'grandson Earl Wm. at North Strynie in Stronsay'. Today no trace is left of the old mansion.

In the eighteenth and nineteenth centuries, the time of the Orkney lairds, we find the main land-owning families installed in Stronsay too: Balfours in Huip, Traills in Houseby and Holland. But the Fea family outshone them all; for 200 years they left their mark on Stronsay. Fea is a Norse name, but nothing is known of their background, except for the fact that they also owned part of the Stove estate in Sanday. In 1591 Earl

Robert Stewart granted the first James Fea a feu charter of Clestrain. Although the family later acquired larger and more valuable property elsewhere, the six consecutive James Feas all used the territorial designation 'of Clestrain'.

It was Patrick Fea, a younger son of James, third of Clestrain, who was the first to make the Fea name notorious. He seems to have commanded a privateer frigate in Charles II's time, and to have made some money in France. He returned to Stronsay to buy the old estate of North Strenzie, or Strynie, and build the house of Whitehall; he also acquired the farm of Airy. He married Barbara Traill of Holland, and over the door of their house was inscribed their initials and the date of 1671. Until he died in 1709, Patrick Fea kept the island entertained by his exploits, such as 'hitting Barbara Cormack for pasturing kyne on his cornes' and 'for chasing and persuing of Wm. Cogill in Strynie with ane drawn whinger swa that the said Cogill being so furiously assaultit and for fear of his lyff was necessitat to run into the sea for his shelter'. But he could also be kind and generous to people in need, if and when his temper did not run away with him.

Towards the end of the seventeenth century Patrick Fea fell out with a man who obviously knew how to stand up for himself. In December 1694 Robert Elphinstone of Lopness in Sanday 'did convocat a great many men in arms and with them invaded Whythall's house in Strynie and chased himself and his son out of the Isle', carried away cattle, crops and furnishings, so that Patrick Fea had 'no manner of bedclowths to lye in when he returned home...'. Because of this H M Treasury in 1700 exonerated him for not paying the duties of Strynie and Airy for the five preceding years, but nothing appears to have happened to the high-handed Sanday laird!

Litigation seems to have been a favourite pastime of Orkney lairds in the eighteenth century, but few carried it so far as Barbara Fea, Patrick Fea's flamboyant daughter. For all of 60 years, long after she herself was dead, the courts were kept busy with the celebrated case that started as one of Fea versus Traill. A contract of marriage had in 1702 been entered into by Barbara Fea and Patrick Traill of Elsness in Sanday, who had been sent by his father to look after their Houseby estate in Stronsay. Patrick Traill was only about 18 years old when their child was born, and he insisted that he had been inveigled by Barbara into signing the contract against his will, whereas she insisted that he had begot her with child under promise of marriage. Patrick fled the county, but Barbara brought matters to a head by going to Houseby, and forcing her way into the house. After that, litigation was carried on for years with the Traill family, with varied success, until Patrick Traill died in 1724 and Barbara herself died in 1731. In 1766, at long last, grandchildren and great-grandchildren of the two unfortunate marriage partners reached a final settlement of the dispute.

Brothers from the Golgotha monastery.

It was Patrick Fea's eldest son James who brought the kelp industry to Orkney in 1721-2, not long after the first experiments had been made on the Scottish mainland. Stronsay quickly became an important supplier of kelp, a raw material for the production of iodine and potassium salts, so that 'to the eye of the passing mariner the smoke from the kilns distinguished Stronsay from the other islands, and gave it the appearance of an active volcano.' (Hossack, 1900). This development was watched with misgiving by the crofters, as they had nothing to gain from it, quite the opposite: they had to do the work, the lairds made the profits. Also, the crofters had been used to 'living off the ebb', catching limpets, cuithes and crabs on the shore for additional food.

In 1762 their patience came to an end. The initiative was taken by the tenants of Dinnatoun and Cleat who started what became known as the Kelp Riot. Helped by other angry crofters they went around the shores destroying the kelp and the kelp-making implements. In court they blamed the kelp industry for dying cattle, horse disease, bad harvests and lack of fish. They were found guilty and fined heavily. The kelp industry went on as before, until it collapsed almost overnight in 1832, when export prices fell drastically because supplies of barilla, a cheap Spanish substitute, became available. Remains of kelp pits and kelp-burning stances can be found even now at Grice Ness and Lamb Head.

The Feas seem to have had Jacobite interests, for at least two of them openly sided with the Stewarts in the 1745 rebellion. One was Patrick Fea of Airy, who for some time worked as a factor at the Bu of Burray for Sir James Steuart, known for his strong Jacobite sympathies. After the Battle of Culloden in 1746, Patrick Fea went into hiding in the caves along the shore from Airy whenever there was a risk of being found by the government troops. He had a narrow escape from drowning, when he miscalculated the rise of the tide. According to tradition he let a friend who helped him have the farm of Hescombe in gratitude. Later he farmed Stove in Sanday, and the diaries he kept of his life and work there in the years 1766-96 have become popular for the light they throw on island customs of the period.

James Fea, sixth of Clestrain, 1694-1756, is probably the best-known bearer of the family name. He was also the most ardent Jacobite of them all. After studying in Edinburgh he travelled in France and while there possibly acquired his political connections. In 1720 he married Janet Buchanan, the richest heiress in Orkney, when she was a child of 11 years or even younger. In that way he acquired the estate of Sound in Shapinsay as well as Carrick House in Eday. He became famous when he captured the pirate John Gow in 1725.

James Fea extended his political sympathies as far as inviting the Jacobites to recruit soldiers in Orkney, and probably he took part in the actual rising – at least he is known to have spent some days in the Prince's camp. After Culloden, James Fea went into hiding in Caithness, and later spent most of his time away from Orkney. He died without an heir, and his estates ultimately passed to Dr James Fea, third of Whitehall, who was then a surgeon in the Navy. He sold everything to Robert Laing, a wealthy merchant who was Provost of Kirkwall from 1788-92. Today there are no Feas or Traills in Stronsay.

There was a wealth of herring to be taken around the North Isles, and the protected waters of Papa Sound provided an excellent harbour. For centuries boats would come from far away for the herring fishing, which was centred in Strenzie. There were Scots, known as Fifers, coming up to fish, but Dutchmen especially came in large numbers. Dutch herring became sought after all over Europe for its quality and flavour. Their boats were known as 'busses' and 'doggers'. Their peak year was 1620, when Strenzie was known as 'Dogger Beach', and the revenue from Dutch landing rights in Stronsay amounted to as much as £800 a year. Patrick Fea built his new house at the head of the pier and called it Whitehall, and this became the name not only of the North Strenzie estate but also of the village that grew up around the fishing activities. When the Dutch no longer came, the herring fishing collapsed.

It was the Laing family who brought the herring boats back in force to the North Isles after they became owners of the estate and the village. In the words of Samuel Laing, 'I brought down six boats with their crews from Fifeshire... I fixed on Papa Sound in Stronsay for my Station for the following reasons; the harbour is good, safe, and of the easiest access to the sea of any in Orkney, as in ten minutes a boat is out at sea free from the tides and currents which are found among the Islands; the place at which the curing could be carried on belonged to my brother Malcolm, and at that time the opposite Island of Papa Stronsay belonged to my brother Gilbert.' For a long time the boats returned empty. 'One fine July morning, I think the 10th July 1816, I was sitting on the rocks in the grey of the morning watching the return of the boats. They appeared through my glass different from usual. I could not understand it. It never occurred to me that they were loaded. Loaded they were with herrings of the finest quality... The Orkney Herring Fishery was established'. (From Samuel Laing's unpublished papers.)

The new settlement became known as the Station. It was carefully planned, with new piers, storehouses, curing yards and cooperages, as well as accommodation for seasonal workers who stayed there throughout the summer fishing season. Among these were a large number of women engaged in gutting and salting. It is said that in the heyday of Whitehall the harbour would be so packed with boats that it was possible to walk dryshod from one deck to another across to Papa Stronsay. At that time the population of Stronsay numbered almost 1000; there were 18 inhabitants on Papa Stronsay and four in Auskerry. By the late 1930s the industry started to fail, then the war and changing fishing methods put an end to the Stronsay herring fishing. Whitehall, with its row of large, two-storeyed houses, remains a unique memorial to this part of island history.

Whitehall remains a unique memorial to the herring fishing.

Stronsay witnessed a fishing revival in the 1960s, now centred on whitefish, lobster and crab. The Stronsay Fish Processing Factory at Whitehall was established in 1981, and was supplied by a few boats based in the island, but it turned out to be a short-lived venture. Although the number of people living in Stronsay was more than halved in the last century, the island still holds its own. Stronsay is perhaps the most fertile of the North Isles and farms are large and well run. Although Orkney farming today is incredibly efficient, a dependable infrastructure in the island is still necessary and may create jobs. Farming has again become the important industry in Stronsay.

The Vat of Kirbuster, the finest natural arch in Orkney.

Westray

Westray is a world of its own, with an aura of self-reliance. Perhaps this is not so strange; the island has many natural advantages, although peat is not one of them, and shortage of fuel was always a problem. But Westray boasts the most varied scenery of the North Isles. Most of its western side is uncultivated, with a ridge of three distinctive hills running parallel to the cliffs, creating a spectacular nature area. All three hills are crowned with prehistoric mounds, which were probably burial markers. At 169 m, Fitty Hill is the highest of the three; the name derives from *viti* that like *varða* means a signal fire, and in Norse times this hill was an obvious location for a beacon. As part of the warning system it would, in time of danger, get fire signals from Wart Holm just south-west of Rapness, which again would be directly in line with Ward Hill in Eday. On a clear day it is possible to see much of Orkney, even glimpses of Shetland, and the Sutherland mountains, from the top of Fitty Hill.

Just north of the two groups of mounds known as Bloody Tuacks, in the saddle between Fitty and Gallo Hills, lies a small valley. In the olden days it was known as 'Doom's Da'. In his Orkney description Jo Ben tells of a legendary battle fought there between Westraymen and raiders from Lewis in the Hebrides. Then, 'being overcome in the battle, the invaders all perished together. One man, however, fought more bravely and fiercely after the others were all slain; having his hamstrings cut, he was brought to his knees when still engaged in the conflict.' The name Highlandman's Hamar is used for a large outcrop of rock just north of the Bloody Tuacks, and this is believed to be where the surviving hero fought in the final stage of the battle. The mounds are close together, and may be the graves of the two groups of people slain in the battle.

The north-west promontory of Noup Head, with its 104 m high North Hill, is now an RSPB nature reserve, with many kinds of birds breeding on the sandstone shelves. The cliffs here give room to an estimated 70,000 guillemots and 50,000 kittiwakes, making it one of the biggest cliff nurseries in Britain. The cliffs are high here, and wildfowling used to be much practised in the nineteenth century, when some even made a living from it. At that time there was a close connection between Westray and the Faroe Islands, and the Faroese method known as 'swapping' was used to catch the auk, or guillemot. It was claimed that in Westray one man alone could catch as many as 300 birds on a good day.

In his *Flora Orcadensis*, published in Kirkwall in 1914, the Orkney botanist Magnus Spence maintains that it was the Faroese who brought *Angelica archangelica* to Westray. It was quite a common plant in the Faroe Islands, and sailors would carry it with them on expeditions, as protection against scurvy. Another rare plant that thrives in Westray is the small *Primula scotica*, found only in northern Scotland. There is also a widespread distribution of the Orkney vole, or *Microtus arvalis orcadensis*, a distinct variety discovered as late as 1904 by J G Millay, and found only in Orkney.

Shipwrecks were common in Westray waters, and in the late nineteenth century the Noup Head Lighthouse was built on a magnificent vertical cliff, to warn passing ships of the dangerous North Shoal, at its foot. Fully automatic, the light switches on whenever the sun is absent, and is visible for some 20 nautical miles.

According to George Low, who travelled through the North Isles in 1778, Westray thrived on farming, 'the crops are good, and the soil well cultivated, the farm houses and Cottages by far the neatest I had yet observed in Orkney, with an air of cleanliness for which many of the other isles are not at all distinguished.'

The best land is found in the south of the island and also on its eastern seaboard. As in Sanday there are sandy bays and beaches, often flanked by level sandy ground known as 'links', and very difficult to cultivate. We learn in the rental of 1492 that skats were reduced that year, because much of the soil in the north end had been 'blawn till Birrowne' – blown to Bergen – while on the west side it was 'blawn till Issland'.

In one of these sandy areas, known as The Links of Noltland, an extensive prehistoric settlement was excavated in 1978-82, by Dr David Clarke of the National Museum of Antiquities of Scotland. The site was only partly excavated, and this village in the dunes may yet turn out to be many times the size of Skara Brae. The Grooved Ware pottery and other artefacts were roughly similar to finds made at the Neolithic houses of Skara Brae and Rinyo. A primitive plough had left furrows in the soil that could still be traced after five millennia; a number of deer skeletons were also found.

During work in the flagstone quarry at Pierowall in 1981 a strikingly decorated stone was discovered. It was over 1 m long and 20 cm thick, the fragment of a carved lintel stone, believed to be some 5000 years old, and today considered the most important example of prehistoric art in

Scotland. The stone came from a low mound at the corner of the quarry. A salvage excavation resulted in the recovery of the other half of the stone, as well as two smaller ones.

The site was occupied during two separate periods, the Neolithic and the early Iron Age. In the former period a large chambered cairn of the Maeshowe type was built, measuring some 18 m in diameter; the lintel stone probably marked the entrance passage to this tomb. It is now in the Tankerness House Museum. In the early Iron-Age period a large roundhouse with 3 m thick walls was built directly over the cairn.

The three stones uncovered in the cairn are all decorated with the same motif, a pair of 'spectacle'-linked spirals arranged back to back. This is a pattern not found anywhere else, although a stone discovered at Eday Manse has a close similarity. Still, it is true to say that in spite of the individuality of these decorated stones, they are part of the general tradition of Megalithic art in Britain and Ireland.

To the Norsemen, the harbour of Pierowall must have been irresistible: sheltered, spacious, with a sandy beach where nousts could easily be dug out for their shallow ships. They called it *Höfn*, meaning the harbour, as it would have been the best and perhaps the only real harbour for them in Orkney. Around the middle of the nineteenth century a number of Norse graves were excavated in the sand dunes between the village and the farm of Gill, mostly by eager amateurs. They left scanty if any reports, so that records are few and vague, but as many as 17 grave-finds seem accounted for. Unfortunately, many of the artefacts cannot be found, as they were sold at the auction of the Kirkwall Museum collection in the 1860s.

A number of the graves were of high status, and judging by descriptions of the artefacts found, some go right back to around 800, and so probably represent the first phase of settlement, while others belong to the later ninth century. An interesting feature is the coffin built of large stones unearthed in some of the graves. The cist-grave may mean that Pictish burial customs were adopted, but it may also signify that there were immigrants in Westray from northern Norway, where such stone cists were fairly common. A considerable Norse immigration into Westray at some point would perhaps explain why there is a certain blood group difference between Westray and Sanday. Of the two island populations, that of Westray shows a blood group pattern more similar to that of Scandinavia.

In describing the prominent families of Orkney in the early twelfth century the *Orkneyinga Saga* also mentions Westray. 'There was a farmer at Rapness on Westray called Kugi, a rich and intelligent man. There was a rich and dependable farmer called Helgi living at a certain hamlet which used to be there on Westray, and yet another farmer on Westray was Thorkel Flayer, a very able man, but overbearing. His sons were Thorstein and Haflidi, both unpopular men.'

We learn from the saga that in 1135 Kali Kolsson, soon to be Earl

Breeding birds on the cliffs at Noup Head.

Rognvald II, was waiting in Shetland for the right moment to launch his campaign in Orkney. The Shetlanders had already gone over to him. Then in April 1136 he invaded Orkney, landing first in Westray. He had bided his time till the spring tide coincided with an easterly wind, 'for in those conditions it is virtually impossible to go between Westray and Mainland, though with the wind easterly one can sail from Shetland to Westray'. He had already seen to it that the beacon system did not work.

The people of Westray accepted Earl Rognvald as their overlord, and he made use of the island as a base for a time. But one night his men became aware of a plot being hatched against Rognvald; they beat up some of the islanders and put shackles on Kugi, accusing him of being the party responsible. Kugi insisted he was innocent, and Rognvald recited to him this light-hearted verse, composed in his own whimsical style:

Bent-iron I see bound
about, night-beast, your
legs, locking them
from leaping away, Kugi:
keep your word, care,
Kugi, for your oath, don't
you dare hold more dark
councils, no more dodges.

All were spared by Rognvald and they again swore an oath of allegiance to him.

Kugi is much deferred to in the saga, and we learn that he hailed from the important farm of Rapness. This south-eastern peninsula was probably one of the pirate stronghold nesses that King Harald Fairhair seized and gave away to the first earl. Not surprisingly this was later the earl's bordland estate, a veizla farm known as the Bu of Rapness. The Point of Peterkirk, close by, indicates that the first Westray church may have been sited on the earl's estate. Earl Paul had entrusted Kugi with raising a levy in Westray, and it was with Kugi he planned to stay when he travelled around the North Isles collecting taxes. Altogether Kugi was in an unenviable position, as he owed allegiance to both earls.

The third chieftain of Westray, Thorkel Flayer, was a rich man who fought for Earl Paul in the Battle of Tankerness, on his own ship. He was burnt to death in Stronsay, and his son Haflidi seems to have become chieftain after his father. In time, he became one of Earl Rognvald's most trusted men. The saga does not tell us where in Westray he comes from, but his estate is believed to have been in the Westside, in the area now known as Tuquoy.

On the very edge of the sea, just west of the Bay of Tuquoy, lie the remains of the twelfth-century Cross Kirk. Its sophisticated chancel archway and lancet window were part of a church building that, according to the archaeologist Dr Raymond Lamb, was one of the most refined of Orkney's medieval churches. It was at first associated with the large, late Norse, settlement and may have been built by Haflidi Thorkelsson, but subsequently the nave was lengthened to make the building into a parish church. The coastline here suffers severe sea erosion, and in 1980 a site adjoining the church was found by Dr Lamb to contain massive stone buildings belonging to a major Norse settlement, among them the impressive remains of Haflidi's hall. The midden of a tenth-century farm has been revealed, but Haflidi's farm complex of the thirteenth century has yet to be discovered.

At some point the greater part of Tuquoy became kingsland. It is possible that Westray suffered some of the same fate as North Ronaldsay after the Battle of Florvåg in 1194. Probably much of the kingsland in Westray was at some point gifted to the church, as by the time of the Reformation the greater part of the land, as much as 68 per cent, belonged to the bishopric, whereas 29 per cent was bordland or kingsland, and only some 3 per cent was odal land. In June 1560, Bishop Bothwell gave all the bishopric land in Westray in feu to Gilbert Balfour and his wife.

On the slope above the Bay of Pierowall lies Noltland Castle, as dominating as ever after more than 400 years. It was built in the 1560s by Gilbert Balfour, a reckless adventurer who in many ways was both master and victim of the turbulent times he lived in.

Gilbert Balfour was one of six sons of the Laird of Monquhanny in Fife. With two of his brothers he took part in the assassination of Cardinal David Beaton in 1546, and was later a prisoner-of-war in Normandy, along with John Knox, who called the brothers 'men without God'. When Mary Queen of Scots returned to Scotland from France, Gilbert Balfour became her 'Maister Household'. He married the sister of Adam Bothwell, the last Catholic and first Protestant Bishop of Orkney, and thereby obtained the extensive bishopric lands of Westray. Balfour also received land in Birsay, Papa Westray and Faray. He became Sheriff of Orkney and Captain of Kirkwall Castle.

Gilbert Balfour was a central figure in the conspiracy to murder Queen Mary's husband, Lord Darnley. The placard which appeared after his death at the Tolbooth in Edinburgh, pointed to her third husband, James Hepburn, fourth Earl of Bothwell, as the murderer, but added, 'and if this be not true, spier at Gilbert Balfour'. In 1571, the Scottish Parliament found him guilty of treason.

Gilbert Balfour is next heard of in Sweden, as part of yet another conspiracy to royal murder. Considered too unstable to rule, Erik XIV Vasa had been deposed as king, and his younger brother, John III Vasa, took over, but tensions existed in court circles. A war was being waged with Russia, and some 3000 Scottish mercenaries were brought in, 'notorious both for ruthlessness and for savage bravery'. Gilbert Balfour

Curtains flap in the deserted community of Netherhouse.

was one of their leaders, and all sources agree that it was due to him that some of the Scottish officers were secretly persuaded to murder King John. Their testimonies, which still exist, are contradictory as to how the murder was to be executed, and the final signal to carry it out was never given. In time, the story got out, and the main characters were arrested. King John wanted to spare Balfour, but an attempt to escape from prison sealed his fate and he was executed in 1576.

In 1597 Earl Patrick Stewart arrived at Noltland Castle with 60 armed men, to seize it from Gilbert Balfour's heir, his nephew Michael, in payment of an alleged debt. When his protests were met with threats to hang him from the rooftree of the Castle, Michael Balfour decided to escape and put his complaint before the Privy Council. But Earl Patrick did things in style, and the magnificent staircase, unrivalled at the time, is said to have been added by him.

The wedding at Noltland Castle of Michael Balfour's daughter Ursilla to James Fea, third of Clestrain in Stronsay, has become an island legend. It was fixed for Martinmas in November of 1632, and guests were invited from all over the islands to celebrate the union of two well-known families. The bride's dress is part of the legend. Made of salmon-pink and green brocaded satin with an antique pattern, it was to become an heirloom worn by 11 successive Balfour brides.

November is normally a stormy month in Orkney, and not really the right time for an island wedding, as Michael Balfour found out to his cost. The wedding party lasted almost three months, until Candlemas in February, by which time the last bull was being served up, and the host said, 'Lord kens whit's to come neist, for we hae eaten the last o' the bull, stoop and roop, the day.' The next day the weather cleared sufficiently for the guests to leave, but Michael Balfour had to dispose of some of his land to buy new livestock, or so it is said.

The Balfours grew in numbers in Westray, most of them taking their title from Trenaby, the main farm of the Rackwick tunship. The name may derive from *þrándar-bær*, the farm of Throndr, and perhaps refer to an early land-take. In the summer of 1746 William Balfour of Trenaby, Archibald Stewart of Cleat, John Traill of Westness in Rousay, and John Traill of Elsness in Sanday, who had all been rash enough to sign an incriminating letter in support of the Jacobites, went into hiding in Westray.

The tales of their hiding in two local caves during the raids of the Hanoverian troops are a colourful part of Westray lore. One of the hiding-places, Gentlemen's Ha, is in a steep cliff-side just south of the Geo of Ginna Guan, on the east coast of Rapness, and when taking refuge in this cave, the fugitives were looked after by the people at the Bu of Rapness. Their other hiding place was The Gentlemen's Cave, just south of Noup Head. The cave cannot be seen from above, but can be reached from the Grip of Monivey, along a fairly broad ledge. At one point, known as the Snud, a part of the ledge is missing, and some climbing, or perhaps clambering, becomes necessary. This was a test of courage for the fugitive lairds, and remained so for Westray youngsters.

It seems the lairds did not stay long at any one time in the western cave, as in rough weather it could become a dangerous trap. Jerome Dennison, Walter Traill Dennison's grandfather, held the lease of Noltland at the time, and lived at the Castle. He saw to it that the tenants of Backaras looked after the lairds, and a skin bag used to bring them food was long preserved in the Dennison family. The government troops raided the Castle in the middle of the night, seeking the fugitives, and according to tradition the roof was pulled off the building as Dennison refused to tell them anything.

At the same time Trenaby and Cleat, the houses of the fugitive

Westray lairds, were burnt down by the troops. Their final place of refuge was Caithness, where they stayed on until the Indemnity Act of 1747 made it safe for them to come back to Orkney. Practically bankrupt, it took William Balfour some eight years to build a modest new house at Trenaby. His luck turned when Sir Lawrence Dundas bought the earldom estates of Orkney in 1766, and engaged Balfour as his factor, first in Shetland, where he introduced kelp making, and then in Orkney. In 1836, his eldest son, John Balfour, third of Trenaby, who had made a fortune abroad, endowed a Trust to fund the building of Balfour Hospital in Kirkwall.

The parish system came late to Orkney, as churches and chapels were privately owned and operated for some three centuries or more after Christianity became officially accepted in the islands in 995. But at some point in pre-Reformation days Westray was divided into the southern parish of the Holy Cross, with a church at Tuquoy, and the northern parish of St Mary, with a church popularly known as Lady Kirk, situated in Pierowall, right on the shore. Parts of Lady Kirk, today a roofless ruin, date back to the thirteenth century. The original version of it may have been built on the site of the older church where Earl Rognvald II attended a service on his first arrival in Westray.

As we have seen, in early Norse times the name of Pierowall was *Höfn*, meaning harbour. Perhaps the harbour as such became less important at some point, at any rate another Norse word, *vágr*, meaning a bay, came into regular use. In Orkney this word was shortened into 'wa', which map-makers assumed was short for wall. The area around the bay was a two-urisland tunship called Wa, so that the origin of the village name must simply be the Pier o' Wa, the pier of the bay.

In his report on the parish of Westray to the *Statistical Account of Orkney, 1795-1798*, the Revd James Izat writes, 'There are none in this parish who earn their bread by fishing.' Although there were quite a few people owning boats in the island, all the fish they caught would be consumed within their own families. This pattern would change during the nineteenth century, so that the name of Westray became almost synonymous with fishing and life at sea. The boats most used in the islands, both for transport and for fishing, were the Orkney yole and the Westray skiff, which were built to withstand the strong tides.

Most of the lore involved the sea. 'The Storm Witch of Westray' is the most colourful story of them all, and the insight it gives into the seventeenth century witch-hunt psychosis is scary. The very visual story begins in 1627, and it is well documented. In that year three young men set out for a sail and never returned. Some years later people stood on shore and watched a strange ship being tossed inexorably on to a sunken rock. No one lifted a finger to help. Then the young Janet Forsyth sprang into her father's boat. She performed the feat of getting on board the ship and bringing it safely to port. Her seamanship in all kinds of weather had already made people call her the 'Storm Witch'. The Westray people, furious at being cheated of a rich booty, charged Janet with witchcraft. Tried in St Magnus Cathedral, she was found guilty and sentenced to be burned at the stake. But the story of Janet Forsyth does not end on Gallow Hill. Her lost sweetheart, who had been picked up by a man-of-war and carried off to take part in the war against France, came home in the nick of time. He contrived to get her guards drunk, and the ship she had rescued took them away from Orkney. Understandably, she never came back.

Another Westray legend is that of the Dons, the survivors of a ship from the Spanish Armada of 1588 that foundered just off North Ronaldsay. They settled along the North Shore, adopted Westray surnames such as Hewison, Reid and Petrie, and though the first generation married local girls, the generations that followed were forbidden to do so, by their own people. The Balfours were also nicknamed 'the Dons', because of a marriage between a Hewison and a Balfour some time in the seventeenth century.

The Dons were known as colourful people and superior seamen. They were also notorious smugglers. In his paper 'Orkney Armada Traditions' which the folklorist Walter Traill Dennison read to the Orkney Natural History Society in 1889, he recounts the story of how a party of five or six Dons were taking a cargo of grain to Norway, when they were captured by a French privateer, taken to Shetland and dumped there. Given weapons by a Shetland laird, they boarded the French vessel while most of the crew were ashore. Later their victims, nine in number, were found floating in the harbour. One of their own men, Hugh Petrie, had drunk so much gin that he just lay there, insensible, and had to be left behind. The ship was seen to stand out of the harbour in full sail, to the horror of the remaining Frenchmen, but it ran into a storm on the way south, and the only Don who survived to tell the tale was Hugh Petrie, who ever since has been known as 'drunken Hugh'. He was an ancestor of Walter Traill Dennison.

The story of the Angels probably takes place in the 1730s, when a ship was wrecked off Aikerness during a storm. A small boy was the only survivor. A piece of wood was washed up from the vessel, bearing the name of the Russian port Archangel, and the child came to be known as Archie Angel. He was taken home and brought up by the islanders who

found him, the Rendalls of the now derelict croft of Seaquoys in Aikerness. The Angel surname died out in the 1930s but several Angel descendants still live in Orkney.

Westray has been prosperous in the years after the Second World War. Pierowall has long been a modern fishing centre, with a fish factory and freezing plant as well as a crab factory in operation since the late 1960s. Some 30 fulltime fishermen have worked out of Pierowall, which in fishing activity is second only to Stromness.

The island boasts two well-known hotels, where people come from Stromness and Kirkwall to get away from it all. One of them features in the *Taste of Scotland 1998*

Lobsters at Pierowall.

guide, as one of four Orkney establishments to have made the grade.

The nineteenth century was the era of large estates, the time of the 'rural multitude'. The Rapness estate, for example, had 30 crofts and operated a mill of its own. Today a large area, where many smaller farms may have been amalgamated, will be run by a farmer and his tractor, perhaps assisted by his family or hired help at harvest time. Thus paradoxically, Westray is back to the starting-point, with the difference that now the crofters are gone, and this time the 'clearances' have been effective and have met with few protests.

There has been growing concern at decline in the Westray population, and true to tradition, the Westray people faced the situation squarely, by holding a conference on the island's future in Pierowall in 1998. It was attended by some 400 people, and many topics were introduced and issues raised. If anyone can turn the tide, it is certainly the people of Westray with their determination and love for their close-knit community.

Knap of Howar, a well-preserved Neolithic farmstead.

Papa Westray

In Orkney the island is called simply Papay and that is how Papa Westray was known to the writer of the *Orkneyinga Saga* as well. To him it stood for the island of the priests, and he spelt it *Papey*. When describing the fall of Earl Rognvald Brusason in 1046, however, he needed to distinguish between two such priest islands, so he called the smaller one where Rognvald was killed, *Papey in lítla*, and the larger island where he was buried, *Papey in meiri*. The names of Papa Westray and Papa Stronsay are in fact fairly modern, and reflect the need of map-makers and bureaucrats to maintain a distinction, even today.

The Westray connection may have been very real in a remote past; it has been suggested that the two islands were once joined together. Ancient oyster shells turn up occasionally on the shore along Papa Sound, and indicate that here was perhaps at one time a sheltered bay where today there is a racing röst. It also seems probable that the Holm of Papa was at one stage merely a long and narrow promontory of the main island, and this need not have been so very long ago. Even now it is possible to wade across Holm Sound at an exceptionally low tide.

Such radical change in the landscape would demonstrate better than anything how exposed the island is to the onslaught of nature; even its cliffs are heavily eroded. In the lee of the wind in one of the sandy bays, on a fine summer day, the island seems peaceful, a place of fertile, pastoral beauty. Yet even then the tidal race of the Bore roars tempestuously past the northern cliffs. It can be dangerous; in fact, when three men of the Harcus family from Westray were out fishing for saithe in 1858, they were sucked into the Bore and drowned.

The northern part of Papay is hilly and heathery, and a haven for birds. It is common grazing land and today is known as The North Hill RSPB Reserve, with a warden available in the summer months. It is one of the main nesting areas of the 'pickie' or Arctic Tern, *Sterna paradisea*, a long-range migrant that each year makes a round trip of thousands of miles to spend winters on the northern fringes of the Antarctic pack ice. In some years as many as 6000 pairs have been observed on North Hill in their nesting period, between mid May and late July, but lately the numbers have been down to about 3000 pairs.

Numerous other birds nest on the Hill, and the walk along the crags is therefore popular with birdwatchers. The bombing bonxie, or great skua, *Catharacta skua*, sees to it that no walkers stray from the path allotted to them. The aggressive skua not only keeps the tourists at bay but also threatens other birds by chasing their chicks. Storm petrels breed on the Holm of Papa, where there is also a large colony of black guillemots. The fields of Papay are home to curlew, snipe and lark.

A small memorial at Fowl Craig reminds us of the fate of the great auk, *Pinguinus impennis*, a relative of the razorbill and the puffin, or 'cooter-neb' and 'tammie-norrie', as they are still called in parts of Orkney. Flightless, but a great swimmer, the great auk or gare-fowl moved clumsily on land and fell easy prey to unrestrained hunting. According to tradition, a pair known as the king and queen of the Auks nested in the cliffs of Fowl Craig. The female died first, and the male, probably the last of its kind in Britain, was shot in 1813. The species became extinct in 1844 when the last great auk was killed in Iceland.

The vegetation of the Hill area is dwarf shrub heath, rich in herbs, of a kind that grows only on Old Red Sandstone. It provides a good habitat for the Scottish primrose, *Primula scotica*, and we find several colonies of this rare plant on the Hill as well as on the links of Moclett in the southern part of the island. This tiny plant has amethyst-coloured flowers with a pale yellow centre, and is found only in the northernmost parts of Scotland, so anybody caught picking it in Orkney will have a lot of explaining to do! There is on the whole a rich variety of habitats in Papay, and as many as 230 different species of plants grow there.

The fertile land and the bird-rich northern cliffs must have been attractive to settlers, as the island was inhabited from a very early date. In fact, Papay has the oldest standing houses in northern Europe. On the west side, facing Papa Sound, lies the Knap of Howar, a well-preserved Neolithic farmstead. A thick blanket of windblown sand covered it. Radiocarbon dating of midden deposits has suggested that the site was in use for some 500 years, probably from about 3600 to about 3100 BC. As the walls have a core of midden deriving from an even earlier period, people must have occupied the site before the houses were built. When lived in, the farm was well inland, as the topography was different in Neolithic times. The masonry is of a very high quality, and the walls are still preserved virtually to roof-level. These houses were obviously built to last. The climate must have been milder and drier in the fourth millennium, allowing wheat to be cultivated.

That there must have been an earlier experimental stage seems natural enough, as these houses seem curiously modern and homelike. They are completely different from the buildings of Skara Brae, as they are rectangular in shape and divided into rooms by crosswise walls. William Traill, the then Laird of Holland, and his friend William Kirkness, who first excavated the farm, realised that all the evidence pointed to a Neolithic date for the site, and were exasperated by the scepticism they met with. Charles Calder surveyed the farm in 1934, and it was then re-excavated in the 1970s by Dr Anna Ritchie, who found among the artefacts the rubber lost there by Calder.

The Knap of Howar site gives valuable knowledge of life in Neolithic times, long before the building of the pyramids. It was probably the home of one family who were self-sufficient in most ways, using the smaller of the two houses as a workshop and storage area, and the larger one for sleeping and cooking. They also made their own pottery, of the kind known as the Unston type, and so far Knap of Howar is the only Unston Ware settlement discovered in Orkney. This type of pottery has otherwise been found only in the chambered tombs known as stalled cairns, and was long believed to be a funerary ware.

The chambered tombs on the Holm of Papa may have been built by

St Boniface's Church.

the farmers at Knap of Howar or by their descendants; the effort put into the construction of the tombs indicates the importance of the dead in Neolithic times. At the same time the tombs are well away from the fertile land. On the whole it seems obvious that it would take a highly organised population to complete construction work of such size and complexity. Knap of Howar is the only settlement site so far discovered on the island, but others may still lie under sand blow.

At the north end of the island we find a stalled cairn that has many features in common with the houses at Knap of Howar. Anna Ritchie excavated it in the 1980s. On a slight rise at the opposite end of the island is a huge cairn, the largest tomb found so far of a Maeshowe design. Known as 'The Disses of the Holm', it was first examined in the winter of 1849 by Captain Thomas, who discovered no human remains or ancient material. The tomb consists of a very long chamber with as many as 12 side cells, still intact. The lintels above the entrances to the cells are decorated with unique carvings.

In the crumbling cliff face below the ancient St Boniface's Church, on the west side of Papay, extensive stone structures interspersed with middens have long been visible. The stonework formed an archaeological layer nearly 3 m high and covering a large area of ground. It was believed to be a broch-type settlement. The name Munkerhoose, from the Norse *munkarhús*, a house for monks, was used for the area alternatively with Binnas Kirk, from *bænahús*, a prayer-house or chapel, but the latter name was also used specifically for a grass-covered mound just north of the site.

A fulmar chick.

A limited-scale excavation took place on this site in 1990, and remains of buildings dating from the early Iron Age to the Middle Ages were discovered, a broch among them. The site may originally have covered about four hectares, and would have been further inland than now, but coastal erosion is fierce, and every trace of the broch is already gone. Two incised cross-slabs of the eighth century have been found in the churchyard. The small twelfth-century church is dedicated to St Boniface, as was the eighth-century church before it.

St Boniface (*c.* 675-754) became known as the 'Apostle of Germany' who cut down the sacred oak of the god Thor and with the timber built a church dedicated to St Peter. Originally given the name of Wynfrid, he became a Benedictine monk in his native Wessex, but obtained from Pope Gregory II the authority to evangelise Germany, provided he used the Roman, rather than the Celtic formula of baptism. The ceremony he performed to anoint Pepin the Short, father of Charlemagne, became the prototype of royal coronations. He brought the whole missionary movement under Rome, but was killed by pagan Frisians on Pentecost Sunday, while he was walking towards them, reading the Scriptures.

Perhaps the first church on the site was built at about the time the news came of St Boniface's death as a martyr. Papay was an important Christian centre in late Pictish times; it may also have been the site of Orkney's first bishopric. Around the year 840, when quite a young man, the Irish St Findan was captured by Vikings, but he managed to escape from them during a stopover in Orkney, probably in South Wick, between Papay and the Holm. He made it ashore and met men who came to his aid and took him to a bishop whose seat was nearby. St Findan stayed with him for two years. Norwegian sources also mention an early bishop in Orkney.

Surrounded by some of the best farming land in Papay is the Loch of St Tredwell. On a small holm that today is connected to the shore, are the remains of St Tredwell's Chapel, also built on a broch site. There used to be a path known as Messigate – the road to church – leading from the chapel down to the Bay of Burland. Boats must have come here through the centuries, bringing in visitors to the chapel from all over the islands.

St Tredwell, whose Latin name was Triduana, was known to the Norsemen as *Trollhæna*. She was a Scottish saint who is surrounded by shadowy legend. According to one version she awakened the passion of King Nechtan of the Picts, who sent messengers to tell her how much he admired the beauty of her eyes. She then committed the astonishing act of tearing out her eyes, and skewering them on a twig for the messengers to take back to the King. Perhaps this was not such a senseless action on her part after all: she realised that this was her only chance of securing her personal freedom.

It is not clear what St Tredwell's connection with Papay was, but there has been some belief that she was buried there, and during an excavation towards the end of the nineteenth century, the skeleton of a woman was actually found on the site. She became associated with eyesight, and the blind and sufferers from eye afflictions came on pilgrimage from near and far. We read in the *Orkneyinga Saga* that in 1201 Earl Harald Maddadarson took Bishop Jon of Caithness captive near the stronghold at Scrabster and had his tongue cut out and a knife driven into his eyes.

> 'Bishop Jon kept praying to the holy virgin St Tredwell, and
> when they set him free he went over to a hillside where he
> asked a woman to help him. She could see the blood
> streaming from his face.
> 'Quiet, my lord', she said, 'I'll help you gladly'.
> The bishop was taken to where St Tredwell rests, and there
> he was restored to health both in speech and sight.'

For a long time people kept on coming to the site, and in the *New Statistical Account* of 1842 the Revd John Armit has this to say about the chapel, 'Such was the veneration entertained by the inhabitants for this ancient saint, that it was with difficulty that the first Presbyterian minister of the parish could restrain them, of a Sunday morning, from paying their devotions at this ruin, previous to their attendance on public worship in the reformed church.'

The whole island must have been considered a church estate by the Norsemen, as they called it Papey. The same name was given to islands in Shetland, as well as to Papa Stronsay, and the Norsemen seem to have left them alone for some time, as no pagan graves have yet been found on them. Thus at the time of St Findan's stay with the bishop, Orkney may already have been a Norse territory.

The placename pattern is unusual, and supports the idea that there was no early Norse takeover in Papay. As Dr Hugh Marwick points out, there are no names ending in -garth, -ston, -by or -bister. Nor do we find any name derived from *varða* or *viti*, for beacon. No tradition of a beacon is remembered, and this may be quite simply because there never was one. The island may not have been strategically placed, or as a religious community it might even have been exempt from beacon duties.

Probably Norse settlement was late in coming, although the farm Holland points to the island being part of the earl's administrative system from at least the early eleventh century. Holland lies in the centre of a fertile agricultural area, with easy access to a landing place for boats. The placenames of Nouster and Skennist also point in this direction. Nouster derives from *naustar*, the plural form of *naust*, which means a boatshed or a berth for a boat on the beach. In Orkney it mostly refers to the latter. At Skennist we still find a row of seven boat nousts. The name Skennist itself is very suggestive, as it derives from *skeiða-naust*, *skeið* meaning a large warship, a fast-sailing longship.

The sanctity of Papay may have continued well into Norse times, and the fact that the body of Earl Rognvald Brusason, who was slain in Papa Stronsay in 1046, was brought to Papay for burial, supports this view. The probable site of his burial was the Church of St Boniface, where the Norse hogback stone, which can still be seen there, may have been a marker to his grave. Today nobody knows where this was.

The Church of St Boniface is the smallest parish church in Orkney, and apart from St Magnus Cathedral it is the only church that survived the Reformation. Nothing more is heard of Munkerhoose, but it may well be that the monks in Westray who were made fun of by Earl Rognvald II in one of his tongue-in-cheek verses, came from neighbouring Papay. The Earl and his men had attended mass in the village then known as *Höfn*, and were standing outside the church, when they saw 'sixteen men, unarmed and with shaven heads, walking by', and

Primula scotica.

wondered who they could be. Then the Earl composed this verse:

> Sixteen I've seen
> stepping together; shaved
> their foreheads, no fur
> growth on their faces.
> We bear witness,
> west on this windswept isle,
> many a proud maid
> parades here, poll-pared.

As in Sanday and North Ronaldsay there are traces of the old system of building on mounds, and the farm of Mayback is built on such a site. There is also a treb-dyke, known as Gairsty, which divides the island into two parts, with roughly the same agricultural value, so that each of them was skatted as two urislands. The two parts are known today as North Yard and South Yard, but in the three early rentals they were called Benorth the Zarde and Besouth the Zarde. The best land is found west of the Loch of St Tredwell.

According to the early rentals, from around 1500, more than half the land at that time belonged to king or earl, while as much as 40 per cent was odal land. Some six per cent was bishopric land; Mayback being the only farm known to have been part of this property. But at the time between a third and a quarter of the land was no longer arable, because it was 'blawin with wattir and sand'. In 1601 there still remained 16 small blocks of odal property, belonging to 14 owners. Of these, the Leasks and the Hewisons had owned their land for a long time.

The first Traill in Orkney was Earl Patrick Stewart's chamberlain, who originally came from Fife. His son Thomas fought on the side of the Swedish King Gustavus Adolphus in the Thirty Years War. He did well, and bought the farm of Holland in Papay in 1636. One by one, the other farms on the island became part of the Holland estate, until in 1820 the Traills owned the entire island, and for seven generations from then on, a Traill named Thomas or George followed the other as laird, until

The Farm of Holland.

Thomas Traill, seventh of Holland, was bankrupted in 1886. Most of the tenants bought their farms in 1924 and became owner-occupiers. The home farm with the main estate buildings was bought back from the trustees in 1928 by a Traill heir, only to be finally sold in 1952. Today none of the Traill family, once so numerous, are left in Orkney.

There were advantages in running a business like kelp production on an estate-owned island, and the Traills did well during the kelp boom; in the early nineteenth century Papay produced 80 tons a year. The Traills then built a new main house, close to the buildings of the home farm, instead of the old mansion house, which stood in a more exposed position. Holland Farm is one of the most interesting traditional steadings in Orkney, featuring both a horse-engine house and a corn-drying kiln.

The Traills acquired a reputation as bad landlords. Thomas, third of Holland, was known as 'the Wicked Laird', and was believed to be in league with the devil. He fell out with the minister, threatening him with physical violence and forcing him to land on the rocks by the 'Minister's Flag', forbidding him to walk on his land. This meant the minister had to walk an extra three kilometres each way every time he came to St Boniface. And George, sixth of Holland, was indeed such a devil with the girls that he was called 'the Parish Bull'. But Thomas, seventh of Holland, did much to improve the land: it was squared, artificial drainage and crop rotation were introduced, and the economy changed from subsistence agriculture to cattle rearing.

Whereas close on 400 people lived on Papay in the nineteenth century, today there are fewer than 100. But the inhabitants have a strong community feeling, and every summer there is a communal outing to the Holm of Papa for the clipping of the sheep, with every family getting a 'sheepie' for the freezer. The Papay people have also worked actively to preserve their way of life and halt the drift away from the island. In 1978 the cooperative scheme they set up was the first in Orkney. But there were crises coming. Because of the drop in population there would no longer be a resident doctor; the health service is not obliged to provide a doctor if the population is below a certain level.

On the bright side, the new transport services made it possible to go across to Westray for medical aid. The air service between Papay and Westray has earned fame as the world's shortest scheduled flight; officially it takes two minutes, but it can be done in an even shorter time.

Another setback was that the old shop at Backaskaill was closing down, and it was crucial to replace it. The local shop was more than just a place to get provisions, it was a social centre for meeting one's neighbours and exchanging news, and it was necessary to carry on this tradition. The Community Cooperative acquired six farm workers' cottages from Holland, and started the work of converting them. Papay Community Shop was opened in 1980, followed by a youth hostel and a small hotel, all run by a committee of islanders. So there is never a dull moment! And where else would you find a notice on the bulletin board asking customers 'A sum of money found in a ditch. Is it yours?'

Eday

The striking shape of Eday bears out its Norse name of *Eiðey*, the isthmus island. Eday's middle part is only some 400 m wide, even less when the Loch of Doomy on its western side is left out of the reckoning. Consequently only a low, exposed area keeps Eday from becoming two islands. The name is therefore apt, and shows the down-to-earth quality of Norse name giving; placenames were oral maps to help the traveller. In the case of the neighbouring Calf of Eday the name sounds more whimsical, but it is in fact a standard type of name often given to a small island lying beside a larger one; it has many parallels along the Norwegian coast.

Visitors who fly to Eday will be amazed to find they have landed at London Airport, right on the isthmus, in what was until recently the sheep run of the farm of Skaill. The present name is only indirectly the work of the Norsemen, as their name for the area was *Lundinn*, the small wood. Remains of trees have been found in the Sands of Mussetter, close by.

The isthmus is the only exception to Eday's upland character, and from afar the island looks like one long, dark, heath-covered hill. A walk through the hill country of the north end is a striking experience – in the distance is the contrast of green Sanday land, but of Eday nothing but heath and peat moss is visible. More than a century ago the Red Head area was the home of the white-tailed sea eagle, or erne, as it is known locally, but intense egg-collecting drove it away. A beautifully made stone dyke runs the length of the ness, and, looking rather like a mini version of the Great Wall of China, it offers the only relief to the dark monotony.

Another boundary wall, the prehistoric treb dyke, runs along the edge of Noup Hill and is also visible in other places, indicating that more traces of a Neolithic culture may still be hidden under the heath. The building of this type of dyke required a special technique and when in use the dyke must have been fairly high. Heavy slabs would be set on edge in two parallel rows and the space in-between filled with small stones. The dyke was then topped with larger stones.

It is not surprising then that not only this northern part of Eday itself, but also the Calf of Eday, are of particular interest from an archaeological point of view, with a time scale through the third and second millennia BC. On Muckle Hill of Linkataing there may be a

The red and grey heads of Eday and the Calf of Eday.

complex of prehistoric houses under the peat, as cists, pavements and lines of wall have been exposed by peat-cutting. On the southern slope of Vinquoy Hill we find a chambered cairn of the Maeshowe type. The tall impressive Stone of Setter seems somehow to act as a marker of Neolithic territory, but the monolith is actually about a millennium younger!

The cluster of prehistoric sites on the south side of the Calf of Eday provides invaluable insight into the history of the area. It was excavated over three seasons in the 1930s by Charles Calder, who found a long stalled tomb from the early Unston period, that is from the fourth millennium BC. There are two other tombs in the vicinity. The settlement expanded through the Bronze Age and seems to have been at its greatest in the second millennium BC, when as many as 20 families may have lived there.

Farther up the slope the Iron-Age people built their roundhouses. In one of them a large quantity of pottery was found. Mixed farming is indicated by the remains of sheep, cattle and deer, as well as the fact that bere was grown with the help of a small plough known as an ard. As wood was scarce in Orkney, ards were made of stone, and many have been found in the Calf settlement. But conditions became so bad that the last inhabitants left some time in the early Iron Age, probably around 2000 years ago.

What happened to make the peat cover the Eday hills like a brown carpet? Peat seems to form naturally as a surface blanket on uplands where summers are moist and cool, especially in stony, acid soils like that of Eday. Thus the growth of peat was probably caused mostly by the climate changes of the Bronze Age, but bad husbandry in the form of unsuitable farming practices would have hastened the process, turning the land into wasteland. Some years ago two Eday men cutting peat in the Cusbay area found two pots, believed to have been made in the later part of the Iron Age, that is in the early centuries AD. They were discovered in a peat bed 1.5 m thick, some 30 cm from the bottom, which probably makes the peat bed some 2000 years old. A simpler way of finding out the age of the Eday peat is of course to have it carbon dated!

After the coming of the peat, centuries of island history are unknown. Eday is the only Orkney island of some size to be without a ruined broch; perhaps there was no fertile land to protect, nor people to build one. The island is not mentioned in the *Orkneyinga Saga*, nor in the early rentals. The placenames are mainly Norse, but they are not of an early settlement origin and they do not give much away. An interesting exception is Veness, the Norse word *vé* meaning a holy place and a sacrificial site. If the name refers to Norse practices, it would point to an early land-taking in this south-eastern part of Eday.

A large mound known as the Castle of Stackel Brae on the south shore has been considered the possible site of a chieftain's stronghold. As it has not been excavated, this must remain guesswork. But it is probable that in Eday the central, administrative farm of the earl would from an early date have been Holland. In the troubled Stewart times Holland was the centre of dramatic events. Today this farm is called by the venerable name of Skaill, from the Norse *skáli*, a designation often given to a large hall used for festive occasions. This is also the site of the old parish church, built close to the sea. Nearby is a mound that is possibly a Viking grave. In fairly recent times Skaill was the residence of the Eday estate's factor.

According to local tradition, the red sandstone used for the building of St Magnus Cathedral came from Eday. The stone was taken off the shore at Whithebeir on the east side, just north of Bay of London. There are numerous other quarries around the island, the best-known being at Fersness on the Westside. This has yielded an excellent light-brown building stone that is believed to have been used for the doorways of the cathedral.

Early records show that Eday paid its rentals in butter and meat, and not in corn, which was the common payment in Orkney. Jo Ben in 1529 comments on the abundance of cattle in the island, but says of farmers that 'scarcely one is there now'. But whether this was true or not, in the years to come the island was sought after, fought over, and changed owners several times.

In the mid sixteenth century the island seems to have been part of the estate of the Bishop of Orkney. In 1560 Bishop Adam Bothwell gave it in feu to his stepfather who then sublet it to his nephew Edward Sinclair. The island was probably only wadset to the Bishop, as according to tradition it was odal land belonging to the Peirson family, and in the most villainous fashion, so the story goes, Edward Sinclair seduced the daughter of the family and obtained the title deeds from her. In the event, with six leading Orkney men arbitrating, in 1564 the island of Eday passed from Peirson hands into Sinclair power. In that same year Robert Stewart was given the Crown estates in Orkney by his sister, Mary Queen of Scots.

The controversy between Earl Patrick Stewart and the Sinclairs of Holland drew Eday into history with a vengeance, as it helped bring about the downfall of Stewart rule in Orkney. In 1604, when Edward Sinclair was close to 100 years old, his son William complained to the Privy Council that the Earl's men had on two occasions invaded his land, thrown him out of Holland and removed the furniture. They had also worked the Fersness quarry, taking out stone for building purposes worth an astonishing £200,000. Probably the lovely, hard Eday freestone was the prime reason; the Earl needed it for his building projects, Scalloway Castle in Shetland and the Earl's Palace in Kirkwall. Both were built by forced labour, and Earl Patrick probably would not or could not pay for the stone either. Earl Patrick, on the other hand, insisted that Edward, 'that auld, decrepit man', feared his son William, and for that reason he had sold all his lands in Eday and elsewhere to the Earl for protection. Whatever the truth of this, the Court of Session in 1609 found in the son's favour. It was during this feud that the house of Holland was wrecked. Today the Old Manse stands on the former

Holland site, built probably of the old stone, as there is no trace of the Holland house.

By 1632 there were Stewarts in Eday after all, as the whole island was then conveyed to Earl Patrick's brother, John, by King Charles I. He was also made the Earl of Carrick, a title which died with him. In younger days he was charged with plotting his brother's death by consulting with Alison Balfour of Stenness, 'ane Wich, for the distructioune of Patrik Erll of Orknay, be poysoning.' Under torture of herself and her family, she confessed to witchcraft, but later retracted her confession. Regardless, she was burnt at the stake. The Earl of Carrick, on the other hand, was acquitted.

The Earl saw the possibilities of Calf Sound, and built a house on what is now known as the Bay of Carrick. His plan was to establish a port there, with a weekly market and two annual fairs, St Peter's on 11 June and St Bride's on 5 October. King Charles awarded the village the status of a Burgh of Barony. On the Calf of Eday the Earl had saltworks built, and the well-preserved remains of two buildings can still be seen there along the southern shore. The salt was used for the fish industry that grew up around Calf Sound, but as there was a heavy tax on salt in the seventeenth century, it could also be sold at a good profit.

As the Earl had no lawful issue, his estate was sold to Sir John Buchanan, who was Sheriff of Orkney. In the early eighteenth century the island, with 'houses, biggins, yards, crofts, town maills, quoys, quoylands, outbrecks, outsetts, annexis, connexis, parts, pendicles, and pertinents,' became the property of Janet Buchanan of Sound, Orkney's richest heiress, who in 1720, at 11 years of age, was married to James Fea of Clestrain. Carrick House was one of their many residences. Because his wife was not feeling well, James Fea was staying with her at Carrick House at the time when John Gow, the Orkney pirate, made a dramatic appearance on board the *Revenge* in 1725.

What Gow had in mind is not clear, but he may have felt that he had an account to settle with James Fea, who was an old schoolmate of his. He had not reckoned with the difficult drifts and eddies of Calf Sound, and his ship ran aground at the Graand on the Calf. Arrogantly he sent a letter to Fea, asking for his assistance in getting afloat again. But Fea cleverly outmanoeuvred him, and the Captain Kidd of Orkney ended up on the London gallows. James Fea found his fame as a pirate-catcher a mixed blessing; although he received some prize-money, he came close to bankruptcy because of all the strange lawsuits trumped up against him.

Some felt that James Fea had been too clever, perhaps even treacherous, in his dealings with Gow. In his return letter to Gow he wrote: 'you shall not want my assistance as far as honour can allow me. No more but that I am your old school comrade, James Fea.'

For some time Eday had more than one owner. Then in 1824 the whole island was acquired by Samuel Laing of Papdale, who had to sell it because of financial difficulties. It was bought by Robert James Hebden, an Englishman, in 1853. He is remembered as being influenced by the temperance movement and therefore making Eday dry, at least officially. This song was written in celebration:

> Ye sons of Eday, stout and strong,
> Come join with me the joyful song,
> And swell the chorus loud and long –
> We have no public houses.
>
> No dram-shop stands upon our shore,
> The drunkard's voice is heard no more,
> Where all was grief and woe before -
> We have no public houses.

Hebden was interested in large-scale sheep farming, and introduced Cheviot sheep, for which land was cleared: four crofts in the south-west, along with the farm of Mussetter and six crofts in the London area. On the other hand, a group of people who had been cleared from North Ronaldsay at about the same time, because of its overpopulation, found crofts in the Cusbay area. About this time Eday had reached its peak population: the 1851 census shows 947 people in 220 households, occupying 177 houses.

Today overpopulation is, however, no longer a problem! The 1951 census showed 198 people, and the decline has continued. Apart from present-day population trends everywhere, there are many reasons for this that are inherent to Eday. At the time of the 1851 census, agriculture was only one of Eday's work possibilities, employing 44 men fulltime. The island then had 19 lobster boats, each with two men, and with Westray it was a centre of cod and ling fishing. As many as 79 men worked as fulltime fishermen, another 42 combined farming and fishing. Some had other occupations; there were seven tailors and six shoemakers. Job possibilities existed for women too; there were as many as 21 dressmakers.

Some cash income also came from more seasonal work, such as kelp burning. Peat has been cut for centuries. The work was mostly a communal summer task, which was important both economically and socially – it called for the brewing of a barrel of special ale! The neighbouring islands of Sanday and North Ronaldsay were for a long time completely dependent on Eday peat for fuel. As early as 1597 Sanday was trading grain for 'Peitts, a kinde of black Mosse'. As the Eday peat is of a good quality it has also been exported to whisky distilleries on the Scottish mainland, such

Rock formations at Sands of Mussetter.

as Glen Morangie at Tain. But today the characteristic peat banks are few and far between.

At the time of the 1861 census there were some 170 small crofts on the island. Just after the First World War the proprietor started selling the crofts to the tenants. Today the holdings are all privately owned, but few of them belong to the original families. Although many of them have been amalgamated, and much of the hill-land of the common has become available for summer grazing, it is still difficult to run a croft without an extra income. With the exception of the farm of Fersness, the land on the west coast of Eday is still divided up into smallholdings. The low-lying eastern side is more fertile, and supports several fair-sized farms. The two large farms on the island, Carrick in the north and Greentoft in the far south, make up the Eday estate, which still belongs to the family of the last Laird of Eday.

'Man is getting to be the endangered species on Eday' was the immediate reaction on the island when it became known in the early 1980s that the Nature Conservancy Council had designated three separate sites on Eday as Sites of Special Scientific Interest. These were Calf of Eday, the Mill Loch and the Doomy-Whitemaw Hill area. The Calf of Eday is famed for its breeding birds, with reputedly more than 30 different species. A large colony of cormorants has nested there for a long time, and the islanders have given them the nickname of 'scarfs'. The island is now a sheep walk where some 450 Shetland ewes run more or less wild. But if visitors are not welcome there during the lambing season, it is also because the fledgling cormorants cannot fly, and can easily fall off the cliffs when disturbed.

The Mill Loch site supports a colony of red-throated divers. Eight pairs usually breed here, and this site is believed to have the densest concentration of this species anywhere in Britain. It is known in Orkney as the 'rain goose'; an old Norn name for it is the loom. The heather moorland of the Doomy-Whitemaw Hill site is home for some eight pairs of whimbrel. This is usually their only habitat in Orkney; of the 150 pairs existing in Britain, the greater part prefer to nest in Shetland. There was strong opposition to the designation of the third site, as it was believed to prohibit the use of the land for agriculture in a large area.

Many speak of Eday as 'the forgotten island'. That is as may be, it is certainly a very lovely and interesting place. Although no great distance separates the east from the west, both sides remain different worlds. The hill country is another world again, with ever-changing views of the surrounding North Isles. For the walker, the birdwatcher, and the nature lover, there are unique experiences.

Faray

Faray and the Holm of Faray are empty today. The Holm has heather moor and was used for grazing; it is connected with Faray by a rock path. The coast around the low-lying islands is a stretch of spectacular stacks, geos, caves and arches, with a foreshore full of jagged outcrops.

Faray is also known as North Faray, as there is a Fara, or South Faray, in Scapa Flow. The Norse form of the name is *Færey*, the sheep island. The name of the Faroe Islands derives from the Norse plural form, *Færeyjar*.

Faray is not mentioned in the *Orkneyinga Saga*, but is known to have formed part of the bishopric estate, before it became the property of the Balfour estate in Westray in the late sixteenth century. Today Faray is owned by the Stewart Mortification for Religious Purposes, which belongs to the Church of Scotland, and is managed by their trustees.

Faray was once a flourishing little island which in 1851 had a population of 69 people. There were eight farms; the largest being Holland which was one of the old earldom farms. The farming land is good, and even Jo Ben was pleased with the island on his visit in 1529. It is 'very convenient for cattle, especially cows, which graze there on the bushes with great satisfaction and the boys sing to the cattle. The whole island is full of corn and fish.'

The wide, straight road that runs the length of Faray, was once metalled, running past well-built houses that are now derelict. It is said that Faray folk were once given the choice of a road or a pier by the County Council, and mistakenly chose the road, and isolation. Perhaps the island was always too small to carry a resident population in a modern society. In 1946 the small school was closed and the homes left empty, when everyone left. Many of the inhabitants settled in Westray.

Since 1972 the island has been used for sheep and cattle by two Westray farmers who work from home, crossing by boat from Rapness. In the 1980s they decided to bring Highland deer to Orkney and try keeping them on Faray. The deer evidently found out they did not like it there, so the stag and two of the hinds struck out for Eday. It is a hard swim and one of the hinds did not make it. The other two were captured and brought back to Faray. Apparently they made the others want to see more of the world, as several hinds subsequently swam to Eday and from there to the Green Holms.

Guarding the entrance to Elwick Bay, the 17th-century Dishan Tower.

Shapinsay

The meaning of the name Shapinsay remains a mystery, in spite of the many fanciful attempts to explain it over the years. The island has a central position in Orkney, and only the narrow stretch of water known as The String separates it from the adjoining Mainland parish of St Ola; here the point closest to Shapinsay is Car Ness. The name probably derives from Old Norse *kallaðar-nes*, the calling ness, the place to call for a boat to come from the other side. And on the Shapinsay side the name of Setter Noust indicates where the boats came from. Many of the travellers would cross Shapinsay to find another boat, from the Noust of Erraby or Ferry Geo, for Eday or Stronsay. Nowadays the island is often considered a suburb of Kirkwall, as the distance is short and the ferry connection is good.

The small island of Helliar Holm makes Elwick a very protected bay, an ideal anchorage, usually without fog. At very low tide Helliar Holm is almost joined to Shapinsay by the natural causeway known as the Riff, but the channel of Holm Sound crosses it and effectively prevents any attempt to walk across. This may not have been so when the island was inhabited in the not too distant past. There are remains of a broch and a cairn on Helliar Holm. According to tradition there may have been a monastery at one stage, and Kirk Geo indicates the presence of a church. The island is shown as Eller Holm on Mackenzie's Chart of 1750.

Shapinsay is mostly low-lying, with gentle slopes. The south-eastern part, known as the east hill or the Craig, is still mostly uncultivated moorland. In the olden days peats were cut here. Today it is a place in which to roam, both for people and birds, as it is blessedly free of barbed wire. According to an old story, the coast here was once struck by a tidal wave which swept as far as the meadows of Harroldsgarth.

A striking feature of the Shapinsay landscape is the three storm beaches or ayres, from the Norse word *aurr*, for gravel. In Veantrow Bay we find Lairo Water shut off from the sea by a narrow ayre, and the tidal loch of the Ouse, which is still partly open. On the west coast The Ayre of Vasa, jutting into the sea as Vasa Point, forms the Loch of Vasa. There are also lovely sandy beaches, such as the Bay of Sandgarth and Veantrow Bay where spoots (razor-shell molluscs) and other shellfish are found.

As in Hoy, there are no voles in Shapinsay. This is the only wild animal native to Orkney, and its absence was first mentioned by the Revd George Barry, minister of Shapinsay, who wrote *The History of the Orkney Islands* in 1805. On the other hand the unwelcome brown rats are plentiful; according to tradition they vacated the island some time in the early nineteenth century, but were back again in the mid 1930s.

The water coming from the Mill Dam, just north of Elwick, was at one time used to power the large meal-mill facing Elwick Bay. Today, the Mill Dam is Orkney's tenth nature reserve and second wetland reserve. Although covering a fairly small area, it is home to a large number of breeding birds, such as ducks, wading birds and black-headed gulls. In the winter, the reserve is visited by many birds – whooper swans and greylag geese among them.

We also find Neolithic remains in Shapinsay, such as Castle Bloody, which is probably a chambered cairn, in the moorland area of the east hill, but no major excavations have been made. The only excavated site is the Iron-Age Broch of Burroughston, from the Norse *Borgstaðir*, the site of the broch, in the north-east part of the island. David Balfour opened it up in the early 1860s, and the interior was cleared with some care so that internal structures were preserved. The work was recorded by the archaeologist Sir Henry Dryden. The broch was well defended by a wall, ditch and rampart which must originally have surrounded the broch entirely. There may have been other structures inside the defences as well.

In AD 84, a Roman fleet sailed north along the Scottish coast to Orkney. The historian Tacitus describes in *Agricola*, the biography which he wrote about his father-in-law, 'how this coast of that remotest sea was first rounded, at this time, by a Roman fleet, which thus established the fact that Britain was an island. At the same time it discovered and subdued the Orkney Islands, hitherto unknown. Thule too was sighted by our men...' Thule is here believed to refer to Shetland. Agricola's name is not mentioned in connection with the northern expedition.

On the west shore of Shapinsay, just south of Vasa Loch where the tides are rapid, we find an area called Agricola, and on the shore are the Noust of Agricola and the Grukalty, originally Grikalty, pier. The Revd Barry has this to say about the possible historical importance of this area, 'Thither, tradition reports, one of Agricola's ships, in his celebrated voyage around the island of Britain, was driven by violence of weather, and stranded; and what seems to evince that the tradition is founded on truth is, that Roman coins are said to have been found here, by the late Mr Fea of Clestrain.'

We have to go to the placenames to find the first traces of the Norse settlers in Shapinsay, as the island is not mentioned in the *Orkneyinga Saga*. In the middle of the beach in the large, beautiful Veantrow Bay, between the Ouse and Lairo Water, lies the large Black Stone of Odin. It is quite different from surrounding stones, and probably was never a standing stone, but has come on an ice sheet in the distant past, much like the Savil Stone in Sanday. Its position, more than anything, will no doubt have impressed the Norsemen. There are traces of pagan worship in the name of Weland, which is almost certainly the same as the Norse *Veland*, meaning holy land or a place used for sacrifice. Later the chapel for the north-west part of the island was at Weland, and it is a well-known fact that the first churches were often built on pagan sites. It is also possible that the first syllable of Veantrow carries the same meaning, but the rest of this name is quite obscure.

The placenames also point to the south-east part of the island as having had great importance in Norse times. The farm of Housebay would have been a large, royal administrative farm for Shapinsay and the

East Mainland; the fact that it is never mentioned in the old rentals and thus was not taxed, supports this idea. Its harbour might have been in the Bay of Sandgarth; there is a church site close by, and perhaps the most important factor of all is the beacon site at Ward Hill.

Mackenzie's Chart of 1750 shows a large area called Holland Town, extending from The Bay of Linton, at that time called Hollandswick, all the way up to Veantrow Bay. The name of Holland has now disappeared completely, but can be found in the rentals until 1739. 'The original tunship of Holland seems to have stretched right across the island at the base of the Ness peninsula, and probably formed a whole urisland of itself', says Dr Hugh Marwick in *Orkney Farm Names*. Holland would have been the earl's administrative farm for Shapinsay. In the Bay of Linton are the remains of an old chapel, which has been compared to the historic twelfth-century chapel, still standing, on the island of Wyre. For a safe anchorage the earl's men probably used the site that is now called Skenstoft in Veantrow Bay. This may derive from the Norse *skeiðar-naust-topt* – the site of a noust for a skeid, or large warship. The name Skennist in Papa Westray is a parallel.

In the moorland between the old Housebay and Holland areas stands the tall Mor Stein. It is visible from afar, a commanding presence. It is also known as the Mör, Meur or Mora Stein, and is probably of Neolithic origin. According to local Shapinsay tradition a Mainland giant threw the stone after his fleeing wife, but such giant stories were fairly common in the islands.

It is more interesting to note that oaths sworn by a standing stone were particularly binding. In Walter Traill Dennison's tale 'Johnie Croy and the Mermaid', which takes place in Sanday, Johnie falls in love with a beautiful mermaid he meets on the beach, and 'he went down on his knees and swore by the meur-steen that he would court this maiden of the deep and win her for his wife, even if it cost him his life–'.

Dennison explains a meur-steen as generally being a standing stone or boulder where district 'things' or public assemblies were held. A similar tradition can be traced to Sweden, to the district of old Uppsala, where the site of the Mora stone was used as a thing site even from pagan times, and a king who was elected by the Mora stone would be lucky and harvest-happy. The tradition of choosing a king by the Mora stone has been compared to the crowning of Scottish kings on the Stone of Destiny. The Swedish Mora stone disappeared in 1457, perhaps for political reasons. But like the Odin stone in Stenness, the Mora stone was also widely used by courting couples, who would come from afar to plight their troth by the stone. The name and the position of the Shapinsay Mor Stein indicates that it may also have been a thing site.

In 1263 Hakon Hakonsson, who had been King of Norway for 46 years, sailed westwards from Bergen to protect the Norwegian possessions of the Isle of Man and the Hebrides against a threatened attack by Alexander III of Scotland. The Icelandic Annals state that his army was 'so great a host that an equally great army is not known ever to have gone from Norway'. He chose Orkney as a base of operations, and in late July his magnificent fleet of more than 100 ships sailed into Elwick Bay. The king himself stayed on board the large ship that had been built for him in Bergen, the *Kristsuðin*. It had 37 rooms, was entirely made of oak, and both stem and stern were decorated with carved and gilded dragons' heads, in the old Viking tradition.

King Hakon must have liked Shapinsay, because he wanted to stay there while some of his men made forays down into the Moray Firth, but they objected to going without him. On 29 July, the day that St Olaf fell in the Battle of Stiklestad, a memorial mass was held in the land-tent, followed by a reception for the people on board the *Kristsuðin*. The royal visit does not seem to have left much popular tradition, although it is possible that the placename Haco's Ness in the south-east of Shapinsay may somehow stem from it.

When King Hakon chose Elwick Bay for the anchorage of his fleet, it may have been because it was well-known as a good harbour, being so close to the royal farm at Housebay. Much of the eastern area seems to have remained the property of king and earl for some time. When feudalisation gained momentum in the period after the Reformation and the Stewart earls, the first feus given in Shapinsay were of the properties of Holland and Ness, which were then apparently still crown lands. And it comes as no surprise that the land was acquired by Patrick Graham of Rothiesholme in Stronsay, the son of Bishop Graham.

However, the largest acquisition of property was made by the Buchanan family. The cultivated land in Shapinsay was divided into nine main tunships: Sound, Waltness, Weland, Holland, Meaness, Burroughston, Sands, Kirbister and Elwick, representing a land value of some six urislands. The Buchanan family obtained the prime land of Sound, Elwick and Weland, as well as some scattered properties in other tunships, constituting an estate of at least three urislands. The fact that Sound was the most important tunship in Shapinsay is emphasised by Bishop Law's rental of 1614 using Sound and not Shapinsay as the name of the parish. There used to be an old church called Lady Kirk just west of Sound.

One of the Buchanan lairds was Sir John, who had to leave court circles when his wife was banished to Orkney for stealing jewels from Anne of Denmark, the Queen of James VI. Sir John Buchanan later extended the estate by acquiring the lands of the Earl of Carrick in Eday.

The right-angled road system.

The estate then passed to Arthur Buchanan, who also owned most of Stronsay and all of North Ronaldsay. On his death his enormous estate was inherited by his little grandniece Janet Buchanan, making her the richest heiress in Orkney. Tradition has it that she was no more than 11 years old when in 1720 she married James Fea, sixth of Clestrain in Stronsay. He was a much-travelled man who became famous for capturing the pirate Gow. At some point he had become an ardent Jacobite, and had met the Young Pretender during the 1745 rising. Afterwards he went to earth in Caithness, and did not return to Orkney until the Act of Indemnity had been passed in 1747.

After the battle of Culloden rumours were rife that several rebels had fled to Sound and were hiding there, and in many ways James Fea was made the scapegoat by other lairds. A naval squadron of four ships of war was despatched to Orkney. Men burst into the house at Sound one night, and brandishing swords and pistols, they broke open all the cupboards and closets in the house in search of the fugitive rebels who were said to be concealed there. They also unceremoniously broke into Janet Buchanan's bedchamber. She had to witness the destruction of her property while placed on a chair before the gate. The house was first pillaged, then set on fire.

In 1784 the estate of Sound was bought by Dr Thomas Balfour (1752-99) and his wife Frances Ligonier. They built an elegant Georgian villa called Cliffdale, on a site east of Sound, to replace the ruined mansion. An extensive garden was laid out at the same time. Thomas Balfour was interested in land improvement, and started growing clover and turnips. At Elwick he built a windmill and the planned village of Shoreside with more than 20 new houses.

When the Balfours inaugurated their new regime, there were no odal owners left in Shapinsay. All the farmers were tenants, and the entire land belonged to one of the three estates: the bishopric lands, a small estate centred around the farm of How and owned by Robert Laing of Papdale, and the Balfour land. Only the Balfours were resident in the island, and the Balfours alone improved their land.

In 1846 the Balfour estate was inherited by David Balfour (1811-87), Dr Thomas Balfour's grandson. David Balfour, who studied law at Edinburgh University, was fifth of Balfour and Trenaby, and also came into his great-uncle John Balfour's enormous Orkney estate. Energetic and also interested in land improvement, he became the most important landowner in Orkney, taking an active part in many agricultural activities, but also finding the time to become Provost of Kirkwall. Assisted by his factor, Marcus Calder, he replaced the old inefficient run-rig system of farming by a system of squared ten-acre field units, separated by open drains. New land was drained and cultivated, so that in the course of a few years the arable acreage was increased from 750 to 2250 acres. A visible result of the improvement schemes which transformed the island is the right-angled road system, which has given Shapinsay the longest straight road in Orkney.

David Balfour engaged David Bryce, an Edinburgh architect, to design a new house that would be both elegant and commodious. The result was the baronial-style building of Balfour Castle that dominates the approach to Shapinsay. The old Cliffdale house partly survives inside the Castle. No expense was spared, and not even a secret passage is missing. The village was extended and centred around the west side of Elwick Bay, where the entrance is guarded by the old Dishan Tower, once a saltwater, or seawater, shower. The Balfour Village has kept its old-world charm and has now been declared a conservation area.

But the changes – no matter how essential – did not occur without controversy. Ironically, David Balfour is the author of *Odal Rights and Feudal Wrongs, Memorial for Orkney* but he does not seem to have realised that only a feudal lord could carry through such far-reaching reorganisation of a whole island. Thus a great number of the Shapinsay farmers were required to quit their farms while the work went on, or pay heavy fines, and according to the factor 'The poor folks...are in a terrible funk about "the new sort of farming" about to be introduced into the island.' Although the smallest holdings disappeared, most of the tenants could come back to the same farms afterwards.

The elders of the United Presbyterian Church, more popularly known as the Secession Church, reprimanded those members of their congregation who had danced at the laird's harvest home party, a 'muckle supper' followed by entertainment. David Balfour regarded the 'Dancing Affair' as a personal insult, and the factor has this comment, 'The young trees are thriving wonderfully well and I hope they will in the course of a few years be sufficiently tall to hang these Secession Elders on'. The confrontation with the laird was bitter, and the elders were not willing to apologise to him. Consequently they were evicted from their homes and many of them emigrated to Australia.

Tribute should still be paid to David Balfour for his life's work. When he started, much of the Balfour family's property on Shapinsay was considered wasteland. Today the island presents a fertile appearance, and is sometimes called the Garden of Orkney. The last of the Balfour lairds sold most of his property in the 1950s, and the Balfour family is now extinct in Orkney. The home farm of Balfour Mains was bought by a Polish man, Captain Zawadski, who had been an officer in the Second World War. He later acquired the Castle as well.

In his well-known *Description of the Orkney Islands* the sixteenth-century traveller Jo Ben writes that Shapinsay people 'are very ignorant; they worship fairies and other wicked beings'. The trow – a close relation of the Norwegian troll, but living in hills and mounds instead of

Balfour Castle.

mountains – may perhaps come into the latter category. The many prehistoric 'knowes' would appeal to the popular imagination. One of the most common Orkney trow stories has been immortalised by a famous writer with Shapinsay roots, and another Orkney writer, George Mackay Brown, tells of how this came about:

> People have been dragged or lured or cajoled to the trows'
> abode inside the hills, and been lost to human ken. The
> midsummer revellers thought they had been gone for half
> an hour or so, but when they emerge into the midsummer
> light again, they find that they are strangers in a familiar
> land. All their generation has vanished or grown so old as
> to be unrecognisable. Only they, the enchanted ones, are
> not a day older than when they entered the trows' castle.
> Nearly two centuries ago a little boy in New York heard his
> father telling him this story – at bedtime no doubt. Being a
> glutton for narrative, the boy made it a part of himself.
> And when he grew up, he wrote a very famous story called
> 'Rip van Winkle'. The theme is immediately recognisable.
> The child's name was Washington Irving, and his father was
> a Shapinsay man.

The theme was used again by George Mackay Brown in his story 'The Two Fiddlers', and set to music by his friend Sir Peter Maxwell Davies.

Washington Irving (1783-1859) was America's first internationally successful writer, born in New York to emigrant parents who loyally named their youngest son after the president of their adopted country. The father, William Irving, came from the farm of Quholme, from the Norse *Hvammr*, in the north-east of Shapinsay, and belonged to an old, distinguished, odal family, the Irvings of Sebay in St Andrews parish on Mainland. They were cleared out of their farm by Earl Robert Stewart in 1584, and settled in Shapinsay.

Irving first became famous for his witty descriptions of life in New York. His satirical *A History of New York* was ostensibly written by a Dutch-American historian named Diedrich Knickerbocker, who makes good-natured fun of the Dutch settlers, but also levels serious criticism at the Thomas Jefferson administration. His best-known and most popular work *The Sketch Book* was written in 1819-20, after the failure of the family firm, and contained a collection of essays and romantic tales, among them 'Rip van Winkle' and 'The Legend of Sleepy Hollow', built on folklore material. It was Sir Walter Scott who suggested he should explore this material in his stories, which became tremendously popular. Washington Irving spent a large part of his life in Europe, but strangely he never made it to Shapinsay, to see the place where his father grew up.

Shapinsay remains essentially an agricultural island. Year after year the island's stock takes the top prizes at the agricultural shows, as well as the top prices in the marts. The island still has its geometrically patterned landscape to show for the upheavals of the nineteenth century. Perhaps Shapinsay people are now reaping the benefits of having had a head start on many other islands.

Rousay

The Norse origin of the name Rousay is *Hrólfsey*, but the saga is silent about who Hrólf might have been and how the island came to bear his name. The name itself is simple when compared to such placenames as the Sinions of Cutclaws and the Camps of Jupiter Fring, hopeless distortions of the original designations that would be down-to-earth and descriptive. 'The name is strange, and would import some Notable Accident, but what it was I could not learn', writes an intrigued James Wallace about the latter name in 1693. The Orkney scholar and philologist, Dr Hugh Marwick, grew up in Rousay and always considered the placenames of his native island 'peculiarly obscure', but then that may be the reason why he became so interested in them!

Rousay offers more varied scenery than all the other islands, with the possible exception of Hoy. A narrow, green and fertile fringe of farmland runs all around the coast. In the north and west the cliffs are precipitous, with tall, natural arches like the Lobust and the Hole of the Horses, the natural homes of all kinds of seafowl. On the maritime heaths of The Brings are some very large colonies of skuas, gulls and waders, as well as some 4000 Arctic terns. Along the coast there are blowholes, or gloups, such as the Kilns of Brin-Novan, and large sea-caves like the Covenanters' Caves, where religious dissidents sought refuge in the seventeenth century. The Covenanters found for themselves a wild, romantic spot under Sacquoy Head, and their caves can only be seen from the sea.

Beyond the cultivated area are steep brown hills, running east to west in two parallel ranges, with Blotchnie Fiold in the south the highest point at 250 m. The peat-covered upland area between the two hill ranges is a hidden, different world, with names like Erne Tower and Loch of Loomachun pointing out the haunts of the eagle and the loon, or red-throated diver. No roads cross this high moorland, and the walker and the birdwatcher have it all to themselves. In places the tussocky clumps known as gowk-heads make the going rather rough.

Some 20 km of hilly road circles the island. The road should be travelled by bicycle, the better to study the variation of the scenery, as well as for the exhilaration of riding down long slopes, and the exercise of going up others! The island has from far back been divided into nine different districts, Wasbister in the north, Scockness, Sourin and

Knarston in the east, Brinnian, Hunclet, and Frotoft in the south, with West Side and Quandal in the west being practically empty today. Until the road was built in the second half of the nineteenth century, the districts were mostly connected by boat.

Rousay has been called 'Egypt of the North' because of the density of its prehistoric sites, and it is true that the concentration of archaeological monuments is impressive. For the interested visitor, exploring the island means taking a step into another historical timescale – into life as it was lived and observed some 5000 years ago. Of course, one reason why this veritable museum has survived intact through the millennia is due to the absence of agricultural interference. The prehistoric chambered tombs were, notably, built in steep and stony hill ground, and were therefore left alone.

Many prehistoric monuments were dug out of their mounds and knowes in the 1930s thanks to the zeal of Walter Gordon Grant (1886-1947), a keen amateur archaeologist. As owner of much of Rousay and director of Highland Park Distillery in Kirkwall, he spent summers at Trumland House, where he entertained such eminent archaeologists as Dr V Gordon Childe and Dr J G Callander. In the years between the world wars, one Stone-Age monument after another was scientifically excavated at W G Grant's initiative and personal expense.

The Rinyo settlement was first discovered by James Yorston in the late 1930s when he became aware of some upright slabs sticking out through the turf in the area called Braes of Rinyo, on the farm of Bigland in Sourin. Till then it had always been thought that the name of this farm referred to Norse *bygg*, for barley, but in fact it could very well derive from the Norse verb *byggja*, to build, and thus point to earlier habitation.

Like the people of Skara Brae, the inhabitants of Rinyo were Grooved Ware users, and the two settlements also had many other factors in common. But the settlers at Rinyo were exceptional in being the only Neolithic builders in Orkney who preferred the hill to the coast. Artificial terraces had been made in the sloping ground to shore up the houses. The site was only partially excavated, and the settlement may have been larger than Skara Brae.

In contrast to the many tombs, Rinyo has been called 'an abode of the living', the only Stone-Age homes so far found in Rousay. The houses were designed roughly like those at Skara Brae, with a central fireplace, a dresser, and beds, but the small square clay-built ovens are exceptional, although it is not clear what they were used for. In the more recent upper layers the first beaker pottery in Orkney was found.

So far 15 chambered tombs have been found in Rousay. They are scattered, and may have represented different settlements. Each cairn was sited so as to be clearly visible to the people of the local community, almost as a marker of their particular domain. Much effort has been spent on the construction of these elaborate houses for the dead, perhaps more than on the houses built for day-to-day domestic life. The population of Rousay must therefore have been quite substantial in Neolithic times.

A number of tombs are open to the public. Of these Blackhammer, Knowe of Yarso, and Midhowe are interesting examples of the Unston type. Midhowe, which was excavated in 1932-3, is a classic stalled, chambered cairn, and the longest in Orkney. The remains of some 25 people were found here, in compartments formed by upright slabs. There were also bones of all kinds of fish, birds, and farm animals, as well as of the Orkney vole! The question that cannot be answered is whether the animals were there as food for the dead on the journey to the other world, or whether the animals were also being given the chance of an afterlife.

There are also cairns of a different kind in Rousay, the so-called Bookan-type. This has cells opening off a central chamber, and the two-storeyed Taversoe Tuick is an example of this kind of tomb. It was discovered quite by chance in 1898 when the owners of Trumland House decided to make a garden seat in the knowe, or mound, where they were wont to sit. This is how Lady Burroughs described her reactions to the find: 'When I went to bed that night I could think of nothing else! There had we sat, during many happy summers, stretched on the purple heather, basking in the sunshine; laughing and talking with the carelessness of youth, little dreaming that barely eight feet below us sat these grim and ghastly skeletons.'

The brochs of the Iron-Age period were defensive structures built and occupied within a millennium time span – roughly between 500 BC and AD 500. Some of them would be used as settlement sites even after that period. In Rousay eight brochs have been identified as such; of these only one has been excavated. Midhowe broch was built on a promontory, and some of the external buildings have been lost through erosion. According

Internal furnishings, Midhowe Broch.

to Anna Ritchie, the well-known archaeologist who has done much work in Orkney, 'the design of the broch and its defences is so compact, with the wall of the broch only a couple of metres from the inner ditch, that there can be no doubt that this was built as a prestigious, fortified family house – the Iron-Age equivalent of the Norse castle on Wyre. The external buildings round the broch were added later, when defence was no longer as vital'.

Apart from the broch known as the Taft o' Faraclett in Scockness, the other seven Rousay broch sites are concentrated along the shore of Eynhallow Sound to a remarkable degree. Beginning with Midhowe broch we find the remains of North Howe broch slightly further west, then moving eastwards along the shore we come across the brochs of South Howe, the Knowe of Swandro, the broch near Viera Lodge, the Knowe of Burrian and the Knowe of Hunclett. They must have been an amazing sight, and one cannot help wondering at the reason for such a building pattern.

In the district of Wasbister, in the north-west of the island, the name Burrian is used for the small island in the Loch of Wasbister. Burrian may of course refer to another broch structure, but no ruins are visible today, and the name may also be just a descriptive term for the holm itself. On the other hand, the round mound on Bretta Ness, on the other side of the Loch, may cover an early chapel, and there is also a rise on the shoreline known as the site of St Colm's Kirk.

The placename pattern in Rousay does not give any clear idea as to how the Norse settlement took place, and the island does not appear in the *Orkneyinga Saga* until the twelfth century. In the early nineteenth century a sword and a shield-boss of Norse origin were ploughed up on the Westness shore. And in 1963 when people on the Westness farm were going to bury a dead cow at Moaness, they happened to hit upon the richly outfitted grave of a woman with her newborn child. Among her grave-goods was a beautiful brooch of the Celtic 'Tara' type, made of silver with gold filigree and inlaid amber; it is now known as the Westness Brooch. Of eighth-century origin it was already well worn when placed in the grave, some time in the ninth century.

It is interesting to note that recent excavations carried out at the low headland of Moaness on the Westness shore by Dr Sigrid Kaland of the Historisk Museum in Bergen, have uncovered a noust, a rich cemetery, and an important farm of Norse origin. The noust lay on the east side of Moaness, where the shore was free of cliffs, and is exceptional in that it is stone-built, with walls up to a metre in height, like a type also known in Iceland.

The cemetery contains some 30 graves of different kinds, both with and without grave-goods. It was in use for several centuries, and consequently has both Pictish and Norse burials. The farm lies slightly to the west of the headland, on the green slope above the Bay of Swandro, and consists of three houses. One is a longhouse of some 35 m in length, divided into two halls with central stone hearths, the others are byres. The farm grew flax, barley, rye and oats.

The Westness area has some of the best farming land in Rousay, and it should come as no surprise that in the twelfth century it was the domain of Sigurd, a chieftain 'of distinguished lineage' and married to Earl Paul Thorfinnsson's granddaughter. He is mentioned five times in the *Orkneyinga Saga* in connection with the dramatic events leading up to the takeover of power by Earl Rognvald Kali Kolsson in the 1130s. Earl Paul Hakonsson had stayed overnight at Westness for 'a feast at Sigurd's', had risen early and gone otter hunting with his men. There Svein Asleifarson of Gairsay fell on them, killing 19 of Earl Paul's men, and abducting the Earl himself, who was taken to Scotland and never heard of again.

It seems obvious from the context that much of the Westness area was earldom property, and that Skaill was the Earl's veizla farm which he would sometimes visit. We are told that 'Earl Paul was at Westness on Rousay when he heard Earl Rognvald had landed in Shetland'. The location of the Ward Hill close by supports this idea. Sigurd of Westness would have been the Earl's *veizlu-maðr*, and as such been responsible for the upkeep of the beacon on Ward Hill and the farm and hall at Skaill, but he was perhaps also a chieftain and farmer in his own right. He may have lived at either side of Skaill. The excavations indicate that in the twelfth century the power centre was moved from Westness to Skaill.

Close to Skaill we find the ruins of the former parish church of St Mary, probably built on the site of an older church, as well as the square tower known as the Wirk. The name of this building derives from the Norse *virki*, a fortification, and it may have been built as a defence structure. It has been compared with Cubbie Roo's Castle on Wyre. Westwards there was also the important farm of Brough, the historic Brugh.

At some later date the Westness land was divided into the odal land of Brough and the bishopric estate of Skaill. In 1500 or so the land in Rousay was valued as six and a half urislands. Of this the Church owned some 52 per cent, the Earl 30 per cent and 18 per cent was in odal ownership. In 1601 there were some 40 landowners in Rousay, but 50 years later the number had already fallen to 18, as many of the odal properties were swallowed up.

The old farm of Brough was once the seat of the Craigies of Brough, and in about 1500 three of them were Lawmen of Orkney. At that time Brough was perhaps the most valuable odal estate in the islands. In 1556 the Craigies sold it to the Revd Magnus Halcro, who Dr Hugh Marwick describes as 'Ablest, most ambitious, least scrupulous, and one of the most immoral of all the Orkney clergy of this epoch'. Earl Robert Stewart may have felt that any land that had at one time been part of the earldom was his by divine right, as in 1584 he just took the estate of Brough for himself. The estate came back into the Halcro family after Earl Robert's death, and remained with them until the Traills took it over. The gable ends as well as a cupboard still remain of the ruinous, eighteenth-century farmhouse at Brough.

The Westness estate was acquired by the first Traill in the early

In the 19th century, Quandal suffered a thorough clearance of crofters.

seventeenth century, and gradually extended to include Woodwick in Evie and North Ronaldsay, in addition to an ever-growing share of Rousay. When all of the second laird's nine children died in infancy, the estate passed into the possession of his nephew John Traill, for 60 years. In his younger days he had Jacobite sympathies, and was one of the four North Isles lairds who went into hiding in the Westray caves. He blamed the rheumatism that later bent his tall body on this adventure. Westness house and farm were burnt down by the Hanoverian troops, and not rebuilt until the end of the eighteenth century.

George William Traill (1792-1847) came from a junior branch of the Traill family, and wanted very much to acquire the ancestral estate. He had been an efficient administrator in India, known as 'King of Kumaon' and had become wealthy in the process. He retired in 1836 and started buying up land in Rousay. By 1845 he had reached his chief goal: he owned the Westness lands and the district of Quandal, and he could begin his plans for a large improved farm. He engaged Robert Scarth, the North Ronaldsay factor, to set about the changes.

The Westness and Quandal districts are very different in character. Quandal is exposed and windswept and faces the open sea. The name of Quandal must refer to the small valley formed by the Burn of Tafts, and will almost certainly derive from the Norse *hvann-dalr*, the valley of hvann, or *Angelica archangelica*. The plant thrives along burns; it was popular with the Norsemen and was much cultivated by them both in the Viking Age and in the later Middle Ages.

In this area are the remains of the house known as Tafts, which is believed to go back to the fifteenth century, but judging by the name, it seems to have succeeded an even older house, which perhaps may have been a hunting lodge, back in the earldom days. It is an unusual kind of house, so strongly built as to be almost a fortress, and is one of the few two-storey houses in Orkney of its period still standing. A miniature mansion house, it differed from the traditional Orkney farm in having the outbuildings, barn, kiln, and byre, quite separate. Tafts was the original nucleus of the old crofting community of Quandal.

Over the hill in Quandal were a large number of small crofts. The township had been a detached part of the Westove estate in Sanday. The crofters had no leases and ran their small community on an egalitarian and to some extent independent basis. In the early nineteenth century there were 215 people living in 28 households, but there was some amalgamation of land, so that when the notice to leave came after the harvest of 1845, it affected the households of 16 crofts.

The change from medieval farming was swift and thorough. In Quandal the land was drained by open ditches and enclosed by stone dykes. Former arable land was reseeded as pasture and a flock of Cheviot sheep was brought in. Still, the old traditional pattern of farmsteads, turf dykes and run-rig holdings is visible. The land of Westness was squared and improved the following year. The old odal farm of Brough was the last farm to be cleared, not for any sentimental reasons, but because it had the longest lease. Altogether it was the most thorough clearance to take place on any Orkney estate, affecting a total of 40 families.

The evictions and clearances were not quite completed when George William Traill died in 1847. He had spent only summers in Orkney, and his heir was an absentee laird for 23 years. General Sir Frederick William Traill Burroughs of Rousay and Viera (1831-1905), was only remotely related to the Orkney Traills, but had also spent much of his life in India. In 1857 he was wounded in the Indian Mutiny. He was recommended for the Victoria Cross because of his 'personal gallantry in the Sikanderbagh and being the first who entered one of the breaches and engaged in personal combat with greatly superior numbers of the enemy in which he was wounded by a sword'. Perhaps he was able to squeeze through the small breach in that bastion because he was really quite a tiny man, who in Orkney earned the nickname of 'The Little General'. It was also the title of one of Edwin Muir's poems.

> Early in spring the little General came
> Across the sound, bringing the island death.

And yet, he was later blamed for evictions that were mostly carried out by his predecessor, and he was branded by the national press as the prototype of the old-fashioned laird. He had invested much capital in the land improvements. But the high-handedness that perhaps came with his military training and his tendency to see slights where none were intended, worked against him in his controversy with the Napier Commission and the political opposition centred on the Sourin Free Church and Manse. He was vindictive in his treatment of James Leonard who led the crofters in their evidence against him and his regime. After the Napier hearings James Leonard and his large family were evicted from their croft of Digro in Sourin, but then, like Burroughs, Leonard was an implacable opponent who showed no mercy.

Trumland House was erected in 1873-6, after Burroughs resigned from the army. It was designed in the baronial style by the very fashionable architect David Bryce, who also constructed Balfour Castle. Burroughs was promised a house for £3000 or less, but the bill, when it came, was for more than three times that amount. Trumland House is set in large grounds and has a lovely view towards some of the inner North Isles.

In 1841, before the clearances began, there were all of 976 people living in Rousay. By 1971 this figure had fallen to only 181, but since then there has again been an increase. The pier that Burroughs built in 1871 to make it possible for his ship, the SS *Lizzie Burroughs*, to go on a route between Rousay and Kirkwall, has now been replaced by a modern pier, and the island is served by an efficient roll-on roll-off ferry from Tingwall in Rendall. There is also a cooperatively owned fish factory at Rousay Pier, where crabs and scallops are processed for the European markets. Lobsters are transported live.

There are still cottages going derelict or being used just as summer cottages, as the process of amalgamation goes on, but nowadays this causes no bitterness.

Eynhallow

Eynhallow is one of Orkney's uninhabited islands, and has been so for a century and a half, but it still retains some of its grip on the popular imagination. Legend has it that Eynhallow was at one time the hidden Hildaland, a vanishing island that came and went, and the summer home of the mysterious Fin Folk. It was an enchanted isle where blood would flow from stalks of corn if they were cut after sunset. Cats, rats and mice could not live there. At one time soil would be brought from Eynhallow and put under haystacks or new houses to keep vermin away.

> Eynhallow frank, Eynhallow free,
> Eynhallow lies in the middle of the sea;
> With a roaring röst on every side –
> Eynhallow lies in the middle of the tide.

As this old nursery rhyme shows, it is the position of Eynhallow that, more than anything, appeals to the popular imagination. The small green island surrounded by heaving, white-foaming rösts, is a truly breathtaking sight. When the tide is running in or out, the channels on either side of Eynhallow become tidal rivers sweeping eastwards or westwards, and the rösts are boiling whirlpools on their course. Close to the island the water is shallow, then the depth plunges sharply, and this uneven sea-bottom causes the mad dance of the rösts.

If we go back in time to the late Iron Age the visual impact of the island and its fierce rösts would have been even more striking. On either side of it, along the Rousay and Evie coasts, the brochs would stand in rows. There were six of them on the Evie side, and seven on the Rousay side; of the latter, South Howe, Midhowe and North Howe were clustered together along a very short coastal strip just opposite Eynhallow. The two lines of brochs along Eynhallow Sound must have impressed the Norsemen.

The name of Burgar Röst derives from *borg*, the Norse word for castle or fortress. The Burgar and Cutlar rösts are notoriously difficult to navigate, and perhaps present a strong enough defence on their own. It makes the density of brochs in this area even more enigmatic. It has been suggested that the purpose of the brochs was domination rather than defence.

The Norsemen named the island *Eyin helga* – the holy island. They described what they found, and something about the island must have

The Burgar Broch and röst.

struck them since they used such a special name. They met with monks
and priests and the early Pictish Christianity in other places in Orkney,
but to name these they used the word papar for priests. It is of course
also possible that the name is translated from a similar Pictish name that
the Norsemen made their own. To this day the inhabitants of Evie have
referred to Eynhallow simply as The Isle.

On the north shore, east of Ramna Geo, are remains of what may
have been a prehistoric settlement. There are other possible prehistoric
sites, but so far they have not been examined. Interest has been focused
more on the island as it was in later times. Eynhallow figures in the
Orkneyinga Saga, in connection with the doings of the Gairsay chieftain
Svein Asleifarson in the year 1155. Svein fell out with two men in
Caithness, captured them and treated them abominably, but let them go.
Their brother was the influential Jon Wing, from Rackwick in Westray.
He did not know what had happened to his brothers, so he went:

> to Eynhallow and captured Olaf, the son of Svein
> Asleifarson and foster-son of Kolbein Hruga, taking him to
> Westray where they ran into Earl Rognvald at Rapness.
> "What brings you here, Olaf?" asked the earl when he saw
> the boy.

Eynhallow Church.

"Jon Wing had better answer that," he said.

The earl looked at Jon. "Why did you bring Olaf here?" he asked.

"Svein took my brothers," answered Jon, "and for all I know he may have killed them".

"Take him back at once," said the earl.

What was Olaf Sveinsson, the son of one important chieftain and the foster-son of another, doing on the small island of Eynhallow? The natural assumption must be that he was being taught by monks there.

For some time 'The Ale of Anehallow' was part of the bishopric and was in feu to the Halcros of Brough in Rousay. In the nineteenth century the island had become the property of the Balfour family. In 1851 a virulent epidemic broke out among the four families who farmed as tenants on Eynhallow. Several people died, and the survivors were taken away by the landowner. In an attempt to stamp out the infection the roofs were taken off the old buildings, and only then was it discovered that one of them was a church.

In the early twentieth century the Norwegian scholar Lorentz Dietrichson (1834-1917), accompanied by the architect Johan Meyer, travelled around Orkney. In 1906 they published the richly illustrated

Monumenta Orcadica. The Norsemen in the Orkneys and the monuments they have left. It was Dietrichson who first maintained that the rest of the farm buildings in Eynhallow were in actual fact an old monastery. He had gone to Eynhallow expecting to find it, as the island had 'a scenery of enchanting beauty, just such as the mediaeval monks were accustomed to choose for the sites of their monasteries'.

Dietrichson believed that the ruins in Eynhallow were of a twelfth-century Cistercian monastery. His ideas met with some opposition, but there is agreement today that the buildings represent a monastic layout, probably of Benedictine origin. The twelfth century seems now to be accepted as the period of construction; it was a time of transition from the massive Romanesque style to the lofty Gothic architectural style, and details from the church at Eynhallow help place it in this period. Whereas the first two doors in the church have rounded Romanesque arches, the choir door has a clumsy, pointed arch, as if in an attempt to imitate a new and fashionable style.

According to the customs and beliefs of the Benedictine order the old monastery would basically have been a work farm; their aim was to make such a religious community both self-sufficient and self-contained. The transition to domestic use of the houses seems to have come sometime in the sixteenth century, and must have come about quite naturally, as farming went on much as before.

Around the coast of Eynhallow are three large caves. In the *Orkneyinga Saga* an island called *Hellisey*, or Island of Caves, is described as a place 'where there are steep sea-cliffs and a great cave in them: at high tide the sea comes right up to the mouth of the cave'. Dr Hugh Marwick believed that this was a mistake made by the scribe, confusing *hellir* for cave with *heilagr* for holy, and that Eynhallow is meant.

In Hellisey Svein Asleifarson and his men sought refuge after having once again fallen out with Earl Harald Maddadarson. 'They got to the cave on the rising tide and hauled the boat up inside, since the cave slopes upwards into the cliff, and the sea rises right up to the mouth of the cave.' Earl Harald spent the day scouring the island for them, but without success.

The historian R P Fereday, who in 1972 examined the three large caves in Eynhallow, found that Cave Geo in the northern line of cliffs, just west of Ramnageo, matches the description of Svein's cave in the

Orkneyinga Saga. On the western side of the island are the two caves known as Twenty Men Hole and Nine Men Hole. The latter is known to have concealed nine Rousay men hiding from the press-gang, but all three caves may have been used for this purpose during the Napoleonic Wars.

Eynhallow was part of the lore connected with the strange Fin Folk whose daughters were the enchanting mermaids. The Fin Folk lived in the town of Finfolkaheem, at the bottom of the sea. It was a town so gorgeous that it might have come from the pages of the *Arabian Nights*. Everything was built of gold and crystal, covered in pearls, and with rugs and hangings in the shimmering colours of the Northern Lights. A vast dancing hall was lit by the phosphorus in the sea. There were those who had been there and could tell the tales.

The summer home of Hildaland was thought of as a beautiful green island with rich farms in the western ocean. Only very rarely was a human being fortunate enough to see Hildaland. It would rise suddenly out of the sea and be gone again as suddenly. To break the spell a man must leap ashore holding steel in his hand. 'There came at last the hour and the man; the vanishing isle was won from the waters and left standing in the middle of the tide.' Hildaland became Eynhallow.

In his story 'The Dancers' the writer Eric Linklater presents his readers with a modern version of this lore. 'For this story, against a real background, rural and sea-girt, that I knew well and described without excessive detail, I invented a "fairy tale", a tale of extra-territorial happenings, and told it with an assumption of realism.' The result is both funny and enchanting.

It is the story of Mr G P Pomfret, the junior partner in a prosperous brewery, who disappeared with five members of his family and became a newspaper sensation. This happened in the 1920s. The Pomfrets rented a house in Orkney for a holiday and went along with their chauffeur and three maids. Some of them fished; Mr Pomfret walked and enquired diligently into local traditions and history.

On Midsummer's Eve, the Pomfrets set sail for Eynhallow, carrying rugs and cushions and a portable gramophone. And that was the last that anybody saw of them. The papers cited the vanishing crew of the *Marie Celeste* as a parallel case. But we, the readers, know better. The Pomfrets are dancing to the music of the Fin Folk, who are in the island for the summer.

The Fin Folk invite the Pomfrets for breakfast, and as though 'it were the most natural thing in the world, the Pomfrets went down rock stairs to a long, sandy hall, lit greenly by the sea, and full, at that time, of the morning song of the North Tide of Eynhallow. They sat down, talking with their hosts, and then two very old little men brought stone cups full of a yellow liquor that smelt like honey and the first wind after frost. – Not one of them had any thought of going, for it was heather ale they drank. – And at night they danced, to the music of the tree-root fiddles and pink shell-drums.'

The last private owner of Eynhallow was the Kirkwall lawyer, naturalist and writer Duncan John Robertson (1860-1941), who recorded his observations on Eynhallow in *Notes from an Orkney Bird Sanctuary*. The island was bought in 1980 by Orkney Islands Council for £60,000 from the trustees of the family estate, to preserve it as a part of the Orcadian heritage.

For a long time now the birds, sheep and seals have had the island to themselves. Aberdeen University has for many years carried out bird research, and has taken a special interest in the fulmars and the way they have spread around Britain's coastline in just a century. Fulmars normally lay just one egg each year, and therefore it is mostly their longevity that makes them multiply as they do; they usually live for an average of 20-25 years. And the fulmars probably survive for so long because they are feared by other birds. When fulmars feel under threat they defend themselves by spitting at long range a foul-smelling oily liquid at any attackers. This sticky substance removes the waterproofing from the attackers' wings, and the other birds therefore leave the fulmars strictly alone.

Faithfully, year after year until 1997, Britain's oldest bird, Flora the fulmar, would show up in Eynhallow for her normal breeding season. The scientists who had been studying her believed that she was about 50 years old, as she was first ringed as an adult bird in 1951. She became so used to the interest of the ornithologists that when they arrived at her breeding ledge to put a new ring on her, she would not spit, but obligingly lift her leg to help them with their task.

St Magnus Church and graveyard.

Egilsay

The tall round tower of the St Magnus Church in Egilsay is a familiar landmark that can be seen from far away. Much of island history and lore is connected with St Magnus's death there in 1117. The story of what happened then is central to *Magnus' Saga* and is also told in the *Orkneyinga Saga*. To the Orkney folklorist Ernest Marwick, who grew up by the Evie shore, the round, pointed tower of the Egilsay church 'was the most beautiful thing within sight, and it rose every day against the sky until it seemed to become a sign in the fable of our lives'.

The interpretation of the island name also depends on its history. Were it not for the saga story the name might quite simply have been seen to mean the domain of a man called Egil, a common Norse name. The Norwegian historian Peter Andreas Munch first suggested that the name might derive from a Celtic name for a church – *eaglais* – from the Latin *ecclesia*. To Jo Ben the island was 'insula ecclesia'.

At the north end of Egilsay lies a small island, known as Kili Holm, which is much exposed to the erosion of sea and wind. The Celtic word *ceall* for cell is believed to be the origin of the name, and this would suggest a monastic connection. But Dr Marwick points out that in his description of Orkney, written in 1633, Robert Monteith gives the name of this island as Ridholme. 'As he was the owner, it is hardly possible that he was making a mistake about the name, although today it is quite unknown. The north point of the island, however, is called the Point of Ridden.' A possible Norse origin of Ridholme might be holm of the *hrið*, or ox, implying that the island was used for grazing, but this remains speculation.

Egilsay has much good land and was skatted as two urislands in the olden days. There is a prolific plant life, reputedly with more than 300 varieties of wild plants. The island is low-lying, but has rocky cliffs and heather-covered hills that offer inviting habitats for a large number of birds. The marshland with small lochs down the east side of the island is especially attractive to ducks and waders such as snipe and redshank. The elusive corncrake still calls at times. The RSPB has bought land that may be turned into a nature reserve.

There are few prehistoric sites in Egilsay, and none that has been excavated. The placenames do not give much away, but the name Weyland at the north end, close to a geo and the only sandy beach in the area, points to pagan connections, as it probably derives from the Norse *vé*, which means a sacred place. And again we find the name Skaill used about an early farm, with the best anchorage, a beacon close by at Warsett, and a church site.

When Earl Thorfinn the Mighty died, some time in the 1060s, he left Orkney to his two sons, Paul and Erlend, to rule together. This they did peacefully until their sons reached manhood. The young earls-to-be never got on, and once again Orkney was divided into two parts, with Earl Paul and his sons Hakon and Erling in the west, and Erlend with his son Magnus in the east. When Hakon and Magnus became earls, the situation grew more and more tense between the two factions. This is the way things once were between Earls Thorfinn and Rognvald Brusason, and the stage is set for the same dramatic ending. A soothsayer's words to Earl Hakon strengthen the feeling of doom, 'During your life you'll be the cause of a crime for which you'll barely be able to atone – perhaps never.'

The writer of the *Orkneyinga Saga* cleverly builds up the tension towards Earl Magnus' ceremonial death on Egilsay in Easter week of 1117. Whereas Magnus believes he is coming to a settlement of peace,

Hakon arrives prepared for force. Still, when Magnus in fairytale style makes his offers of surrender, Hakon is prepared to accept the third and most extreme one, but the Orkney chieftains object – they want a final solution – and Earl Magnus bends to receive the blow from the axe. According to old Norse laws this was not murder, and even by Christian law it is perhaps more of an execution.

The saga gives no reason why Egilsay was chosen as a meeting place for the earls. It has a central position, and it may have been the seat of Orkney's first Norse bishop, known as William The Old because he held the office for more than 60 years. With two earls in power, it may have been difficult to choose either Birsay or Kirkwall as a residence. But there were two bishops in power as well; *c.*1112 bishop Rodulf was appointed by the archbishop of York. Egilsay would therefore be a neutral area for many reasons, yet in the twelfth century the islands of Egilsay, Wyre and Gairsay seem to have become a kind of power region. The saga makes frequent references to the bishop being visited in Egilsay; probably his residence was at Skaill with its good harbour. Although Bishop William is not mentioned in connection with Earl Magnus' death, it is possible that he was present in Egilsay.

When rumours started to circulate of miracles attributed to Magnus, these were discouraged by Bishop William, who seems always to have preferred Hakon. But after a visit to Norway *c.*1134, Bishop William changed his mind and began actively advocating Magnus' sainthood, probably won over by Rognvald Kali Kolsson's promise to build a minster in Kirkwall, should he become earl.

It is possible that the existing church of St Magnus was built in the years 1135-8, while Bishop William was still living in the island, to replace the old church that gave the island its name. If so, it will be the oldest building now extant in Orkney. The chancel was once two-storeyed, and the nave was roofed with flagstone. The arches of both doors and windows are said to be a combination of Grecian and Roman, but rather clumsily made. The circular tower is on the west end, and is today some 15 m high, but was originally higher. There were at one time several such distinctive, round-towered churches in the Northern Isles, the old church in Deerness among them, but the church of St Magnus in Egilsay is now the only remaining one. It was used for services until the early part of the nineteenth century.

In the olden days people used to call the small room above the choir

Egilsay from the air.

the grief-house, and believed that it had been used as a kind of jail. It is more likely that grief is a corruption of the Norse word *grið*, which meant peace or sanctuary, and applied to the church and the thing in session.

Some distance away from the church, a stone pillar marks the site where St Magnus was killed. It was erected on the initiative of the vicar of St Magnus Church in London.

In early Norse times Egilsay was probably earldom land but was given to the bishopric at some point, along with the district of Sourin in Rousay. The link between the two communities continued for a long time, and in the seventeenth century the Sourin people refused to help to pay for the repairs to the church at Westness, as they never attended service there. They always went by boat across the Sound to the St Magnus Church in Egilsay, as it was shorter and easier and this is what they had always done.

When Earl Robert Stewart took over all the bishopric land in Orkney, he feued land in Egilsay to Patrick Monteith (1564-97), who was one of his followers. Patrick Monteith's nephew Robert was the first to use the designation 'of Egilsay'. Robert Monteith was a colourful character, and fell out with Earl Patrick Stewart, who declared him an outlaw. Monteith was therefore forced to leave the islands, but in his absence, Earl Patrick plundered his property, invading his Egilsay estate and stripping it of anything of value. The ensuing legal actions went on for eight years.

In 1633 Robert Monteith wrote *A Description of the Isles of Orkney*, which was published much later by Sir Robert Sibbald as part of his book on the topography of Scotland. This is the first work on Orkney written by an Orcadian, and therefore he may perhaps be forgiven for being mostly interested in identifying the lairds in the various islands and evaluating their estates.

A rather picturesque old manor house at Howan, on the east side of Egilsay, is the seventeenth-century laird's house of the Monteiths. It is a two-storey, three-bay traditional house of harled rubble flagstone with a flag slate roof, and forms part of a U-plan courtyard. Howan House stands on top of a small mound in the otherwise flat landscape, and has not been inhabited for a long time. It is in a rather tumbled-down condition today, and has been used as a byre. It has been listed by the Scottish Civic Trust as a building worth saving, so hopefully it will be given a new lease of life.

Robert Monteith, second of Egilsay, had no sons, so in 1674 the estate was inherited by his son-in-law William Douglas of Spynie. It was between 1648 and 1667, while William Douglas was commissioner for Lord Morton, that most of the odal land in Orkney passed into feudal tenure. The Douglases of Egilsay prospered as a merchant and administrative family, and Sir Alexander Douglas, second of Egilsay, became Sheriff of Orkney and tacksman of bishopric rents. History repeated itself when the estate again passed to others through marriage. The heiress Janet Douglas, daughter of the deceased Sir William Douglas, in 1736 married James Baikie, sixth of Tankerness, who was made provost of Kirkwall soon afterwards. The estate then remained with the Baikie family.

For a long time the islands of Rousay, Egilsay, Eynhallow and Wyre have been united, and according to J Storer Clouston there 'is no corner of Orkney more steeped in history than this parish'. In his report to the *Statistical Account of Orkney, 1795-98*, the Revd James Leslie gives a unique description of eighteenth-century Orkney life where he writes this about the manners of his parishioners,

> There is no difference in manners and habits between the cottager and the master of the farm. The master often turns

to cottager, and the cottager sometimes becomes the master. They all take social snuff together. Their houses and their furniture are exactly the same. They all, without distinction, sit at the oar in their boats; and at land they all jointly perform the same labour and work. Youth and old age constitute the only distinction of rank. The old often are so reduced, that they betake themselves to going from house to house for sustenance; and then they are well received; and it is not accounted beggary when they do so.

During the Napoleonic Wars (1792-1814) young, able-bodied men in the Northern Isles were always in danger of being captured by the press-gang, as they were known as good sailors. If we are to believe the numerous stories and lore of the time, Orcadians became adept at eluding the press-gang.

An Egilsay story tells of Hugh Hourston, who lived at the farm of Sound, in the north-western part of the island. He made a lot of money from acting as a pilot to ships going through Howie Sound, and did so well that a jealous rival decided it would suit him better if Hourston were off fighting the French, and therefore managed to get him captured. Then the frigate that was taking Hourston away was in danger of being lost when going through Hoy Sound. Hugh Hourston offered to act as pilot, and the captain was so grateful to him for bringing the vessel safely into port, that he gave him liberty to go ashore.

In the last few decades of the twentieth century the social and communal structure of Egilsay went through rapid change. From having had a population of more than 200 people in the olden days, it was suddenly in danger of becoming depopulated. Farms that had been in families for generations were sold, some were integrated so as to make more workable units, others were taken over by incomers, known as 'ferryloupers', and the rest simply left unoccupied. This exodus occurred all in the space of a few years, in the late 1970s. The trend was apparent in many islands, but for some reason it had a stronger impact in Egilsay than elsewhere.

Today the island has mains electricity and better transport and community facilities. It takes time to adjust to such radical change and build a new communal basis, but it now seems as though the islanders will succeed in charting a new way of life in Egilsay.

Wyre

The flat and fertile island of Wyre was known as *Vigr* in Norse times. There is an island called Vigra off the north-west coast of Norway and we find a *Vigrafjörður* on Snaefellsness in western Iceland. The word *vigr* signified a spear or javelin in Norse. Neither of the two islands looks anything like a spear, but they have the common feature of long, pointed nesses, making it clear that a spearhead is meant. The name was latinised to Viera by the historian George Buchanan in the sixteenth century, but Veira became the accepted version, until it was finally dropped in the 1930s.

Very little is known of the island's early history. In the rocky moorland area just north of Skirmieclett are a number of stone-built enclosures. Though very well-preserved, their purpose is not known. In this area we find also the tiny Loch of Oorns, perhaps at one time a haunt of eagles. From the long, narrow Taing – the spearhead of the island name – comes the atonal singing of seals.

The old chapel of St Mary, built sometime in the twelfth century, has also been called Peter's Kirk, and according to Jo Ben, the island of Wyre was dedicated to this apostle. It is possible there *were* two churches on the site, one succeeding the other, the older of the two being perhaps one of the early Christian churches of the Picts. The area east of the chapel could have been an early Norse land-take in the island, probably centred on the farm of Onziebust, which had good land and occupied a strategic position, between the beacon at the Point of the Wart, and the best harbour. The meaning of the name is not known, but it is interesting to find the same designation also in the south of Egilsay.

Wyre was skatted for a land value of 12d in the old rentals, which describe it as old kingsland. It does not appear in the *Orkneyinga Saga* till the middle of the twelfth century, and then only as a background for the chieftain Kolbein Hruga, who by then had apparently taken over the whole island. He was a Norwegian from Sunnfjord, in the fjord country north of Bergen. The saga speaks of Kolbein Hruga as a very able man, who had a fine stone fort – a *steinkastala* – built on Wyre, 'a really solid stronghold', but the saga is silent about why he should have found it necessary to build a fortification near his farm of the Bu.

The stronghold appears again in the *Saga of Hakon Hakonsson* in 1230-31 as a refuge for Hanef Ungi, King Hakon's sysselman in Orkney and a distant relation of Kolbein Hruga. This was after he had taken part in the killing of Earl Jon Haraldsson during a drunken brawl in Thurso. Hanef and his men sheltered their stores and cattle behind the outworks and prepared for a siege. 'When the earl's friends in Orkney learned of this, they gathered a lot of men who went to Vigr and surrounded the castle. But it was a difficult place to attack'. Jon Haraldsson was the last Norse Earl of Orkney.

The castle of Wyre is the earliest stone-built castle in Orkney, if not in Scotland. It is of Norse design and consists of a small keep, which forms almost a perfect square and is surrounded by a circular ditch. The castle long remained just a grass-grown mound, until it was excavated in 1929. The original structure would have been some three storeys high and must have been quite impressive, commanding a view of everything going on in the island and around it. Today only the ground floor survives. The Romanesque chapel of St Mary consists of a nave and a chancel, and was probably built in connection with the castle.

Kolbein Hruga must have been a large man, as his nickname of Hruga means a pile or a heap, and must have referred to his stature. He has passed into folklore as the giant Cubbie Roo, who would walk with enormous strides from one island to another, always losing on the way the stones he carried for bridge-building. Thus nobody knows whether the stones he used to shore up Straenia Water on Rothiesholm in Stronsay were placed there by design or by accident! But as the historian Wallace puts it in 1693, 'Of this Cubbirow, the common people report many idle fables, not fit to be inserted here'. Many a naughty child would be told, 'Cubbie Roo'll get thee!'

The Revd George Barry, in his *History of the Orkney Islands*, which was published in 1805, writes of Wyre: 'In directing the eye over the island, the first object that arrests the attention is the ruins of the castle of Cubberow on an eminence; an ancient chapel afterwards attracts some notice, especially as there is a churchyard around it, in which most of the graves are seven feet long, since the present inhabitants, that amount to a hundred and fifty, are many of them above the ordinary stature'.

Some of these long graves may of course belong to the descendants of Kolbein Hruga and his wife Herbjorg, who was the great-granddaughter of Earl Paul Thorfinnsson. They had five children, and they are all described in the *Orkneyinga Saga* as outstanding characters. Their only daughter Frida married the son of the 'ultimate Viking', Svein

The old Chapel of St Mary and Cubbie Roo's Castle.

Asleifarson of Gairsay. But it was their second son, Bjarni Kolbeinsson, bishop and skald, that left his mark on Orkney. He was probably born around the 1150s, as he succeeded William The Old as Bishop of Orkney in 1188, and remained in this office until his death in Bergen in 1223.

Nothing is known of his early life or education. His first major task as a bishop was to obtain papal permission to have Earl Rognvald's remains moved from Caithness, where he was murdered, to St Magnus Cathedral in Kirkwall. He succeeded also in the incredible feat of having Earl Rognvald canonised in 1192. But then he must have been a very special man, with a gift for mediation and peace-making, perhaps also for politics. It was inevitable that when King Sverrir of Norway threatened a punitive expedition to Orkney after the Battle of Florvåg in 1194, Bjarni accompanied Earl Harald Maddadarson to Bergen as a peacemaker, and when King Sverrir was banned by the pope for opposing the power of the Church, he supported him in an appeal to Rome.

Earl Rognvald and his father had started the work on St Magnus Cathedral, but it had come to a standstill. This was resumed by Bjarni after he became bishop, and the second great building period began.

Apart from the west front, Earl Rognvald's original design for the Cathedral was carried out in Bjarni's lifetime. The twelfth-century Kirkwall Grammar School drew its revenues from land in Wyre, so it seems probable that this was founded by Bishop Bjarni.

Research has established that the *Orkneyinga Saga* must have been written by an Icelander, but Bishop Bjarni may have supplied much of the information for it, and he is known to have had Icelanders spend the winter in Orkney as his guests. The *Orkneyinga Saga* first introduces Kolbein Hruga's second son as the poet. The only work that can with certainty be ascribed to him is *Jómsvíkingadrápa* – 'The Lay of the Jomsvikings.' Its form is simple, and the poet seems set on defying the rigid rules of skaldic poetry – in a way an Icelander probably would not have done. He begins by saying 'I ask no armed warrior for silence for my lay' and goes on to explain why he cannot do so:

> *Varkak fróðr und forsum*
> I did not grow wise under waterfalls,
> *fór ek alldri at goldrum*
> I never went to magicians
> *...ollungis nam ek eigi*
> never did I learn
> *Yggjar feng und hanga.*
> Ygg's prize – skaldic poetry – under the hanged.

Being a Christian, Bjarni has not learned the art of poetry 'under the hanged', that is from Odin. He also complains of unrequited love, in a way which makes the reader wonder if he is also making fun of the romantic troubadour style.

The subject of the lay is the expedition of the Jomsvikings, warriors from the castellated town of Jomsborg in the estuary of the river Oder in northern Germany, who after too many beers decided to sail for Norway in midwinter to fight against Earl Hakon. They were thoroughly beaten in the Battle of Hjørungavåg in 986, but then they never stood a chance, as the earl had the trolls on his side. The story has a clear parallel: the expedition of the Eyjarskeggjar – the Island Beardies – to Norway and the Battle of Florvåg.

Probably Bishop Bjarni is also the author of *Málsháttakvæði*, as there are points of similarity in style. It is a collection of proverbs and words of wisdom running to 29 verses, very well worked together in a poem. On the surface the poem is written in an extremely simple style, but there are plays on words and double meanings. The work reads very well, because of its easy rhythm. His attitude to life and to his work, expressed in a laid-back, humorous, but clever style, has much in common with that of an earlier Orkney poet, Earl Rognvald Kali Kolsson.

A letter written in 1223 by Bishop Bjarni still exists. It is in Norwegian, and is a kind of will where he leaves his property Holand in Dalsfjord, in the Sunnfjord region, to Munkeliv monastery in Bergen on condition that a woman named Agnes shall live there till she dies. The early thirteenth-century stone church at Dale in Luster, in the same region, has many features in common with the St Magnus Cathedral in Kirkwall, and its form is believed to have been inspired by Bishop Bjarni. Such an idea is not strange; his father Kolbein Hruga came from Sunnfjord, and there would have been family connections. According to local tradition, much of the work was done by Scots masons.

More than seven centuries after Kolbein Hruga's children grew up at the Bu, another poet in the making spent his early childhood there. Edwin Muir was born in Deerness in 1887, but his family moved to Wyre when he was about two years old. In his *An Autobiography* of 1954 he draws an enchanting picture of a childhood spent in a pastoral setting:

> When I think of our winters at the Bu they turn into one
> long winter evening round the stove – it was a black iron
> stove with scrollwork on the sides, standing well into the
> kitchen – playing draughts, or listening to the fiddle or the
> melodeon, or sitting still while my father told of his witches
> and fairicks. The winter gathered us into one room as it
> gathered the cattle into the stable and the byre; the sky
> came closer; the lamps were lit at three or four in the
> afternoon, and then the great evening lay before us like a
> world: an evening filled with talk, stories, games, music,
> and lamplight.

Perhaps Bishop Bjarni would have recognised this description as rather similar to his own childhood, but Edwin Muir was not a chieftain's son, and the whole island had by then become the property of the Westness estate in Rousay, so that the Bu was a tenant farm. His father fell out with the laird, General Burroughs, and the family had to leave. They tried for some time to run a farm in St Ola, but gave it up, and in 1901 moved to Glasgow. Edwin Muir saw the change in his life as being plunged from order into chaos.

The move to the big city proved a nightmarish collision with an unknown culture, and within two years his parents and two of his brothers had died. To Muir the island of his childhood naturally enough became idealised, but he also came to see his later life as an ordeal by fire from which he stood to gain in strength. This is how he expresses it in his well-known poem, 'One Foot in Eden',

> But famished field and blackened tree
> Bear flowers in Eden never known.
> Blossoms of grief and charity
> Bloom in these darkened fields alone.

Edwin Muir later had a distinguished literary and scholarly career. With his wife Willa Anderson he lived abroad for a number of years, and together they translated works by Kafka. He was also a visiting professor of poetry at Harvard University. As a warden of Newbattle Abbey College Edwin Muir was a mentor to George Mackay Brown in his student days; they remained close friends.

About a hundred people lived in Wyre in the nineteenth century, and a school was opened in 1877, but closed down soon after it had celebrated its centenary. Today the children cross by boat to Rousay.

The Wyre Band was formed in the 1950s, and began with four members, all from Wyre. It initially played only at local dances in Wyre and Rousay, but with improved ferry connections and increased interest in traditional dancing, their lively old Orkney dances are much in demand all over the islands.

Deerness

Deerness is the most easterly parish on the Mainland, a peninsula that narrowly misses being an island. Only a narrow strip of sand dunes, the road past Dingieshowe, separates St Peter's Pool from the North Sea. The parish plays an important part in the *Orkneyinga Saga*, where it is called Dyrness, the Norse word *dýr* being used mostly of elk, hart and deer. The name of Deerness has generally been taken to refer to red deer, whose bones have been found in peat-bogs, but it may also simply be an oral map which points out the most striking geographical landmark, Mull Head. It is possible that the name Duirinish in the Isle of Skye derives from the same root.

South-east of Deerness lies the island of Copinsay, from the Norse *Kolbeinsey*, also the black rock called the Horse of Copinsay rising steeply from the sea, and the tidal islands known as Corn Holm, Black Holm and Wart Holm. 'Hawks and Falcons have their Nests in Copinsay', writes James Wallace in 1693. George Low went to Copinsay on his tour in 1774, and was impressed by the number and variety of birds he found there. He noticed 'a single pair of a large species of Hawk which the people told me build in one spot of the rock and have done so past memory of man. This kind is much valued and sought after by the falconer, who gives the people 5*sh.* for the nest, which they procure by letting one another over the precipice.' To the family farming at Copinsay in the old days, the value of the seabird harvest was important. The last residents at the farm left soon after the Second World War, but the lighthouse keepers were there until automation came in 1991.

The Deerness peninsula itself is rather flat, rising in the centre part to 87 m at The Ward. Deerness is fortunate in its climate, which is dry for Orkney. It has fertile land, with soil consisting of deep black earth, clay and fine sand, and farms are intensively cultivated but not large compared to other parts of Orkney. The eastward slope down to the sea is especially striking. Not so long ago, bere and oats were produced, but today mostly barley and grass for cattle are grown. Deerness is all cultivated except in the Mull Head area and the Kirbister Moss.

The cliffs around the coast are awe-inspiring, and are seen at their best from the sea. This is especially true of the Gloup, a deep chasm in the eastern line of high cliffs. Such a gloup is usually due to a geological fault that could no longer withstand the hammering of the waves. The

Gloup of Deerness forms a long cave into the rock, some 50 m long, with the noise of the churning sea below often quite deafening, as well as frightening. The inner part of the roof has collapsed, and the Gloup could therefore be very dangerous, were it not well marked.

Mull Head forms the northern point of the parish; it is a conspicuous landmark which can be seen from far away. The Norse *múli* means both the mouth of an animal and a broad, high promontory. George Low tells us that close to the Mull 'is the Mulhead, a perpendicular rock, in which the most remarkable inhabitants are a couple of Sea Eagles which time immemorial have possessed it without disturbance'. Today the Mull Head is a Nature Reserve.

Deer Sound is almost a landlocked bay, which was a safe anchorage for sailing ships, but Low tells us that it was 'not much frequented except by the Iceland fishing fleet, which some time ago consisted of between 20 and 30 sail, and constantly touched here to hire some part of their hands, and trade with the people for fresh provisions, feathers, stockings, gloves, linen, white stuff, and the like'. At the inner end of the sound, adjoining the large sandy beach at Dingieshowe and well protected from North Sea winds, is St Peter's Pool. It is a favourite resort with all kinds of wild duck and many migrants.

In nearby Campston, in St Andrews, was once a Pictish church, dedicated to St Peter, which clearly has also given its name to the inner parts of Deer Sound. It probably dated back to the eighth century, and was one of the very first Christian churches in Orkney.

The Brough of Deerness was long cast in somewhat the same role, that of being the site of an old, probably Celtic monastery with a Norse church added on to it later. The beautiful, almost inaccessible headland is a place that appeals to the imagination, and earlier visitors had no difficulty believing in the stories of Celtic anchorites who wanted to seek God 'in the untravelled ocean'. Today archaeologists question most of the myths surrounding the Brough, and justly so, as only the chapel has so far been excavated. We must see the Brough of Deerness as an appeal to the imagination, not only for its beauty and its isolation, but as much for the many questions it poses.

The southward end of the Brough is edged by an old massive wall, thought to have been a so-called *vallum monasterii* whose purpose was to isolate the monastery from the world. But the wall may just as well be a relic of a prehistoric fort, an idea first suggested by George Low.

'Towards the land this rock is fenced with a very strong stone wall, and within many foundations of small huts, which plainly demonstrate that this has served more purposes than that of religion, which in all probability has been but the latest – it surely has been a rock fort'.

The cells seem to indicate a monastic community, but until they have been examined more closely, the site cannot for certain be ascribed to any period of history. The chapel was excavated by the archaeologist Christopher D Morris who thinks it should be associated with the late Norse period, rather than the Viking period. The chapel is surrounded by a churchyard where four graves were found, two of them being infants' graves placed next to the east wall of the chapel.

Jo Ben's description from the Brough of Deerness gives an eyewitness account of how it remained a site of pilgrimage for Orkney people into the sixteenth century, as well as the earliest record of the chapel.

> On it is a chapel called the Bairns of Brough. Hither flock together from various islands men, youths and boys, old people and servants innumerable, in truth coming with naked feet, as formerly related; they ascend praying, where none except one at a time can come to the chapel. Here is a well, pure and sparkling, which is indeed wonderful. Then the people on bended knees and with clasped hands, without confidence in the God that is, supplicate the Bairns of Brough with many incantations, throwing stones and water behind them and walking twice and thrice round the chapel.

The word Bairns may be a corruption of the Norse *bænahús*; prayer-house, or chapel.

On the north side of the Brough is a small hiding place hewn out of the cliffs. Tradition has it that during the Napoleonic Wars this was a sanctuary for the men of Deerness hiding from the press-gang. And the small circular depressions south of the chapel, once seen as cells, are now believed to be the result of gunnery practice during the Second World War, when a splayed east window and an aumbry in the north wall of the chapel were probably also destroyed.

North of Sandside Bay, at the end of a footpath, lies a small cliffbound bay, where a long, narrow ness known as Riggan of Kami runs out towards the stack called the Moustag. A very broad mound, some 1.5 m high, hinders the access to the ness itself. Portions of wall can be seen within a mound, but it is clear from the shape that this was not a broch, but a fort.

Deerness plays an important part in the Orkney history of the early eleventh century, as described in the *Orkneyinga Saga*. The stories centre round Earl Thorfinn the Mighty and his friend and foster-father Thorkel Amundason who was nicknamed 'The Fosterer'. Most of the events take place at Sandwick, the sandy bay, which today is known as Sandside Bay. Thorkel's farm was called *Hlaupandanes*. The name means 'the running ness' and may refer to the long ness that today can be clearly seen only at low tide. Conditions in the Viking Age might have been different. At some point the farm became known as Skaill.

Thorkel the Fosterer had become involved in the endless strife between the heirs to the earldom, his loyalty lying always with Earl Thorfinn. Attempting reconciliation, Earl Einar Wrymouth and Thorkel each agreed on alternate banquets. Thorkel would host the first, then they would foregather to Einar's feast. But Thorkel soon suspected that Einar was not playing fair, so he killed the Earl in the drinking hall of his own farm at Sandwick, as the Earl sat beside the fire. This happened in 1020.

Later an important naval battle took place off Deerness. The King of Scots, Thorfinn's grandfather, had died, and 'the next man to take over power in Scotland was Karl Hundason'. Thorfinn fell out with Karl Hundason over the right to Caithness. On the way to Sandwick Thorfinn and his crew are surprised by the enemy, with 11 ships. The battle that followed was long and hard, and for some time no one could tell how it would end.

> singing the bows spilt
> blood, steel bit; bright
> though the quick points quaked,
> no quenching Thorfinn.

This is how the Icelander Arnor Thordarson Jarlaskald, the Earls' Poet, describes the battle, and he is right, Thorfinn and his crew are winning – 'south of Sandwick shone the lord's battle sun' – Karl retreated to Moray Firth.

The saga tells us that Skaill was an important farm in Norse Orkney, and excavations there show that people have lived and worked at the same site continuously since at least the early Iron Age and up to the sixteenth century. The work began in 1963, and was carried out by the late Peter Gelling for Birmingham University. Skaill was a so-called high status site, where chieftains or community leaders would have lived.

The Skaill hogsback tombstone dating back to the late 11th century.

There seems to be a marked change around AD 600: a Pictish phase began, with pottery of a much finer quality than previously, and well-built stone walls, partly at right angles. The Pictish buildings were then abandoned, to be followed by a strongly contrasting phase with Norse structures of poor quality. It was not until the eleventh century that houses were again built with skill to a more elaborate plan.

Was there a dramatic social upheaval at the top levels of society? Peter Gelling speculates that there could have been an official Pictish residence at Skaill, whose occupiers would have been more prepared to return to some part of the Pictish heartland when their control over Orkney was lost. The sense of a clean break, and of a change for the worse in many material respects, is very strong at Skaill.

The first chapel at Skaill was perhaps built by Thorkel the Fosterer in the early eleventh century. A hogback monument, probably going back to the eleventh century, was found in the churchyard. A pre-Reformation church, dedicated to St Mary, was declared 'too small, ruinous, and irreparable' and replaced in 1796 by the present church. George Low was so struck by the old church on his tour in 1774 that he drew three sketches of it. It had two tall, circular steeples, not unlike the tower of St Magnus' Church on Egilsay. According to local tradition a lady living at

The Brough of Deerness.

Sandside lost her two sons when they were drowned, a little south-east of the church. The twin towers were erected in their memory.

The present church is named after the SS *St Ninian* that grounded itself on a sandbank in the bay in 1903, while on the way from Lerwick to Kirkwall with 30 passengers on board. Visibility was poor, and the ship missed the entrance to The String. Instead the steamer ended up on a sandbank near the church at Skaill, having narrowly missed running on some nasty rocks, and could be towed off undamaged. The parish minister persuaded the passengers on board to pay for a bell to be placed in the belfry of the church, for the purpose of warning future voyagers off the rocks.

Another excavation site is Newark Bay, where an early Christian cemetery was gradually eroding into the sea. About 250 people were examined; infant mortality was found to be high.

In the rental of 1595 Deerness is estimated as six urislands, of which the bishopric had some 40 per cent, the earldom share was 23 per cent and the rest was odal property. The land was divided into six tunships, each consisting of a whole urisland: Braebister, Kirbister, Sandwick, Skeatoun, Watland and South End.

Deerness seems to have been a district of well-run farms, but few large estates. Newark, by the bay of the same name, emerged as an estate in the seventeenth century. In 1716 it was taken over by John Covingtree who was Provost of Kirkwall 1718-30, and known as an astute, but not over-scrupulous merchant laird. The estate also owned a large part of Lady parish in Sanday, as well as Eynhallow with its valuable kelp shores. When the estate was taken over in 1778 by the Balfours of Trenaby in Westray, it was worth £1734 a year clear.

The former urisland farm of Braebister was for a long time the largest farm in Deerness. The Reids of Braebister were among the best-known families in Orkney in the nineteenth century. Samuel Reid, who was considered 'the founder of the family', was a merchant and shipowner, as well as Provost of Kirkwall 1876-87. He modernised the farm, and in 1888 built a striking three-storey house in local stone, with a tennis court, as his country residence.

Another well-known nineteenth-century Deernessian was David Vedder (1790-1854), a prolific writer, popularly known as the sailor poet of Orkney. His schooling was sketchy and he was nearly grown up before he was able to read and write. At the age of 12 Vedder went to sea as a cabin boy and as quite a young man got the command of a trading vessel. Later he worked mostly as a journalist, and was long on the staff of *Blackwood's Magazine*, where much of his best work appeared. His works include *Orcadian Sketches* and *Poems, Legendary, Lyrical, and Descriptive.*

It is part of Deerness lore that Napoleon, after his defeat at Waterloo in 1815, surrendered to Acting Lieutenant James Tait from the farm of South Windbrake in Deerness. On parting, Napoleon gave his greatcoat to Tait, who brought it back to Deerness, where it was a ten-day wonder. Unfortunately, with time its origin was forgotten, somebody borrowed it on a cold winter's day, and it was never seen again.

East of the Ward a long footpath leads down to Scarva Taing, where the ship *Crown* was grounded on 10 December 1679. Some 200 people lost their lives, and most of them were buried at Scarva Taing, which is named after the shags that habitually nest there. The story of the ship and its passengers is stark and tragic; the passengers, who were religious objectors known as Covenanters, were prisoners captured after the Battle of Bothwell Brig, 22 June 1679.

A religious controversy had become a war. Most of the prisoners were freed after five months in prison, but the hard core who stubbornly refused to give in, were put on board the *Crown*, to be deported to the colonies. There were ugly rumours that the ship was never meant to reach harbour and that the shipwreck was no accident, as significantly there were no provisions on board for such a long voyage. It is believed that some 50 people were saved, as they managed to find passage on a ship bound for Holland.

Other shipwrecks occurred, and Deerness lore is full of them. The writer Edwin Muir, born in Deerness, grew up with legends and local tradition. His first autobiography tells the tale of his Orkney childhood, and is aptly called *The Story and the Fable*. In this book he points out that in the islands of his childhood there was no great distinction between the ordinary and the fabulous; a man he knew 'once sailed out in a boat to look for a mermaid, and claimed afterwards that he had talked to her.'

Edwin Muir tells the story of what happened to Elizabeth Cormack, his own mother, when she lived with her family at Skaill. When a young girl of 18, 'she was home alone; the rest of the family had gone up to the Free Kirk, two miles away, for an evening prayer meeting. It was a wild night of wind and sleet, and she was sitting in the kitchen reading, when the door opened and ten tall men, dripping with water, came in and sat round the fire. They spoke to her, but she could not tell what they were saying. She sat on in a corner, dumb with terror, until the family came back two hours later. The men were Danes, and their ship had split on a rock at the end of the bay.'

The Gloup of Deerness forms a long cave into the rock.

Holm and Paplay

The southernmost parish on Mainland is Holm, but it is also known as Holm and Paplay. The old rentals dealt with the districts separately, as two parishes, but administratively they have been one unit. Although Holm has long been the official name, Holm and Paplay has lingered on as the way of referring to the whole parish.

The designation Holm is obscure. It might naturally be taken to refer to the two holms in Holm Sound, were it not for the pronunciation, which has always been 'ham'. Probably the original name was *Höfn*, a haven or sheltered bay. By comparison, the place in Caithness where Earl Hlodvir Thorfinnsson was laid to rest some time in the late tenth century, is called Höfn in the saga and known as Ham today. Paplay is called Papuli in the saga, and is no doubt a contraction of the Norse *Papa-byli*, a settlement of papae, or early clergy. There is a Papley in South Ronaldsay. Lamb Holm, known as Laman on old maps, is also a part of Holm parish.

The interior area of East Mainland is still largely uncultivated heath; from there the landscape slopes down towards the sea. This is reflected in the name of Hamly Hill, derived from the Norse *hafnar-hlið*, the haven slope. The southern part of the district is very fertile and well cultivated. In the east we find the striking headland of Rose Ness. The name may derive from the Norse word *hreysi*, a pile of stones or scree, and may refer to the pile-up of stones known today as The Riff on the western edge of the ness. Another possibility is that it points to the cairn that is such a prominent feature on the rocky shore, at the southernmost point of Mainland. The eastern coastline boasts some dramatic crag scenery, with geos and natural arches, and it can be easily walked all the way to Stembister or Dingieshowe.

In 1774, George Low wandered around Holm, while waiting for an opportunity to go to Shetland, and he had this to say about its birdlife:

> Great part of this parish is Moss, which yields fine Peat and shelter for Moorfowl, Plover, Redshank, Lapwing, and I have heard of straying Woodcocks found here, but this cannot affirm with certainty, as I myself have never observed any of this species in Orkney. Feldfares are frequent here in autumn; they come in small flocks of half-a-dozen, but continue very shy till they go off. I have shot several Godwits

about the shores of Holm, being not at all shy, and easily
come at; this species is but scarce in Orkney, flying in flocks
of a dozen, only seen in winter.

Around the two small lochs on the southern seaboard, Loch of
Graemeshall and Loch of Ayre, can be found specimens of some
interesting plants, as well as wintering birds. On the north bank of Loch
of Ayre, not far from the main road, lie the remains of the Broch of Ayre.
Probably the ayre, or shingle bar, that separates the loch from the sea, is
comparatively recent, which indicates that the broch originally stood on
the seashore. The remains of at least three individuals were found when
the broch was excavated, rather amateurishly, in the early twentieth
century by Alexander Sutherland Graeme, eighth of Graemeshall.

Still, the Broch of Ayre seems to be the only Holm site so far
excavated, although as George Low points out, there may be others,
'particularly Pights' houses, the ruins of several yet appearing round the
shores, in the form of pretty large hillocks, called by the inhabitants
Howies, as Castle-howie'. Any unidentified mound was at one time
referred to as 'Picts' houses' in Orkney.

Castle Howe in Paplay has some resemblance to Cubbie Roo's stone
castle in Wyre, mostly perhaps because it is square and fairly large, but
on the other hand it seems to have been built on top of a broch. As it has
not been professionally excavated, it is difficult to say definitely that it
once served as a Norse stronghold, but going by the name and the
location, it seems probable. The Scandinavians would often use the word
kastali when talking about fortifications of some size, often close to a
church site, whereas *vígi* seems to have been used more of a smaller
defence structure, perhaps on a hill or in a field. Up on the hill is the farm
of Vigga, and down on the shore by Howes Wick was the site of the old
church, dedicated to St Nicholas.

The district of Paplay is mentioned several times in the *Orkneyinga
Saga*. In the early twelfth century there seems to be a special connection
between Paplay and the family of Earl Erlend Thorfinnsson. His
daughter Gunnhild's dowry included a farm in Paplay; when his widow
Thora married again, she lived with her new husband at a farm in Paplay.
Thora was descended from one of the first settlers of Iceland, Hrollaug,
natural son of Earl Rognvald of Møre.

The story of the feast at Paplay is a poignant part of the *Orkneyinga
Saga*. The feast was meant to celebrate the peace agreement reached at

The Three Graces at Graemeshall.

the meeting in Egilsay between the Earls Hakon and Magnus. Only Hakon turned up, with his men. Thora herself attended to the guests, serving drinks to the men who had participated in killing her son. When the drink was beginning to work on Earl Hakon, Thora asked him to let her son be taken to church. Then the Earl fell silent and began to think it over. She had asked him so gently that now he began to feel the burden of his crime. He looked at her, and wept. 'Bury your son,' he said, 'wherever you wish.' Soon afterwards Magnus's body was brought to Christ Church in Birsay.

Although Kirkwall would have been the centre of the eastern half of the earldom, Paplay may have been the private property of Earl Erlend, and a favourite residence. In the rental of 1492 there is a farm in Paplay called The Bow of Scale, which was later known as Upper and Nether Bu. This is believed to have been the residence of the old Paplay family, which remained one of Orkney's most distinguished families for several centuries. In an arched recess in the south nave of St Magnus Cathedral are a tomb and a tombstone bearing the Paplay arms. These date from the fourteenth century, and are therefore the oldest armorial remains in the cathedral.

In the mid fifteenth century Earl William Sinclair acquired most of Paplay from the heiress Edane Paplay and her husband Criste Irving in exchange for the Sebay property in St Andrews. The farms were rearranged and Greenwall became the central farm of the substantial area known as 'the grange' or Paplay estate, which remained in Sinclair hands for some time.

The whole parish consisted of five tunships of which Paplay was one, the others being Aikerbister, Netherton or Swartaquoy, Hensbister, and Easter- and Westerbister, all of one urisland each. George Low speaks of the people of the parish as industrious, and the Revd J Wallace, writing in 1685, has this to say, 'By reason of the Temperance of their dyet, and wholesomeness of the air, the People usually live to a good age. A man in the parish of Ham died not many years ago and had lived upward of four score years with his wife in a married state.'

George Graham became Bishop of Orkney in 1615, and seriously set about the business of acquiring land, which he seems to have done to some extent at the expense of the Church. His son Patrick was given the estate of Rothiesholm in Stronsay by his father, and by pestering its Sinclair owner, or so it is said, he also acquired Greenwall. According to tradition the old house was built on the site of an old Franciscan monastery, and the ghost of a monk has been seen at Greenwall, dressed in white robes. In 1656 Patrick Graham built an impressive house at Greenwall, which still stands.

Soon after moving to Orkney, the bishop acquired the property of Meil, a fairly large farm in the Aikerbister tunship. The sixteenth-century house of Meil, from the Norse *melr* for sand, was rebuilt by Bishop Graham in 1626 and after an interval this estate was also acquired by Patrick Graham, who moved there from Greenwall and named it Graham's Hall. By that time he owned more than nine-tenths of the lands of Holm and Paplay. The house of Greenwall became a dower house. A later Graham changed the spelling of his name to Graeme, and the estate name accordingly to Graemeshall.

Patrick Graeme (1739-1786), who was Sheriff of Orkney, actively encouraged the production of linen in Orkney. The main drawback of the flax was the difficulty of saving seed for the following year, but Patrick Graeme saw to it that lint seed was purchased from another source and supplied the spinners with the necessary equipment, collecting and paying for the produce. Around the 1760s linen production in Orkney provided work for some 200 people who spun, wove or dressed flax, both in their homes and in mills. Thousands of yards of fine and coarse linen were woven for the British market. But the French wars put a stop to this, as lint seed could no longer be obtained.

Through the following century the Graeme Lairds were mostly absentee landlords. One of them was Admiral Alexander Graeme (1741-1818), who was born at Greenwall but at most paid three or four short visits to his estate. For generations the estate was administered by factors of the Petrie family, who in 1827, at the order of the Graemes and their family trustee, began the first estate improvement in Orkney. The run-rig system was abolished, the land was enclosed and laid out in individual farm-holdings. Crop rotation was introduced, and the commonties were divided. For better or worse, Graemeshall was a vanguard estate. The house was at one point extensively rebuilt, and today it houses the large collection of antiques that was built up by Norris Wood over a number of years.

From Holmsound Bay, where the village of St Mary's now stands, a badly equipped army left for the Scottish mainland in April 1650. The Marquis of Montrose was a refugee in Norway when he learnt about the execution of King Charles I, and came back to avenge him. Raw Orkney recruits made up most of his army, which was annihilated at Carbisdale in Sutherland.

At the east end of St Mary's is the old storehouse of the Graemeshall estate, with crow-stepped gables and an outside stone stairway. It was built in 1649, in the early years of the estate, and was raided by French privateers in 1694. The beacons were lit, and the French chased off, but not before they had taken what they wanted.

St Mary's developed as a result of the herring fishing which started up in Holmsound Bay at the beginning of the nineteenth century. By 1829 there were as many as 20 Holm-owned smacks going to the herring fishing. Small plots of land along the shore were given in 99-year leases to 'hands making fishing their occupation', and the line of pleasant cottages still so typical of the village, was the result. A large deep-water pier was built, and St Mary's became a well-known fishing-station. Then the blockships came with the First World War, and the Churchill Barriers with the Second, and a way of life that had been built up in St Mary's over so many years came to an end.

On the other hand, it may be said that the Churchill Barriers have caused an extended Mainland area by joining it with Lamb Holm, Burray and South Ronaldsay. Lamb Holm, the island to get the first barrier, was at one time inhabited, but had long been empty. The work was ordered by Winston Churchill after Captain Günther Prien's passage into Scapa Flow in October 1939, which had made it only too obvious that the old blockage was no longer adequate. Much of the heavy construction work was begun by Orcadians and Scots under civilian contract, but the work gathered speed when they were assisted by 550 Italian prisoners-of-war. The Italians had been captured in the Western Desert of North Africa, during General Wavell's successful campaign.

The Italians lived in what was known as Camp 60 on Lamb Holm. In the middle of the war they there began the work of turning two Nissen huts, made of corrugated iron, into a Roman Catholic chapel. They used scrap materials and their own considerable skills. One was a gifted painter and another a metal worker; the result is a beautiful and unique chapel. One of the driving forces behind the work was Domenico Chiocchetti, who twice returned to restore the paintwork in the church. After his death in May 1999, a memorial requiem mass was held in the chapel on Lamb Holm.

The HMS Royal Oak *buoy.*

In the sheltered waters between the Italian Chapel and the Churchill Barrier lie the buildings of Orkney Seafoods Ltd, a modern fish farm for salmon. It is run by three young brothers from Bergen, the third generation of the Sekkingstad family to work in fish-farming and trading. The same family have since 1971 traded with lobster from Orkney. Three times a week, at peak season, a plane takes off from Grimsetter for Bergen Airport, loaded with first-class Orkney lobster for the Norwegian market.

Until the mid eighteenth century the road from St Mary's to Kirkwall was the only thoroughfare of any length in the islands. It gives a clear view of Scapa Flow and the surrounding islands, and as we approach the Gaitnip area, the land grows higher, reaching 100 m at Markstone Moss, the highest point in the East Mainland. In this area was the saga farm of *Jaddvararstaðir*, named for its eleventh-century owner, *Jaddvör*, who was the natural daughter of Earl Erlend II and half-sister of St Magnus. The farm is also referred to as Geitaberg, which may be the origin of Gaitnip.

Under the cliffs of Gaitnip, right on the parish border with St Ola, lies the wreck of HMS *Royal Oak*, which is now an official war grave. On the night of 13-14 October 1939, the German U-boat *U 47*, under the

Bishop Mario Conti after the memorial requiem mass.

command of Günther Prien, managed to find a way past the blockships of Holm Sound into Scapa Flow. The HMS *Royal Oak* was moored under Gaitnip, so that the U-boat just needed to follow the coastline to find her.

The Northern Lights were bright that night, making it possible for the crew of *U 47* to fire at the ship from a distance of 3000 m. HMS *Royal Oak* sank within 15 minutes, and 833 men went down with her. This was the first major enemy strike against Britain, and one of the great submarine exploits of all time. For a long time people refused to believe that the enemy had been inside the Flow, but when the propeller of a German torpedo was located close to HMS *Royal Oak* by a local diver, sabotage theories had to be laid to rest. Every year a memorial requiem mass is held over the wreck.

St Andrews

St Andrews is named after the parish church that once stood just north of the Hall of Tankerness. First mentioned in the rental of 1492 as *Parochia Sancti Andræa*, it is a large parish that is composed of the three main districts of Tankerness, Toab and Upper Sanday. Today Upper Sanday seems more and more to be becoming a part of Toab. In earlier times the Tankerness peninsula comprised the four tunships or small districts of Linksness, Yinsta, Essonquoy and Tankerness.

St Andrews is a sprawling parish, bordered on the north side by the sea, and in the south by large heathery hills which form a natural boundary with the neighbouring parish of Holm and Paplay. The main road through St Andrews runs roughly parallel with this parish border. In the east the narrow neck of land that the Norsemen aptly called *sand-eið*, the sandy isthmus, divides St Andrews from Deerness. Through much of history these two parishes have been united. In the west the parish border neatly divides Kirkwall Airport at Grimsetter in two.

Along the western side of the Tankerness peninsula are the strange lochs of Weethick, where narrow ayres have formed one loch beside the other. Nousts can still be seen on the northern bank of the larger loch, which may have been considered a safe haven for boats in old times. The name probably derives from the Norse *við-vík*, the bay of driftwood. The nearby Loch of Tankerness lies in a very fertile area, and is popular as a feeding and breeding area for a variety of birds.

One of the four brochs in the St Andrews area was placed on a small peninsula in the Loch of Tankerness. Like so many other brochs it was seen as a handy supply of building stone, and this fact is commented on in the report on the united parishes of St Andrews and Deerness in *The Statistical Account of Orkney, 1795-1798*. It is written 'By a friend to Statistical Inquiries'. In the report we are told that the Tankerness broch:

> is placed on a small neck of land jutting out into a fresh-
> water lake behind the minister's house. Its form is now
> semicircular. The wall is nine feet thick, in which, there
> seem to have been no apartments, or if there have, they are
> now filled with rubbish. Some pieces of wall have been
> found on the outside, but their use or form cannot be
> ascertained. Bones and shells of various kinds of animals,
> with peat-ashes, have been found in different apartments on

> the outside of the great wall. The minister, who considers
> modern inclosures, as more ornamental and useful in a
> country, than ancient ruins, has taken a great number of
> the stones of this building for inclosing his glebe.

St Peter's Church was roofless, the manse was 'scarce habitable', and the minister had the whole glebe enclosed at his own expense, at a cost of some 100 guineas. All these complaints are common in the parish accounts, only the St Andrews writer uses more subtle ways to get his views across. And he must have succeeded, as the once elegant Old Manse was enlarged and improved towards the end of the eighteenth century, but is now rapidly becoming derelict.

Today only ruins are left of St Peter's Church, one of the early Pictish churches which were built on broch sites. Its age and importance are apparent from the names of St Peter's Bay and St Peter's Pool, used about the inner parts of Deer Sound. There is another broch site in the Campston peninsula, but the best-known site in St Andrews is Dingieshowe in Upper Sanday, a notable mound in a striking situation. The name implies that the mound, the *þinghaugr* of the Norsemen, once served as a place for meetings of the thing. The name Tingwall in Rendall is the only other name of this kind in Orkney, whereas such names are common in Shetland.

The fertile land of Upper Sanday seems to have attracted settlement from an early age. Close to the eastern shore we find a large standing stone in a striking situation, and the farm of Stembister, from the Norse *stein-bólstaðr*, takes its name from the stone. To the east, in Copinsay, there is a large boulder known as the Giant Stone, which according to legend was flung there from Stembister by a local giant. At the nearby farm of Greens, a Pictish sculptured stone was found in 1923. Among the characteristic symbols incised on the stone was that of the crescent and V-shaped rod.

At Hamly Hill in the Toab district was the *varða* or beacon for the ancient system of signal fires. It is interesting to find that this system was still expected to function as late as 1666, when an entry in the bailie-court book of St Andrews and Deerness begins like this, 'Ordaines all householderis within the said perochin to furnis the Wart Hill called Hamnihill above the house of Horrie with heather and peattis according to thair proportione'. The parishioners were obviously expected to keep the beacon on Hamly Hill in working order.

It would seem that the beacon was lit in the summer of 1136, when men were gathering to fight an approaching enemy. Earl Paul was at the time the sole ruler of Orkney, and refused to share his power with any other claimant. From Sutherland came Olvir Rosta, described in the saga as 'an exceptionally big and powerful man, a great troublemaker and a killer'. He had no claim to the earldom, but was hoping to share it with earl-to-be Rognvald Kali Kolsson, who was waiting in Shetland.

Events are dramatically described in the saga. Earl Paul was told that warships were steering along the eastern coast, and set out to meet them with his fleet of five large longships. They first lay at anchor in Deer Sound, but were rowing east of Tankerness when Olvir Rosta's fleet of 12 Hebridean galleys rounded the Mull and bore down on them. Paul and his men roped their ships together, and the battle began.

Olvir had more men but his ships were smaller; Paul's longships had higher sides and this gave his fleet an advantage. But Olvir himself commanded a large ship and he laid this so hard against the earl's ship, that all the forecastlemen were forced behind the mast. Olvir urged his men to board the ship and he himself was the first up. Everything seemed to be going Olvir's way when he hurled a throwing-spear at the earl and it struck his shield so hard that he fell on the deck. 'There was a lot of shouting and just at that moment Svein Breast-Rope picked up a large piece of rock. He flung it at Olvir, hitting him such a blow on the chest that he was knocked overboard into the sea.' The battle was over.

The piece of rock used in the battle had been provided by the chieftain Erling of Tankerness and his men. In the saga survey of leading Orkney families there is this brief mention of him, 'A man called Erling who farmed at Tankerness on Mainland had four sons, all of them fine men.' Erling offered to help in the battle, but the ships were crowded already, so the Earl asked Erling and his men to collect rocks for them instead.

In the old rentals the name of Tankerness appears as Tannskaraness and Tangskeriness. It has been suggested that the name might refer to a man's nickname. Given the fertile land of the farm and the other advantages of its situation, it would surely have been among the first sites taken, and bearing in mind the map function of the early placenames we should look for an explanation in the surrounding landscape. Close by we find a low, narrow tongue of land; the natural Norse name for this would be *tangi*. Next to this tongue of land we find the Skerries of Lakequoy; the latter name obviously being quite recent.

The standing stone at Stembister overlooking Copinsay.

We can therefore hazard a guess that the name was originally composed of these three elements, *tangi-skerja-nes*, which perhaps would make a good road sign for the traveller.

The older Hall of Tankerness, which now is being used as a barn, was built some time in the mid sixteenth century by a Dutchman called Willem de Groot, brother of the de Groot known from John o' Groats. In 1630 the property was bought by Robert Baikie, of Norse stock, whose family came originally from Isbister in Birsay. He was a young man who persevered and did well, and when he died at the age of 85 in 1675, he was probably the wealthiest man in Orkney. He also acquired the lovely Tankerness House in Kirkwall. The arms of Archdeacon Foulzie, who built the house, and his wife, are still over the gateway.

The Baikies carried on as lairds and merchants, and held on to their lands through changing fortunes for more than 300 years. Many of them were of outstanding ability; some were also politically interested and became Provosts of Kirkwall, where they would spend the winter. The change came in the twentieth century when a large part of the estate was disposed of after the First World War. Robert Baikie, twelfth of Tankerness, sold the rest in 1951.

The area of Linksness, north of the Hall of Tankerness, was once the property of Sir James Sinclair, famous as the victor of the Battle of Summerdale in 1529. He was the natural son of Sir William Sinclair of Warsetter in Sanday, and the Hall of Linksness was once his residence. He was knighted by King James V, and styled Sir James of Sanday and Stronsay. The title seems doubtful, as much of the land was still odal property. He was believed to have committed suicide by throwing himself off the Linksness cliffs, and his estate was forfeited for that reason. His widow, Lady Barbara Stewart, was granted instead bishopric lands in Burray by Bishop Adam Bothwell.

Today nothing is known of the Hall of Linksness. But along the eastern cliffs, close to Rerwick Head, coastal defence installations guarded the entrance to Shapinsay Sound during the Second World War, and the relics are still there. Along the cliff edge are Covenanters' graves, as well as caves where tradition has it they were hiding. At the very edge of Rerwick Point is a curious stone structure, resembling a pier or breakwater and enclosing a tiny harbour. Whether it is artificial or natural has not been ascertained, but the latter would perhaps have been assumed, were it not for the almost similar structures in Sanday and Papa Westray, as well as in Stronsay, where it is known as the Danes' Pier.

The historical farm of Sebay, one of the largest and best farms in the East Mainland, is also closely connected with the sea, as its name shows, Sebay being derived from the Norse *sæ-bær*, sea-farm. The ending *–bær* indicates that it probably was an early settlement farm. It is possible that Sebay is the unidentified saga farm of Flydruness where a man called Thorstein lived with his sons Thorkel Hook-Eye and Blann, and, says the saga, 'all three of them were overbearing men'. Within the old bounds of Sebay we find the placename Point of Liddie, or Liddieness, which is believed to derive from Flydruness, the name of Thorstein's old residence.

The farm of Sebay was earldom property, but it was not bordland and therefore not a veizla farm. In the fifteenth century it was given by Earl William Sinclair to Edane Paplay and her husband, Christe Irving, in exchange for Paplay in Holm. The property flourished, and in the early sixteenth century the Irvings of Sebay had the largest estate in Orkney, including, as it did, the property of Yesnabie in Sandwick, as well as other lands.

The Sebay estate was confiscated by Earl Robert Stewart in 1584,

Farming scene, Upper Sanday.

described by the Orkney historian J Storer Clouston as his 'vintage year'. But in this case 'he seems to have had a suspicion himself that there might be trouble ahead, for he astutely handed over his prize (for a substantial consideration) to his "servitor" William Irving, youngest brother of the family, and let him stand the subsequent racket'. The older brothers Magnus, Gilbert and Edward Irving had to leave Sebay; Magnus Irving settled in Shapinsay and was an ancestor of Washington Irving, the American writer.

Before the era of overland transport much of St Andrews life and work centred on Deer Sound, and for that reason farms mostly face the sea. At the Tankerness Pier we find the relics of a nineteenth-century herring fishing station, and there used to be another across the Sound, at Mirkady Point in Deerness. In the heyday of herring fishing the Deer Sound area would have supported a large number of boats and been a hive of activity.

St Ola

The old name of the parish was *Parochia Sancti Olavi*, the parish of St Olaf. The name derived from that of the church Earl Rognvald Brusason (*c.*1011-1046) built in Kirkwall and dedicated to St Olaf, his foster-father. In his young Viking days in England Olaf Haraldsson had become a Christian, and as King of Norway he tried to christianise the country. He met with opposition, and fell in the Battle of Stiklestad, in which the young Earl Rognvald also took part.

Earl Rognvald evidently knew what he was doing when he chose the central

The Pickaquoy Centre.

part of St Ola as his residence. The parish has a strategic position between east and west Mainland, and the two bays of Kirkwall and Scapa, with the comparatively narrow isthmus of the Scapa Gap between them, make it possible for ships to escape both the enemy and the weather. Communication with the North and the South Isles became relatively easy.

Placenames indicate that Earl Rognvald was not the first to appreciate the area. The valley of Papdale, with a burn running down into Kirkwall, must still have had *papae*, the Christian priests or monks, in residence when the Norsemen arrived. And there is Pickaquoy, on the opposite side of the town, today the site of Orkney's Millennium project, the Pickaquoy Sports and Health Centre, but at one time a home for the Picts, whose presence perhaps was rare enough at the time to be pointed out specially, through placenames.

In the north-eastern part of the parish the wide expanse of Inganess Bay was much sought as a harbour in the old days, as it provided anchorage and shelter for the heaviest of vessels. In his novel *The Pirate*, Sir Walter Scott has his main character, Captain Cleveland, anchor his ship in Inganess Bay. In his *History of the Orkney Islands* of 1805, George Barry writes that the bay 'is so well sheltered from the west wind, which here is commonly the most violent, and so commodious in other respects, that some seafaring men of reputation prefer it as a harbour even to the road of Kirkwall.'

The peninsula that gave Inganess Bay its name is probably the one directly to the north of it, leading to the Head of Holland. Much of the Red Sandstone was taken from here for St Magnus Cathedral, and brought by boat to Kirkwall. Here once lay one of the earl's veizla farms of Holland, with an early chapel. To the west was Papdale, and further west was the farm and bay of Weyland, the name probably deriving from the Norse *vé*, meaning holy. The name of Inganess itself may have a religious origin, as the name could refer to *Yngvi-Freyr*, a Nordic god of fertility.

To the west, a ridge running parallel to the parish border, rises from 81 m at Coal Hill on the Scapa coast, through Upper Berryhill at 85 m, Burrey Brae at 148 m to end at 225 m on Wideford Hill. The view from the summit is in itself a lesson in geography; all the islands can be seen and recognised, and in fair weather it is even possible to have a glimpse of distant Fair Isle. It seems only natural that this is where the main beacon would be situated; the name of Wideford derives from the Norse *vita-vörð*, meaning beacon-watch.

The drawback of the old chain-reactive beacon system was that it could not be stopped once it was alerted. It was replaced later by a centrally based and manned beacon to supervise the others, and it was only when this gave the signal, that action would follow. Again there are Jo Ben's observations to confirm this: 'Here is a very great hill called Whytford where all Pomona and all the islands are to be seen, and it is the criterion of war for the Orkneys when the fountain at the summit is seen to gush forth.'

Neolithic man was also attracted to Wideford Hill, and perched high on the hillside is a chambered cairn dating back to about 2500 BC. Archaeological interest in Orkney began in earnest with the excavation of this tomb in 1849. The pioneer work was carried out by George Petrie, who was an interested amateur archaeologist as well as a local historian.

Petrie found a communal tomb of the so-called Maeshowe type. It had been filled with earth and stones, obviously to seal it off when no longer in use. There were no human remains, but a large quantity of animal bones were found beneath the rubble and earth filling the chamber. The entrance faces west over the Bay of Firth, towards Cuween Cairn in Firth. The striking location of the tombs suggests that their sites were chosen, as in Rousay, for the purpose of maximum visibility within a certain area.

Further down the slope, on its northern side, is the Quanterness chambered tomb which goes all the way back to the fourth millennium BC. In his book, George Barry describes a visit to the tomb 'which has been lately discovered'. He gives a detailed description of the tomb, with measurements, but is greatly puzzled about what might have been its use. Believing it to be what he calls a Picts-house, he never tumbles to its being a burial chamber.

Nothing is known of this first exploration at Quanterness, but when Dr Colin Renfrew excavated the chambered tomb in the 1970s, he found that its contents had not been removed. The tomb still retained a mass of bones, and Dr Renfrew suggests that a community of some 20 people may have used it for about 1000 years. Many bones of the corkwing wrasse were found at Quanterness; this is a fish that is rare in Orkney waters today, indicating that the sea must have been warmer in Neolithic times.

In the earliest Iron Age, some 2000 years after the tomb went out of use, its entrance passage was breached by roundhouse builders. At that time the cairn would perhaps have seemed just a handy supply of building stone. A large circular house was built into the entrance area of the tomb. Roundhouses seem to have become fashionable in the first millennium BC, and the one at Quanterness is the earliest one of its kind so far found in Orkney, dating to around 700 BC.

At Head of Work, with its eye-catching view of the narrow String, is a rather unusual horned burial cairn that has not so far been excavated. The name of Work derives from the Norse *virki*, for fortification, and it is possible that the farm is built on some defence structure. At Grain, near Hatston, an earth-house can be seen, rather like the one at Rennibister. It consists of an entrance stair and a passage leading down to a subterranean chamber; this kind of structure has so far been found

Wideford Hill chambered cairn, looking over the Bay of Firth.

only in Orkney and Shetland. The earth-house at Grain was first discovered in 1827, and some years ago an extensive Iron-Age settlement was found quite close to it.

Archeological finds are still made, some quite dramatically, like the discovery in the summer of 1998 of a Neolithic burial chamber at Crantit, between Kirkwall and Scapa Bay. During ploughing, the tractor driver noticed a large hole in the field he was preparing for a crop of barley. The tomb is thought to be of the so-called Bookan type, of which Taversoe Tuick in Rousay is a well-known example. Two Bronze-Age cists were discovered to the south and north of the Neolithic tomb, which had disappointingly few contents, apart from some human skeletal remains.

An unexpected, very interesting feature of the tomb more than made up for the meagreness of its contents. This is popularly known among the archaeologists as The Crantit Light Box. While working inside the chamber they noticed that a shaft of light was shining in through a gap in the entrance passage. A 'notched' lintel allowed the sunlight to shine on the rear wall. According to calculation, this would, in the Neolithic period, have occurred around 16 February. It is possible that illuminating the interior of a chambered cairn by sunlight at a particular time of the year, as at Maeshowe, was of crucial importance.

Along the banks of Scapa Bay there is a lovely footpath, going past the fields of Lingro. Here until a few decades ago stood the Broch of Lingro, like the Broch of Gurness a defended village that may have housed up to 250 people. Similar to the Broch of Clickhimin in Shetland it had ditches and earthworks of a very involved character. Perhaps the most interesting find made in the broch was some Roman coins. Then one day a visiting archaeologist went to Lingro to see the broch, and found only a field of barley!

In the upset that followed there was anger because a scheduled monument, part of Orkney's heritage, had been

5000-year-old tomb at Crantit.

ruined, but the farmer, for his part, insisted that the broch was 'serving no real purpose' and had not been visited by anybody for years. This echoes an old conflict of interests going all the way back to the Odin stone of Stenness in the early nineteenth century, illustrating to some extent why farmers dread the idea of finding a prehistoric monument on their land.

In Norse times the farm of *Knarrarstaðir*, later known as Knarston, and today a part of Lingro, was earldom property and played a part in the *Orkneyinga Saga*. Just before Christmas of 1136, Svein Asleifarson escaped from Caithness, where his father had been burned to death, 'to Knarston on Scapa, where the farmer was called Arnkel and had two sons, Hanef and Sigurd', who both went with Svein to seek Earl Paul at Orphir.

When Earl Rognvald had ruled over Orkney for two years he held a Christmas feast on his farm at Knarston. On the sixth day of Christmas a ship was seen sailing north across the Pentland Firth. On board was

Bishop Jon of Atholl, and Earl Rognvald 'set the bishop on his own high-seat and he himself served at table as cup-bearer'.

Some years later Earl Rognvald's farm at Knarston was being looked after by Botolf the Stubborn, an Icelandic skald, and it was there the Earl sought shelter one night, while hotly pursued by Svein Asleifarson and the young Earl Erlend. They soon turned up at Knarston, demanding to know where the Earl was. Botolf pointed to the fence and answered in this way:

> Out after eating-birds!
> Fine archers, the earl's men;
> hard for the hen-bird
> the head-shot on the hill.
> Excellent the aim
> of the elm-bows, savage
> the grouse-hunt, grim
> the guardian of the land.

All the while, Earl Rognvald was safely inside, fast asleep.

Further inland, at Caldale, in 1774, a large silver hoard was found by a man digging peat. It consisted of several pieces of silver with some armlets among them, but the most interesting part of the find was the 300 silver coins from the time of Canute the Great. A number of such silver hoards from the period 1016-35 have been discovered in Britain, and are believed to be part of Canute's system of political bribery.

During the First World War there was a Royal Air Force station in the Caldale valley, known as Caldale Airship Station. Besides airships the base also stored reconnaissance balloons carried by the warships. They would be inflated at the Caldale base and towed to Scapa Flow. Remains of some of the camp huts are still visible.

It was here, on the south side of Wideford Hill, that most of the market activities of the great Lammas Fair took place every summer. In *The Pirate*, Sir Walter Scott describes the bustle of preparations for the Market, on the open heath

> ...to the northward of the ancient Burgh of Saint Magnus.
> The plain at the foot of the hill was already occupied by
> numbers of persons who were engaged in making
> preparations for the Fair of Saint Olla, to be held upon the
> ensuing day, and which forms a general rendezvous to all
> the neighbouring islands of Orkney, and is even frequented
> by many persons from the more distant archipelago of

Zetland. It is, in the words of the Proclamation, 'a free
Mercat and Fair, holden at the good Burgh of Kirkwall on
the third of August, being St Olla's day', and continuing for
an indefinite space thereafter, extending from three days to
a week, and upwards.

St Ola is a fertile parish and was skatted as seven urislands in the old
rentals. At some point much of the land was made a part of the
temporality of the bishopric, as around 1500 it had a very large
concentration of bishopric land, as much as 85 per cent, while some ten
per cent belonged to the Earl and only five per cent was odal property.
Earl Robert Stewart later established himself at the Bu of Corse.

To the south-east, at the top of the steep road now called Clay Loan,
is the hill that used to be known as Gallowha'. This is where convicted
witches and criminals were executed in the old days, and the site was
meant to be visible from a distance, to discourage others from taking up
witchcraft. Gallowha' was the name of the only house on the hill. It was
the home of the hangman whose function was passed on from father to
son. The witches were sentenced to be 'worried' to death, which seems to
have meant that they were first strangled, then burned.

The Battle of Papdale, known as Orkney's forgotten battle, was
fought on 13 August 1557. There was anger in the islands directed
against both Lewismen and English fishermen, bound for the Iceland
fisheries, who would at times raid the North Isles and carry off some of
the people. As a result, when an English naval force was sent into the
area with the mission 'to annoy the Scots and protect the homecoming
Iceland fleet of fishing vessels', the scene was all set for trouble. Under
the Summerdale veteran Edward Sinclair, some 3000 Orkneymen
attacked the English landing party, killing close on 100 of the English
invaders, including three of the ships' captains. The Admiral, Sir John
Clere of Ormesby, was drowned while trying to get back to his ship.

Today the venerable Kirkwall Grammar School, with its roots going
back to the twelfth century, has become a large, state-of-the-art complex
in Papdale valley.

The farm of Papdale was bought by the talented Laing family, who built
their townhouse at the top of the valley. They had property in Sanday and
Stronsay as well, and were known as experimental farmers willing to
introduce new methods and breeds. The first owner was Malcolm Laing
(1762-1818) who represented Orkney and Shetland in Parliament, but is

better known for his *History of Scotland*, which became a classic.

Samuel Laing (1780-1868), a younger brother, had an exciting and adventurous life abroad before he came back to Orkney and started the Stronsay herring fishing in 1816. He took over Papdale House after his brother's death, and became a very popular Provost of Kirkwall. Then in 1833, he found himself a loser in the parliamentary election in which he had been considered a sure winner. To add to his woes, his financial affairs had gone all wrong and he was bankrupt, his wife had died and his two children had left home.

Samuel Laing decided to go to Norway, where he stayed for two years in Verdalen, renting the hill farm of Midtgrunnan. He wrote *Journal of a Residence in Norway during the Years 1834, 1835 & 1836*. He went on to write a book about Sweden as well, *A Tour in Sweden in 1838*, where he describes the Swedes as the most immoral people in Europe, for forcing the Norwegian people into a political union.

This was too much for the Swedish ambassador to Britain, Count Magnus Björnstjerna, who wrote *On the Moral and Political Union of Sweden and Norway in Answer to Mr S. Laing's Statement*, a book of 65 pages, printed in London, in which he accused Laing of libelling the Swedish nation. Not to be daunted, Samuel Laing wrote a bitingly sarcastic and offensive reply to 'this genius behind sixty-five manuscript pages'. Norway itself could hardly have fostered a greater chauvinist for its cause than Samuel Laing.

His greatest achievement had yet to come: in 1844 he published his translation into English of the *Heimskringla*, the sagas of the Kings of Norway written by the Icelander Snorri Sturluson. For more than a hundred years this remained the standard translation, and in 1964 it was published in the popular series 'Everyman's Library'.

Kirkwall, from the air.

Kirkwall

In Orkney, all roads lead to Kirkwall. It is the undisputed centre of the islands, both geographically and otherwise, although Stromness people would like to think differently. The best approach is from the east, along the Holm road. The view from the hill, before dropping down into the town, is striking. Kirkwall is spread out beneath, snug between two glittering bays, grey and old, with the cathedral tower its most commanding feature, and the western hills forming a fine amphitheatre.

The approach from the west crosses the tidal basin called the Oyce, popularly known as the Peerie Sea. A spit of shingle called the Ayre forms a barrier against the sea and once made the Peerie Sea a perfect haven for Viking ships. St Magnus Cathedral was built close to the shore. Since then the Peerie Sea has been reduced in size, as land has been reclaimed and the town has grown westwards. The houses along Shore Street were among the oldest in the town, until the powers-that-be demolished them all, in order to make space for an oil depot that completely ruins the western view of the town.

'Earl Rognvald took up residence at Kirkwall and gathered in all the provisions he needed for the winter there. He had a great retinue and lived in grand style.' This is the first time the town is mentioned in the *Orkneyinga Saga*, and the passage describes plans for a future that never came about, as Earl Rognvald was killed in Papa Stronsay before Christmas that same year. According to tradition Earl Rognvald, 'the most able of the Orkney earls', built a church in Kirkwall to the memory of his foster-father, St Olaf, around 1040. This may have been the church that gave the bay its name of *Kirkjuvágr* – church bay – but most probably there would have been an even earlier church in the vicinity. Later the name became Kirkwall.

There would have been a Christian settlement in the valley of Papdale, when the first Norsemen arrived. It probably belonged to the Roman Church which was introduced from southern Pictland, and was active in Orkney in the early eighth century. It is quite possible that they had established a chapel or church in the bay area. By the time Earl Rognvald built his church to St Olaf some 300 years had passed, and the new church may even have been erected on the foundations of the old one. The church of St Olaf stood on consecrated ground between the harbour and the Burn of Papdale. A doorway from the church can still be seen in St Olaf's Wynd.

The village of Kirkwall grew in importance, as a trading centre, and also because of its church dedicated to a saint who was growing in stature all over the Nordic world. The popularity of the Lammas Fair held on St Olla's day early in August each year probably came very soon. The historic Kirkwall was built according to the plan of early medieval Norwegian towns like Bergen and Stavanger. The moving of St Magnus' relics from Birsay to Kirkwall heralded a new era in the history of the town and the earldom.

Earl Rognvald II knew what he was doing when he promised to build a minster to St Magnus in Kirkwall, although it may at first have been the idea of Bishop William the Old, the first resident bishop of Orkney. It was Earl Rognvald's father, Kol Kalason, who supervised the building of the Cathedral of St Magnus. The work started soon after Rognvald was established as Earl of Orkney, and took several centuries to complete. The style reflects the various stages of the building process. The cathedral was built entirely in Orkney stone, by masons brought in from Durham; probably the same school of masons who built the

Cathedral of Trondheim in Norway.

The building of the cathedral transformed Kirkwall into a place of religious pilgrimage and brought about the wealth and increased population caused by such a status. The twelfth century was a time of optimism, one might say almost of exuberance, with the Earl and Bishop William setting off on a crusade to the Holy Land, with poetry writing and Gregorian music. Two schools were founded; the Sang School attached to St Magnus Cathedral, and, later, Kirkwall Grammar School.

With the building of the cathedral the village developed into a town, with much the same plan it has today. The main street follows the outline that the Peerie Sea once had. The old houses of Shore Street were probably built to accommodate the cathedral workmen. The area south of the cathedral was assigned to the church and its dignitaries, and was known as the Laverock. North of the cathedral was the Burgh, where all kinds of trade were carried on, and where the ordinary townspeople lived. The boundary was the Kirk Green in front of the Cathedral. The division was deep; it is commemorated in the Ba', the annual football game played on Christmas Day and also on New Year's Day between the Uppies and Doonies, or the earl's men and the bishop's men.

There seem to have been alehouses too in Kirkwall at the time, as we hear in the saga about the two men Thorarin and Thorkel falling out during a drinking session in the town. Thorarin kills his drinking mate, then seeks refuge in the cathedral, where he is pursued by Thorkel's friends. Earl Rognvald stops them, but not before he has had an argument with them about the church's right to give sanctuary.

Where would Earl Rognvald's residence have been? Kirkwall was the administrative centre of the earldom, and there must have been a hall for the earls somewhere in the vicinity of the cathedral, but there is no record of such a building. The first bishop's palace was probably built for William The Old, perhaps while he was away on the crusade. Some remains of a very old building can still be seen at the site of the Bishop's Palace, and the masonry corresponds to the oldest parts of the cathedral. Its resemblance to the stone hall of the archbishop of Trondheim has also been commented on.

On 16 December 1263 King Hakon Hakonsson of Norway died in the Bishop's Palace. It was the sad ending to a grand undertaking. He had left Bergen in the summer with the largest fleet ever gathered in Norway, to go 'west over sea' in order to strengthen the Norse ties with the Isle of

Nave bays and piers with triforium above.

Man and the Western Isles, but had lost the fight against weather and foe. His body was taken to St Magnus Cathedral and placed there. This is how the *Saga of Hakon Hakonsson* tells the story:

> On the Tuesday the body of king Hakon was placed in a
> coffin with such ceremony as is fit and proper for a
> crowned king. He was buried in the chancel of the
> Cathedral of St Magnus in the raised floor before the shrine
> of earl Magnus the Saint. Then they replaced the stone on
> the coffin and covered it with a cloth.

In the gallery of the cathedral there was until recently an open coffin, probably of medieval origin, of a stone unknown in Orkney. A vague oral tradition has connected it with the death of King Hakon. The coffin is now in the Tankerness House Museum.

In 1987, to commemorate the 850th anniversary of the founding of the cathedral, a new west window was installed. It was designed by Crear McCartney.

When Henry St Clair became Earl of Orkney in 1379, the conditions attached to his grant from King Hakon VI were quite explicit; he 'should build no fort or stronghold within the precincts of the earldom without the royal consent'. There seems to have been political tension between the Bishop, who had accommodation for a large garrison, and the Earl. The building of the massive Kirkwall Castle around 1380 restored the balance of power between them, but it meant going against the royal command.

The castle withstood attacks in the centuries that followed, and at one point made an Earl of Caithness exclaim in frustration, 'I protest to God, the house has never been biggit without the consent of the devil, for it is one of the strongest holds in Britain'. Today only the name of Castle Street recalls the stronghold that once dominated the town.

With the Scottish earls came an influx of Scottish settlers, and the character of the town changed. The earl would entertain his court at the castle in the manner of a feudal baron, and Kirkwall at an early stage became the winter quarters of well-to-do landowners who built houses in the town. Kirkwall itself became a social centre, with the earl's court described as 'the most elegant and refined in northern Europe'.

In 1486 Kirkwall was granted a royal charter by King James III, and made a royal burgh. Under Scots law it then assumed complete monopoly over trade and crafts throughout Orkney. At the same time the King handed over the St Magnus Cathedral as a gift to the burghers of Kirkwall; this status was confirmed in later royal charters. Until recently Kirkwall was one of the Northern Burghs that sent a representative to Parliament.

Bishop Robert Reid, an outstanding churchman, gave new impetus to the bishopric and to religious life in the islands. Bishop of Orkney from 1541 to 1558, he reorganised the Sang School and the Grammar School, he reconstructed St Olaf's Church and as well as restoring he extended St Magnus Cathedral. He completely rebuilt the Bishop's Palace, and added the strong and massive tower, circular on the outside, and square inside. It is known as the Moosie Too'er, and outside bears Bishop Reid's effigy in the form of a rather roughly cut statuette in sandstone.

The Bishop's Palace was locally known as the 'Palace of the Yards' because it had courtyards towards the east. Some time later Earl Patrick Stewart built his own palace close to the bishop's residence. It was long known as the 'New Wark of the Yairdis', and the two buildings probably formed a single complex at the time.

Earl Patrick's palace was built by forced labour, but even so it was instrumental in bankrupting him. The palace building shows that he must have been a man of definite artistic taste; perhaps his one redeeming quality. The palace assumes the character of a castle and palace. The great banqueting hall with its chimneys at either end is obviously meant to dispense generous hospitality; it is reached by a spacious and elegant staircase. The palace has inspired much admiration; it has been called an architectural gem and the finest and most mature Renaissance building in Scotland.

During Cromwell's occupation of Scotland in the 1650s, an English garrison was established at Kirkwall, and one of their forts was built at the Weyland shore. The cathedral was used as a stable for army horses. Although the soldiers and the Kirkwallians seem to have got along well, one of the soldiers wrote a rather ironic *Poetical Description of Orkney*, as he found it:

> Their schooles of learning are in every house,
> And their first lesson is to hunt the louse.

With changing times the political and ecclesiastic importance of Kirkwall may have declined, but its importance as a social centre and a commercial town grew. With the income from kelp the wealthy lairds built town houses along the winding historic street with its oddly nondescript names. By the early nineteenth century the town had a population of some 2000 inhabitants. According to the Revd Barry, writing in 1805, the government of the town 'is in the hands of a Provost, four Magistrates, a Dean of Guild, Treasurer, and fifteen other members, which together compose a Council, that meets at Michaelmas every year for the purpose of alternatively electing and being elected, and at other times to collect and dispense the public funds'.

Visitors to the town have reacted differently. Jo Ben on his 1529 travels in Orkney found that 'the women here are given to excess in carnal pleasures'. In 1806 the Revd Jas Hall attended a ball in Kirkwall and was greatly impressed, 'Though I have seen assemblies at Edinburgh, London, Bath etc., yet I scarcely ever saw more mirth, innocence, elegant dancing, or more handsome and elegantly dressed ladies in my life.' But Sir Walter Scott, who visited in 1814, did not agree:

> We have now got to Kirkwall & needs I must stare
> When I think that in verse I have once called it fair
> 'Tis a base little burgh both dirty and mean
> There's nothing to hear & there's nought to be seen
> Save a Church where of old times a prelate harangued
> And a palace that's built by an Earl that was hanged.

Many of the old houses have not survived, some are disguised as shops or have become hotels, but Tankerness House has so far survived all upheavals. The house is known to have existed in 1574, but may be older. Originally a cathedral property, it was reputedly saved from destruction at the time of the Reformation because the cathedral's last archdeacon, Gilbert Foulzie, managed to secure the building for himself. In 1644 the Baikie family of Tankerness in St Andrews bought the house, and later added on to it several other houses that had previously served as manses for cathedral dignitaries. Tankerness House remained in the possession of the Baikie family until they sold all their property in Orkney, and the whole complex was turned into a museum. Its beautiful walled garden is now a public park.

Some chose to build their houses on the outskirts of the town, notably Buckham Hugh Hossack who in 1900 published his standard work *Kirkwall in the Orkneys*, involving enormous research and much enthusiasm, as well as love for his native islands. His residence, Craigiefield, just north-east along the bay, was the work of the local architect, T S Peace, who also designed many other houses in Orkney.

So much history, lore and tradition is connected with the old town of Kirkwall, and through it all runs a vein of tolerance and good humour. According to one old story a cup was kept at Scapa, and when any new bishop landed there, it was filled with strong ale and offered to him to drink. If he happened to drink it off with good cheer, it promised a noble bishop, and many good years in his time.

Perhaps surprisingly, whisky production is one of Orkney's most important sources of income, second only to agriculture. At one time there were three whisky distilleries in Orkney, but the Old Orkney distillery at Stromness is now only a distant memory. Not far from where the bishop would come ashore is Scapa Distillery, founded in 1885. Up on the hillside is Highland Park, which celebrated its bi-centenary in 1998. Highland Park is thus not only the most northern Scotch Whisky distillery, noted for its single 'malt' but it is also one of the oldest established distilleries in Scotland.

The distillery has won many awards, and has its own faithful devotees. One of them is Jan Guillou, a popular Swedish writer of modern suspense fiction. He has his hero saying, 'When I'm with people, I drink Macallan, when I'm alone I drink Highland Park, it speaks to me!'

Legend has it that Highland Park Distillery was founded by Magnus

Eunson, a renowned smuggler and producer of illicit whisky. With great ingenuity he led a double life; in the daytime he was a popular preacher at his local kirk and a respectable member of society, at night he plied a more lucrative trade in whisky. The stories of how Mansie, as he was affectionately known, fooled the excise men, are the stuff of legend in Orkney.

Detail of west window,
St Magnus Cathedral.

The high quality of Mansie's home-produced whisky was believed to be due to the water from the Cattie Maggie spring near his home on the eastern hill slope above Kirkwall. The distillery still draws water from the same spring and the distilling process has remained almost entirely the same. The distillery malts its own barley, and the malt is dried in kilns fired with peat and heather from its own peat banks at Hobbister in Orphir.

Another old Kirkwall firm was established in 1798, namely the Kirkwall Press, which from 1854 also published the weekly newspaper *The Orcadian*. The firm began as an importer into Orkney of religious books in sheet form which they bound and sold throughout the islands. It has been said that one firm had a spiritual beginning and the other a spirituous one, and that 1798 was a good vintage year for Kirkwall enterprise.

The St Magnus Festival was first held in 1977 and now takes place every year in June. Although it centres on St Magnus Cathedral and Kirkwall, many of the events also take place in Stromness, George Mackay Brown's home town. The music drama 'The Martyrdom of St Magnus' opened the first St Magnus Festival, performed in the saint's own cathedral in Kirkwall. The libretto was built on Brown's novel *Magnus*, the music composed by Sir Peter Maxwell Davies. These two, the writer and the composer, later produced many other works based on local tradition, to be performed at the St Magnus Festival.

Waulkmill Bay and the Loch of Kirbister.

Orphir

Orphir has been a separate parish ever since 1614. The name derives from the Norse *ørfjara*, a word used about a place that is dry at ebb tide. There is an island called Ørfirisey in Iceland, a name that would also apply to the Holm of Houton, as the western entrance to the Bay of Houton is completely dry at ebb tide. The name of Orphir as a district name was probably first used about a Norse land-take of the area from Houton Head to Orphir Bay, including the old tunships of Houth, Midland and Orphir. The name of Midland suggests that it may at one time have been the middle part of an estate.

Orphir is a large parish, but only the coastal slope is fertile land, representing a mere four urislands in the old rentals. The inner part of Orphir consists of hills and moorland, rising sharply towards Ward Hill and Mid Hill, at 268 m and 275 m respectively, the two highest hills on Mainland. The two neighbouring parishes of Stenness and Orphir actually have to share the right to them, as the parish boundary runs right along their summits.

Several paths lead up to Ward Hill, and the view alone is well worth the climb, but the hill is also interesting in a botanical sense. The Revd Liddell, writing for the *Statistical Account of Orkney,* 1795-98, describes how 'at one view, 25 islands and 23 parishes, including most of the Orkney islands, and part of the island of Great Britain', can be seen.

The hill area is home to many birds, the hen harrier and the grouse among them. The hen harrier is also a visitor to the Bird Reserve of Hobbister Hill, the area where Highland Park Distillery finds its peat. There are waders in Waulkmill Bay. The Loch of Kirbister has been known for the quality of its trout and for its rare plants, thus the pond weed *Zannichellia polycarpa* and the sedge *Carex fulva* for a long time had status as British plants only from being found in or around this loch.

The parish has also been a healthy place for people, or so at least the Revd Liddell tells us. 'The ague is not known here, and scorbutic complaints seldom occur; owing, perhaps, to the abundance of fuel, to the frequent use of vegetables, and of malt liquor; and above all, to the salubrious sea breezes, which cool the air in summer, and counteract the frosts in winter, and render the climate, upon the whole, more temporate, than in many places of a more southerly latitude upon the continent.'

The fertile coast-belt forms the most thickly inhabited area; in the old days this was divided into ten different tunships. With the exception of Hobbister, they all had their own chapel, and to some extent the tunships were all independent of each other. The Orphir coast-belt stretches all the way from Moo Taing, facing Hoy Sound, to the border of St Ola parish at Coal Hill.

The old tunship of Clestrain was divided into two parts, Clestrain benorth and besouth the burn. An old spelling is Klatestrand, meaning the shore of crags. The name of Clestrain is found in Stronsay as well. In the old northern tunship we find the Hall of Clestrain, a finely proportioned house and one of the historically most interesting buildings in Orkney. Unfortunately it is going to rack and ruin rapidly. The late George Mackay Brown was saddened by its state, and thought that 'such a famous house – and so gracious too, even in decay – ought to be preserved as a keystone in our heritage'.

The Hall of Clestrain was the old seat of the Honyman family. Robert Honyman (1676-1737) became the Laird of Graemsay when he bought the island in 1699, but he always resided at the Hall. Family members did well, as lawyers and MPs for Orkney. The present Georgian mansion was built for Patrick Honyman in 1769. The last resident laird was

William Honyman (1756-1825), who became a baronet in 1804. In the early decades of the nineteenth century the Honyman estate was second only to the earldom lands in value, and brought in a rental of some £4000 a year, but in 1827 the Honyman heir sold the estate to the Balfours.

In the winter of 1725 the Honyman mansion was looted by the pirate John Gow (1697-1725). The son of a Stromness merchant, he had led a mutiny the year before on the 26-gun ship *The George*, while in the Mediterranean. The ship was renamed *Revenge*, and turned up one day in Stromness, where John Gow and his crew at first were warmly received. Then rumours began to spread, and Gow must have felt he had nothing much to lose by pursuing his piracy. But they did not find anything much at Clestrain, as Mrs Honyman had seen them coming and had hidden everything of any value in the attic, underneath a large pile of feathers.

The famous Arctic explorer, John Rae (1813-93), grew up at Clestrain, as his father was the factor of the Honyman estate. He graduated in medicine from the University of Edinburgh at the age of 20, and became a surgeon on board one of the Hudson's Bay Company's ships. From 1846-7 he set forth on the first of his four research expeditions to explore the Canadian Arctic. His task was to link up the coastline between Ross's discoveries in Boothia and those of Parry at Fury and Hecla Strait.

In 1845 the English explorer Sir John Franklin (1786-1847) had with his two ships the *Erebus* and the *Terror* and a crew of handpicked men, made Stromness his last port of call on his way to the waters west of Greenland. He had been chosen to lead another British attempt to search for the Northwest Passage. His vessels were last sighted by a Scottish whaler at the entrance to Lancaster Sound, north of Baffin Island, before they disappeared for ever.

In the next few years one expedition after the other was sent off to find out what had happened. Dr Rae in 1847 joined the first land expedition to search for Franklin between the Mackenzie and Coppermine rivers. Two years later he was given command of another search party who travelled some 8500 km and mapped much of Victoria Island. Dr Rae's fourth and final expedition, which was organised by the Hudson's Bay Company in 1853, took him to the Boothia Peninsula where Eskimos finally gave him information of Sir John Franklin's fate,

Bay of Houton, known since Norse times for its excellent harbour.

and sold him relics of the unfortunate Franklin party.

The vessels of the Franklin expedition had got stuck in the ice in September 1846, and after Franklin's death in June 1847, the rest of the men left ship, but died on their way to the Back River; 'they fell down and died as they walked', an old Eskimo woman said. The skeletons were found in 1930.

Dr Rae was known for his ability to live off the land on his expeditions, and also for his physical stamina; on his expeditions in the Arctic he walked an estimated 35,000 km on foot. He spent the last part of his life in London, but is buried in St Magnus Cathedral.

The south-western part of Orphir is known today as Petertown. According to the Revd Liddell "Romish chapels are to be met with in every district of the parish"; in Petertown the old chapel was known as Orakirk. The name means the kirk by the river, and it lay on the north bank of the Burn of Coubister, almost at the mouth. It was probably dedicated to St Peter, thus also giving the district its name. The district was at one time called Coubister, and was named after the estate of the same name. The Halcros of Coubister had the largest estate in Orphir until it was divided among heirs in 1820.

J Storer Clouston tells the story of the first owner of Coubister:

In the latter part of the 17th century the two riotous sons
of Hugh Sinclair of Damsay, David of Ryssay and Thomas
of Smoogro, lived in, and probably built the old houses of
Coubister and Smoogro, of which the last named still
stands. Sallying from their mansions, sword in hand and
well charged with liquor, these gentlemen seem to have run
amuck through the adjacent parishes, "ryving" their
neighbours' hair, hurling them "furth of their chairs" at
meals, and occasionally running them through with their
sword-blades; with the consequence that at one sheriff
court held in Stromness in 1677, David had to pay £90 in
fines and Thomas £80.

Houton derives from the Norse *höfuð-tún*, meaning the tunship of the
headland. In 1500 the district was known as Howth, and this name
survives in the old historical house of Howth in the bay area, probably
built by the Halcros in the early eighteenth century. The site of the old
chapel, The Kirkhouse, was right on the beach at Houton Head, and
remains are still visible.

The Bay of Houton is an excellent harbour, and over the centuries a
colourful pageant of ships and sailors have come and gone there. In
Norse times the harbour was known as *Meðallandshöfn*, the Midland
haven, and it was on the shore here that King Hakon Hakonsson of
Norway beached his ships during his stay in Orkney in the autumn of
1263. His ship the *Kristsúðin* was the largest ship ever built in Norway,
and quite new. It was made especially for his western campaign.
Although bearing a Christian name, the ship was equipped with dragon's
heads fore and aft, in the old tradition. In the spring of 1264 the
Kristsúðin carried the King's body back to Bergen for burial.

During both world wars the bay was a hive of military activity, as a
ferry terminal second in importance only to Scapa. On the whole, people
living on the southern shore of Orphir had a ringside view of events in
Scapa Flow, such as the scuttling of the German fleet in June 1919. Today
the Bay of Houton is still a very busy place, as it is the terminal of the
ferries for Flotta and the Walls area of Hoy.

The Midland chapel was known as Kirk o' Myre; it was located near
the present farm of Myre, and any remains will have been swamped by
the gun emplacements of two world wars. The Hill of Midland is full of
old quarry sites. The district was at one time renowned for the quality of

its sandstone; in the seventeenth century the Midland stone especially was in great demand all over Orkney, to be used for tombstones and plaques.

The island of Cava in the Scapa Flow belongs to the parish of Orphir, as does the small skerry known as the Barrel of Butter. Cava is in old sources described as belonging to the Blackfriars of Inverness. The chapel was in ruins even in the Revd Liddell's time, but he emphasises that the three families living on the island frequent the parish church in Orphir regularly. The island used to produce a good crop, but today the brown slopes of Cava are the domain of sheep. The strange name of the Barrel of Butter refers to the price once paid for the right to slaughter seals there. The original name was Carlin Skerry.

The central district of Orphir is mentioned in the *Orkneyinga Saga* in connection with events at the farm of the Bu, a main seat of the earls. We learn that Earl Hakon Paulsson dies peacefully in his bed, probably in the year 1122, and having learnt nothing from his own troubled history, leaves his earldom to his two sons Harald and Paul, who have nothing in common. They soon fall out, but try to make up by having a Christmas party together at the Bu in Orphir, the home of Harald.

Just before the party, in rather a fairytale manner, Earl Harald puts on a shirt his sisters are making for his half-brother, Earl Paul. He collapses in agony and dies. Earl Paul understands that the poisoned shirt was meant for himself, and sends his sisters and their friends packing to Caithness and Sutherland where they came from.

History repeats itself some years later. Earl Paul decides to have a Christmas feast at Orphir, and Svein Asleifarson is among the invited guests. 'There was a great drinking-hall at Orphir, with a door in the south wall near the eastern gable, and in front of the hall, just a few paces down from it, stood a fine church. On the left as you came into the hall was a large stone slab, with a lot of big ale vats behind it, and opposite the door was the living-room.' There was much drink, and Svein ends up killing Earl Paul's forecastleman, his namesake Svein Breast-Rope, then manages to escape.

The fine church alluded to in the saga, where Matins were being sung while blood ran in the hall, was the Round Church of St Nicholas. It was probably built by Earl Hakon in the years after his return from an expiatory pilgrimage to the Holy Land around 1118. It is an imitation of the church of the Holy Sepulchre in Jerusalem, but all that remains today is the chancel and part of the nave. The remains of a Norse hall have been found nearby.

There is a lovely walk from Orphir Bay past the small hamlet of The Breck and the old chapel site at Cairns of Piggar. A broch, the Hillock of Breakna, marks the entrance to the rather lush Swanbister valley.

The mansion house of Smoogro was the home of J Storer Clouston (1870-1944), after he retired from a legal career in Scotland. His family originally came from Nisthouse in Harray. Storer Clouston became a well-known novelist, with a reputation as a humorist, his books being described in one paper as having 'many complications of the gloriously ridiculous kind' that the public seemed to love. He was the author of *Our member Mr Muttlebury*, and *Button Brains*, which was hailed by the *Daily Mail* as 'the most diverting book Mr Clouston has written for some time'. *The Spy in Black* was in 1939 made into a successful film. Some of the most dramatic scenes, including the sinking of the *St Ola*, were filmed on location in Orkney.

J Storer Clouston took an interest in local affairs in Orkney and became County Convener in 1930. He also developed a passionate interest in Orkney history and was a founder member of the Orkney Antiquarian Society, and contributed many scholarly papers to its proceedings in the years between the two world wars. His masterpiece was *A History of Orkney* in 1932; his highly readable account is perhaps at its best when he relates the saga exploits, as he specialised in early historical material.

Past Smoogro, at the point of Ve Ness, there is a place known as Copland's Cleevie. This is the spot where two Copland brothers fell out, and the quarrel ended by one brother knifing the other and then flinging his body over the cliff. J Storer Clouston tells the story:

> A few years ago I came by chance across a document: It was the indictment of Harie Copland, lawful son to Robert Copland in Craiga in Orphir, for murdering John Copland, his eldest lawful brother, on the 2nd Aug. 1629, upon the 'Ness of Smowgrow', by striking him with a knife in the 'womb and ribs, and thereafter tiring of him and casting him into the sea'. He was tried on the 3rd of Oct. in Orphir kirk and condemned to death.

The name of Ve Ness implies pagan connections in the distant past, as the Norse *vé* means holy. It is interesting to find this name so close to the

The Round Church of St Nicholas.

farm of Kirbister, whose name derives from the Norse *kirkju-bólstaðr*, church farm. There was an old chapel by the farm, known as Kirk o' Lian. The first Christian churches were often built close to, or even on top of a pagan place of worship. The Loch of Kirbister area is very fertile, and would have appealed to early settlers. The old Hall of Hobbister was the head house of the Fletts, who were the greatest odallers in Orphir until the middle of the seventeenth century. The farm must have got its name, *Haugbolstaðr*, the farm of the mound, from a very conspicuous site, which is probably a burial mound.

Between the farms of Hobbister and Groundwater the Burn of Swartaback runs through a lovely little valley. Behind that, the hill slope rises gradually upwards to Keelylang Hill, another challenge for the walker.

Stenness

The parish name derives from the Norse *steinnes*, a stony promontory, and was originally given to the ness between the two lochs of Harray and Stenness. The Norsemen would have been filled with incredulity and awe when first seeing this prehistoric setting. Thus the name must at first have applied to the ness alone, and only later been given to the whole parish.

When the name was given by the Norsemen, the ness was probably not yet connected to the other side, but the old farm of Brodgar, from the Norse *brúar-garðr*,

The Watch Stone between two lochs.

meaning farm by the bridge, may have been built quite early. This is the farm that gave its name to the Ring of Brodgar. It is situated on the narrow neck of land known as the Ness of Brodgar. The water is shallow here, so stepping stones may have been sufficient at one time, but today there is an artificial causeway across.

Apart from the ness, the parish of Stenness follows the natural coastline from the Long Holm in the Loch of Harray, along the Loch of Stenness and the Bay of Ireland to Moo Taing. A row of high hills separates Stenness from Orphir, creating a hinterland of little dales, like Russa Dale, the valley of horses. Close by are Bigswell, the sacred well, and Happy Valley, one man's effort to create enchanted woodland.

The northern end of Stenness opens naturally towards the two lochs.

The land is low here, around Tormiston Mill the road is actually below sea level in places. The best agricultural land in Stenness is found along the Bay of Ireland and the two large lochs, where the climate seems favourable; there is rarely fog over Stenness. In about 1500 the land value represented 3.5 urislands, of which the odal share was 54 per cent, that of earl or king 5 per cent and that of the church 41 per cent.

The broad estuary between the Loch of Stenness and the Bay of Ireland is known as the Bush; through this a number of different kinds of fish sometimes enter the loch, such as cod, skate, coalfish and trout. Both lochs are important for wintering wildfowl. The water of the two lochs varies from salt through brackish to fresh water, in a way that is unique in Britain. Sluices have been installed to limit the inflow of saltwater into the Loch of Harray. The rare plant known as the tassel weed or *Ruppia maritima* grows in the Loch of Stenness, as does its close relative, the spiral tassel weed, or *Cirrhosa maritima*, which has status as a rare British species.

The beautiful lochs, divided by the narrow ness and surrounded by hills, must have seemed to prehistoric man an enclosed world, a sanctified landscape. Through the third millennium he did his best to turn it into a ceremonial area for a faith and a culture that we today can see as impressive, but are not able to understand or appreciate fully.

Still, the spectacular setting has appealed to the romantic imagination, and has been immortalised by visiting artists and writers. Around 1814 the artist William Daniell visited Orkney, and the Ring of Brodgar is one of the sites he made known through his aquatints. In the same year Sir Walter Scott visited Orkney; he used the two great stone circles as the setting of one of the climactic scenes of his novel *The Pirate*, letting his imagination run riot when he sees his heroine Minna in the role of high priestess to Druids.

As always, nobody beats Jo Ben when it comes to an original approach,

> Stenhouse is another parish, where there is a large lake, 24 miles in circuit. There on a little hill near to the lake, in a tomb, was found the bones of a man, which indeed were connected together, in length 14 feet as the author affirmed, and money was found under the head of the dead man; and indeed I viewed the tomb. There beside the lake are stones high and broad, in height equal to a spear, and in an equal circle half a mile.

The Stones of Stenness have been radiocarbon dated to c.3000 BC; the early date came as a surprise because it is earlier than that of many henge monuments in mainland Britain. Today the stones are four in number and are the remains of a rather compact circle of 12 tall stones. The nearby Barnhouse settlement dates from the same period as the Stones of Stenness and is so close to the circle that it is natural to see them as related to each other. Close by there are also several isolated stones; one of these is the Watch Stone by the Brig of Brodgar. Another was the Stone of Odin, with its legendary hold on the local imagination.

The Stone of Odin was sought by local people both for curing diseases and for making contractual promises. It had a rather large hole in its centre, big enough to pass babies through if something ailed them, or for old people to put their heads through to cure headaches. Lovers stood on either side of the stone, clasped hands inside, and swore an oath known as the Oath of Odin. This oath was absolute unless their hands met again; thus we are told that Miss Gordon of Stromness, who became engaged to marry the pirate John Gow in 1724, travelled to London to find him and touch his hand after he was hanged.

A member of the Stanley expedition wrote in his diary in 1789, after visiting Orkney, 'We were told that the young Country Lovers meet here and join hands thro this hole, and having agreed to go together, for Life they consider the ceremony equally binding as that by the Priest himself, no instances being found of infidelity on either side after this.'

Only a few months after Sir Walter Scott's visit in 1814, the Stone of Odin was demolished, as was one of the Stones of Stenness. A third one was merely toppled, but was probably meant to go the same way. The perpetrator was an incomer to Orkney, a Captain Mackay, who was a tenant of the neighbouring farm. He was restrained from doing any more damage by the threat of action against him in the Sheriff Court; he promised to 'desist from his operations' and even apologised. But local feeling against him was strong, and according to tradition two different attempts were later made to set fire to his farm buildings.

The chambered cairn of Maeshowe has no precise scientific dating, but due to its size and sophistication it is seen as the culmination of a long architectural development, and consequently dated rather late. A tentative dating is c.2800 BC. The precision of its interior stonework is incredible; a low passage leads into the central chamber where large, smooth slabs of sandstone rise into a square, corbelled ceiling. The room seems strangely modern.

The Stones of Stenness.

The entrance passage of the tomb is constructed so that it will catch the setting sun on the day of winter solstice. George Mackay Brown described how seeing this impressed him.

> You come to a wide plain between the hills and the two lochs. In few other places even in Orkney can you see the wide hemisphere of sky in all its plenitude. The winter sun hangs just over the ridge of the Coolags. Its setting will seal the shortest day of the year, the winter solstice. At this season the sun is a pale wick between two gulfs of darkness. One of the light rays is caught in this stone web of death. Through the long corridor it has found its way; it splashes the far wall of the chamber. Winter after winter, I never cease to wonder at the way primitive man arranged, in hewn stone, such powerful symbolism.

The people who built and used the chamber left us no art, but the Vikings who broke into the tomb in 1152, almost 4000 years later, had no qualms about leaving a profusion of graffiti. They were waiting to go on a crusade with Earl Rognvald II and the Norwegian Earl Erling Wry-Neck, and whiled away the time by carving runic inscriptions and small drawings. They keep on about a treasure found in the chamber that took them three days to carry away, but surely they must be joking, for what prehistoric treasure could possibly interest a Viking, used to precious metals?

Another inscription reads, 'These runes were carved by the man who is most skilled in runes in the western sea with the axe that belonged to Gauk Trandilsson in the south [of Iceland].' Gauk Trandilsson is mentioned in *The Saga of Burnt Njal*, and lived in the second half of the tenth century. Even now these Maeshowe inscriptions represent the largest surviving collection of runes on stone.

The Ring of Brodgar.

Only a couple of years later, during 'the War of the Three Earls' another group sought refuge in the tomb. Earl Harald Maddadarson wanted to take Earl Erlend by surprise at his Damsay castle, and 'set out for Orkney at Christmas with four ships and a hundred men. He lay for two days off Graemsay, then put in at Hamnavoe on Mainland, and on the thirteenth day of Christmas they travelled on foot over to Firth. During a snowstorm they took shelter in Maeshowe, and there two of them went insane, which slowed them down badly, so that by the time they reached Firth it was night-time.' One can only wonder how 100 men could get into the tomb; it is perhaps strange that they did not all go insane.

The two twelfth-century entries into Maeshowe are supported by the archaeological evidence. The tomb is surrounded by an outer ditch. It has been suggested that the ditch might be comparatively recent, and that the Maeshowe mound served as a central 'thing' in early Norse times. Such a theory would perhaps explain the name for Maeshowe which the Norsemen carved in runes inside the tomb. They called it *Orkahaug*, the Orkney mound.

The builders of the Ring of Brodgar chose a dramatic site, on a gentle slope with a view of water in every direction. A ceremonial way was at some time built between the two circles. Although the stones of the second circle are not so high as those of the Stones of Stenness, the circumference of the Ring of Brodgar is much larger. Today there are 27 upright stones, but originally there must have been as many as 60, forming a perfect circle with a diameter of 103.7 m. This would indicate that the circle was constructed according to the standard unit known as the 'megalithic yard' of 0.829 m. The diameter would then be exactly 125 megalithic yards.

The Orkney botanist and antiquarian Magnus Spence (1853-1919), author of *Flora Orcadensis*, was for some time headmaster of the Stenness school. He carried out investigations into the origin and purpose of the Ring of Brodgar. It was his belief that it was part of an enormous complex of ancient measuring stones relating to a calendrical system used by the people who lived in the Stenness area, the heartland of Neolithic Orkney.

The stalled cairn on the low promontory of Unston, projecting into the Loch of Stenness, also dates from the third millennium BC. It is unique, as it has features of both of the two main types of cairn, namely stalls made by large stone slabs on the one hand, and a cell opening off from a main chamber on the other. The tomb was excavated in 1884, and was found to contain shards from more than 30 bowls. The finely decorated pottery, popularly known as Unston Ware, has since been found in a number of chambered tombs, as well as at Knap of Howar in Westray. The distribution of the two types of pottery, Grooved Ware and Unston Ware, is a puzzling question in Orkney archaeology.

In Norse times one of the most important districts in Stenness seems to have been Ireland. Its Norse form *eyrland* derives from *eyrr* which is used about a gravelly beach, but in this case it might refer specially to the spit of land at the back of the Bay of Ireland. The farm known as the Bu, now the Hall, of Ireland was wholly odal property, and at the time of the old rentals, around 1500, this was one of the two greatest odal Bus in Orkney. There was a chapel close to the farm.

The historian J Storer Clouston identifies the chieftain Havard Gunnason and his family with Ireland. Havard was married to Bergljot, Earl Thorfinn the Mighty's great-granddaughter, and they had four sons. The family belonged to the circle closest to the earls, and may have been informants to the writer of the *Orkneyinga Saga*.

The saga describes how Earl Hakon in 1117 is on his way to Egilsay in order to settle the strife between Earl Magnus and himself, by betrayal and death. 'Havard Gunnason, friend and adviser to the earls and loyal to them both, was on Hakon's ship, which is why Hakon concealed his schemes from him as Havard would never have agreed to them. As soon as he learned of the earl's intention Havard jumped overboard and swam to an uninhabited island.'

Havard's oldest son Magnus seems to have inherited his father's integral loyalty. He goes on the pilgrimage to the Holy Land with Earl Rognvald II, in command of one of his ships, and later brings justice to bear on his killer. The second son, Hakon Klo, or Claw, probably built the early twelfth-century castle on the ness at Nether Bigging; the castle had its own chapel, as well as a drinking *skáli* or hall in the courtyard. The district of Clouston, *Klóstaðir*, may have been named after Hakon Klo, and he may have had his home at the now vanished Bu, or Mains, of Stenness.

An old tradition tells the story of the old odal woman known as 'The Lady of Stenness'. She may have descended from Hakon Klo, as she owned the tunship of Stenness. She was still remembered for giving her estate to the parish church of Stenness, on condition that she was buried inside it. The rental of 1503 confirms the gift of the land. When the church was restored in the 1920s, her coffin was found before the altar.

In the 1560s Bishop Adam Bothwell gave large parts of the Stenness and Evie parishes in feu to his uncle Patrick Bellenden. The Stenness part of the estate included the eastern districts of Hobbister, Tormiston and Colston. The family had their residence at Aikerness in Evie, but the land was known as the Stenness estate, and was owned by them for almost 200 years, until it was sold because of bankruptcy in 1744. The estate was very valuable, bringing in an income of £1400 a year, but the last of the Bellendens was 'vicious and improvident'.

The last pitched battle to be fought in Orkney took place in the hills of Stenness in the summer of 1529. It was the culmination of a conflict that had flared up between the Sinclairs of Orkney and the Sinclairs of Caithness. The brothers James and Edward Sinclair, natural sons of Sir William Sinclair of Warsetter in Sanday, had with their Orkney troops stormed the Castle of Kirkwall in 1528, killing some of their close Sinclair relatives in the process, and ejecting Lord William Sinclair from Orkney. The brothers had held the Castle ever since.

The invading Caithness army in 1529 was led by the returning Lord Sinclair and the Earl of Caithness, who was another Sinclair. At

The Bush and the Bridge of Waithe.

Summerdale, the *suðr-merki-dalr* or south boundary valley, just over the parish border from Orphir, they were attacked by the Orkneymen and completely routed. According to local figures, The Earl of Caithness was killed along with 500 men. Lord William Sinclair, who seems to have been the only survivor, himself admitted a loss of more than 300 men. Local tradition knows of only one Orkney casualty, a man mistakenly killed by his own mother who took him for the enemy.

The Orkneymen, driven by fury and frustration, would have fought bravely and hard. Still, the battle raises many puzzling questions. What was the Caithness army doing in the Stenness hills? And how was it the Orkney troops were there to meet them? And why would Sir James Sinclair commit suicide in 1535, by throwing himself into the Gloup of Linksness in St Andrews, just when King James V of Scotland was coming on a visit to Orkney?

More than 400 years later other raiders appeared in Orkney, when one day in March 1940, German planes carrying high explosive and incendiary bombs appeared over Scapa Flow. When British fighters came to attack, the bombers were:

> Flying doon the twa lochs
> Following the sheen o' the water —
> And they winned at last to the brig

where they jettisoned their cargo. Several of the bombs hit the Bridge of Waithe at the estuary of the Loch of Stenness and killed James Isbister at his home close by. Aged 27, he became the first civilian air raid casualty in Britain of the Second World War. In her poem 'The Brig o' Waith' the young Orcadian writer Ann Scott-Moncrieff (1914-1943) expresses the shock that everyone felt at how death had come to Bridge of Waithe:

The low entrance passage to Maeshowe.

> But Maeshowe's round and safe, bad sakes on it;
> The Standing Stones are standing yet
> And I wish they werena.

Firth

The parish of Firth is encircled by a long range of hills, which is broken only by the Binscarth valley. Broad lowland slopes curve around the Bay of Firth, which gave the parish its name. The Norse name of the bay was *Aurriðafjörðr*, the fjord of the trout (*Salmo trutta*), Firth probably deriving from its dative form of *firði*.

The hills of Firth are a walker's delight. From the valley of Settiscarth in the north, where an ancient track known as The Lyde Road crosses into Harray, there is a continuous ridge stretching south along the parish border, breached only by the Binscarth valley. The Ward of Redland is the highest point of the Firth hills, and a pillar was built there by Captain Thomas, the surveyor, in 1848.

Especially lovely is the area sloping down from Burrien Hill to the Loch of Wasdale on the western side. Here is Little Eskadale, which according to the local writer John Firth 'abounds with ferns, pink and white wild roses, and is a favourite rendezvous of lovers'. The burn of Little Eskadale joins the Burn of Syradale, where the vegetation is lush, with wild fuchsia bushes growing along the sides of the burn.

Between the two dales lie the Hamars of Syradale which John Firth describes as a rocky precipice. In the wintertime it is 'a foaming cataract, but in summer, save for a slight trickle, it is comparatively dry. It repays the student of nature to climb these rocks and see the curious effects wrought by the action of the water. Many rare specimens of ferns can be seen in the crannies'.

But others besides students of nature might find the Hamars of Syradale interesting, as they reputedly have a curing effect on toothache. The idea was to go there with a pin between the aching teeth, drop it into a hole, and then walk away backwards, without looking behind. To make absolutely sure of being cured, these 'toothache lines' should be written on a piece of paper and tied round the neck:

Peter sat on a marble stone weeping.

Christ came past and said 'What aileth thee, Peter?'

'Oh, my Lord, my God, my tooth doth ache!'

'Arise, oh Peter! go thy way, thy tooth shall ache no more.'

Further along the ridge, the Hill of Heddle rises above the Bay of Firth as a familiar landmark. The Orkney poet George Mackay Brown called it 'the beautiful Hill of Heddle' and it still is, when seen from the right angle. But a limestone quarry is taking big bites out of the hill and changing its profile in the process. On the other side of the hill is the cairn known as Buckle's Tower, a kind of folly put up by a local herd boy.

On Cuween Hill can be found a very well-preserved chambered cairn of the Maeshowe type, dating to the third millennium BC. It was first opened and examined in 1901. The entrance passage is low, but the chamber itself is quite impressive, with walls more than 2 m high. Four cells branch off from this central chamber, which is of irregular form. Much of the cairn was cut into the bedrock of the sloping hillside. Strangely, the skulls of no fewer than two dozen dogs were found on the floor of the chamber.

Early one morning in November 1926 as a threshing machine was coming out of the stackyard gate at the farm of Rennibister, the ground suddenly gave way under it, revealing another earth-house. It is very similar to the one at Grain, near Kirkwall, and dates back to the first millennium BC. Believed to be storehouses, they are also known as souterrains. The chamber at Rennibister is oval, and on excavation was found to contain the remains of 18 individuals.

The chain of coastline brochs in Evie and Rendall continues into Firth, where at least four are known. The Broch of Redland was excavated by James Farrer in 1858. Its most noticeable feature was the thin walls. It was demolished some years later. At the site of the Broch of Burness, called the Chapel Knowe, an interesting sculptured stone was found. There is also a large green mound, The Hillock, by the Oyce in Finstown. The Broch of Ingashowe near Rennibister was exceptional, being more like Mousa Broch in Shetland. As early as the mid eighteenth century much of this broch had been destroyed by the encroachment of the sea, and since has been used also as a quarry, so little of it is left today.

There are two small islands in the Bay of Firth. The Holm of Grimbister is close to the Mainland shore, and at low tide it is possible to take a tractor across from the farm there. The small island of Damsay is deserted today, but it plays a central role in some of the events in the *Orkneyinga Saga*. When Svein Asleifarson had to escape in a hurry from the earl's hall in Orphir, he went to Damsay. There was a castle in the island, and we learn that the man in charge of it was a chieftain's son, who ferried Svein north to Bishop William on Egilsay.

Some time later the young impetuous Earl Erlend Haraldsson seized the ships of his fellow earls and went with his men to Damsay, 'where they spent each day drinking in a great hall', but they took no chances and slept on board their ships at night. Then one night Earls Rognvald and Harald arrived, taking Earl Erlend so totally by surprise 'that neither the watchmen ashore, nor those on board, knew a thing until the enemy had boarded their ships'. And young Erlend was too drunk to know what was happening to him. Probably the earls had living quarters and a farm on Damsay, as we learn that Earl Rognvald spent Yule there after the killing of young Erlend. He also saw to it that Earl Erlend received a mural burial in the south choir aisle of St Magnus Cathedral, as behoved an earl, no matter how foolish.

Robert Monteith of Egilsay wrote about Damsay in his 1633 *A Description of the Isles of Orkney* that 'Anciently a Nunnery was here sited, it holds from the Arch Dean of Orkney'. In his own inimitable way Jo Ben confirms this idea:

> Here there are no hills, and it is the most pleasant of all, and called Tempe. The church in this island is dedicated to the Virgin Mary, to which many pregnant women make pilgrimage. No frogs, toads, or other noxious terrestrial animals whatever are ever found here. The women here are sterile, and if they do become pregnant never live to bring forth. It is related that sometimes the haughty are carried away for the space of an hour, but truly afterwards restored.

By the middle of the nineteenth century the pilgrimage chapel of St Mary was a ruin. Its site was by a small loch in the north-east of the island, where the ruins can still be seen.

At the head of the Bay of Firth parts of the old farm of Thickbigging can still be seen, the chief farm in the old tunship of Firth. Not far away from Thickbigging lie the remains of a small structure, known as the Black Chapel. The parish church, probably built on the remains of another chapel, is also close.

According to not-so-ancient a legend, the village of Finstown was founded by an Irishman called David Phin. A veteran of the Napoleonic Wars, he was stationed in Orkney where he taught at the school for a while and married a local woman. In partnership with the owner of the Mill of Firth he ran a small inn soon to be known as The Toddy Hole. It became very popular, not least for David Phin's story-telling genius, but

Loch of Wasdale.

after four years he fell out with his partner and left Orkney.

For a long time the inn was known as 'Phin's', and as the village grew it had to find itself a name and Finstown seemed the obvious choice. The inn may have been a focal point, although the village is more likely to have originated as a base for the herring fishing. There were also some good oyster beds in the Bay, and as early as 1529 Jo Ben remarked on these resources, 'Firth is another parish where oysters are taken in abundance.' The main reason for Finstown's growth today is no doubt its central location. The village is a meeting-place of important roads, it has a green, sheltered setting among the Firth hills, and today it is favoured as a residence for people working in Kirkwall and also by retired people.

North of Finstown, against a backdrop of hills, fertile land slopes down to the sea. This is the North Side district of Firth, consisting of the old tunships of Redland and Burness. In 1920 life in this area was vividly described in *Reminiscences of an Orkney Parish*, one of the most interesting books written about the old country life in Orkney.

The writer was John Firth (1838-1922) who was born in Estaben in Redland and who grew up in a period when the common grazing had not yet been divided. At that time the tunship of Redland consisted of seven farms and four cothouses, and was enclosed north, east and west by a turf dyke which was kept up till 1860, when the commons were divided. John Firth describes the community he knew as a young man, before the changes came. Today most of the old tunship is part of the farm of Redland.

A glacial drift created the dip in the hills which today is known as the Binscarth gap, and filled the whole area westwards with hummocks. Such a gap between hills is a scarth, which is an element in many Orkney names. The name of Binscarth probably derives from the Norse *bærinn í skarði*, meaning the farm in the gap.

The farm of Binscarth was bought by Robert Scarth (1799-1879) in 1841. At the time the land amounted to some 60 acres, but only about half of it was under the plough. When the commonty of Firth was about to be divided, Binscarth qualified only for a small share of it. But the strong-willed Robert Scarth succeeded in getting the proportionate commonty allotment of his other lands in Firth added directly to his Binscarth farm.

By the time Robert Scarth acquired Binscarth, he already had a long career as an estate factor behind him. Although feared, even hated, by the many that were affected by his work, he carried out a task of agricultural improvement that was difficult but in the long run beneficial. He is perhaps best-known for the changes made in North Ronaldsay and Rousay; the planned clearances of the Quandal area in Rousay were also to make him notorious.

The house at Binscarth was built around the middle of the nineteenth century, and Robert Scarth took no chances when planning its exact location. He had 12 tatterflags put up to find the most sheltered spot, and this method was later adopted for forest planting by the Forestry Commission. Even so the wood of mixed trees that Robert Scarth planted with such care at Binscarth, suffered severely in the great hurricane of 1953. Today these trees are large and make a lovely plantation, which would seem a forest to an Orcadian, but more like a copse to a Scandinavian!

Across from the Holm of Grimbister lie the remains of the Hall of Cursiter, at one time perhaps the most interesting old house in the parish. It was two-storey and thatched, with a solid stone staircase inside, but it has not been lived in since the late eighteenth century, and has been going to rack and ruin ever since. The house was probably built in 1587, and is traditionally remembered as the old manse, where the first minister of the independent parish of Firth established himself. Earlier Firth, Stenness and Orphir had shared a minister.

Later, the minister moved further up the hill, and the old Church of Scotland Manse of Firth made a nineteenth-century visitor quite lyrical, 'The manse is beautifully situated, on an eminence, at the foot of an amphitheatre of hills that slope gradually away to the south and west. The Manse of Firth commands one of the sweetest and most romantic prospects, both of land and water, to be found in these northern shores.'

This is also the style of the romantic, though melancholy, soldier-poet John Malcolm (1795-1835), who was the son of a minister and grew up in the Firth manse. He took part in the Peninsular War and was seriously wounded at Toulouse. John Malcolm was one of the editors of *The Orkney and Shetland Chronicle*, an interesting magazine that unfortunately extended only to 19 issues. Later he became Editor of the *Edinburgh Observer*, but never really recovered from his war injuries.

In 1952 the manse became the home of Laura and Jo Grimond, who originally were 'ferryloupers' from 'doon sooth'. Jo Grimond represented the Orkney and Shetland constituency in the House of Commons from 1950 until 1983, when he was raised to the peerage. For a long period he was also the leader of the Liberal Party, which he set out to revitalize. In this he greatly succeeded, although perhaps not to the extent he had hoped.

Having had first-hand experience of living in it, Jo Grimond is more down to earth in his description, 'Like many Orkney manses it is unnecessarily tall. Since it is perched on a spur of high ground it catches the full force of all the gales – and there are many. As it is largely one room thick the wind rushes through, no window or door will stop it. But it commands views, south to the long, dark, heathery flank of Keely Lang hill and north over the Bay of Firth.'

Rendall

The small parish of Rendall lies along the West Mainland seashore, linked to Evie in the north and to Firth in the south. It is separated from Birsay and Harray by a fairly large borderland area of heath-covered hills. Rendall is an interesting area for walking, as the scenery is so varied. Away from the main road there is a network of narrower sea roads that also lead among fairly high hills, such as Enyas Hill at 141 m and Gorseness Hill at 124 m. A hill-road running up to Fibla

The old church of Hackland.

Fiold on the boundary between Rendall and Harray gives impressive views of the surrounding landscape.

A little further south, at Starling Hill in Dale of Cottascarth, is perhaps the best place in Orkney for seeing hen harriers. The RSPB has established an important bird reserve in the area. But it is also possible to see bird-life along the shores. The Loch of Brockan near the Bay of Isbister is visited by both migrant and wintering birds. Otters swim along the low banks of the Bay of Puldrite shore, and a little further along there is a large colony of Arctic terns on the Holm of Rendall. Ravens nest in the tower of the old church of Hackland.

The name of Rendall appears in old sources as Rennadalr or Rennudalr. The original meaning is uncertain, but the name may derive from the small brook that runs down past the Hall of Rendall, as the Norse verb *renna* means to flow, and *Renná* is a river name. From being the name of a tunship, Rendall came to be used for the whole parish.

As at Evie the brochs in Rendall were all situated along the shore. Five brochs have been found, but none of them has been professionally excavated. Over the centuries much of the stone has been taken for building purposes. Right on the shore and close to the parish border is the broch site known as the Knowe of Midgarth, which is in a better state of preservation than any of the others. In the old northern tunship of Tingwall, there is a prehistoric mound believed to contain a broch. Further south, in Wass Wick, is another broch in the middle of marshland. Close to the shore, north-east of the Hall of Rendall, are the remains of a broch, and on the land of the farm of North Aititt is the mound called the Knowe of Dishero, known to contain a fairly complete lower section of a broch. The southern area of the parish has a number of tumuli, and some of these were examined in 1998 and found to contain Bronze-Age burials.

The second element of the farm name of Aititt is the Norse *topt*, which usually refers to a site that has been used or built on before, so it should come as no surprise that at North Aititt remains of prehistoric structures can be traced on the site of the farm buildings. Flints have been found in the fields of North Aititt too, but the really rich finds have been made in South Aititt, suggesting that there was a flint quarry here in the distant past. The flint itself is of poor quality, but even so the artefacts found show that it was used for arrow-points and knives, to the extent that it might perhaps be called a flint industry!

In addition to the island of Gairsay, which may at one time have been a parish of its own, Rendall had three main districts. The North Side reached from the Evie border to the large district of Gorseness. Isbister and Cottascarth made up the third district. Dr Hugh Marwick suggests that the whole seaboard area of Gorseness and North Side, representing three urislands of good land, may originally have been one large early settlement or land-taking, and that the striking twelfth-century saga characters of this area are the descendants and heritors of the original land-taker or settler.

The larger-than-life character of Svein Asleifarson of Gairsay dominates parts of the *Orkneyinga Saga*, but we only learn indirectly of life in Rendall. After a revenge expedition to Rousay, Svein goes to his uncle Helgi's farm at Tingwall and 'stayed there in hiding for the first part of the Christmas season'. After Svein's death in 1171, his sons put his great hall in Gairsay out of commission by erecting a wall across it.

It seems evident that the Bu, later known as the Hall, of Rendall then became the main family seat.

Svein's son Andres married the daughter of Kolbein Hruga of Wyre, and the Kolbein of Rendall who appears in *The Saga of Hakon Hakonsson*, is probably their son. He was the leading kinsman of the Wyre family then, and the man who in 1230 had to do the peacemaking with King Hakon after Hanef Ungi, the King's sysselman in Orkney as well as being another family member, had killed Earl Jon in a drunken brawl in Thurso.

The name of Tingwall is interesting, as in Norse times this may have been the meeting-place of the old thing, or local parliament. There are no records of meetings here, nor any other indication of meetings being held than the name, which derives from the Norse *þingvöllr*, site of the thing. We learn of a thing-meeting held before the death of Earl Magnus Erlendsson in Egilsay, but we are not told where this was held. In earldom days the island administration seems to have been restricted rather to the Earl himself and the men around him.

The whole parish of Rendall was skatted as five urislands, and at the time of the early rentals 54.7 per cent of the land was part of the earldom estate, 34.3 per cent was odal and the rest belonged to the local church. It is interesting to note that at that time Rendall was the only Mainland parish without any bishopric land.

The old parish church lay on the Gorseness seashore. There was also a church dedicated to St Thomas near the Hall of Rendall, as well as a St Mary's chapel at Skaill in Isbister. These three were all situated on the largest farm of each district. In addition there may have been a chapel for the North Side at the site known as Kirkabreck in Tingwall. Tradition also points to an old chapel at Cottascarth, known as the Kirk of Cot.

Close to the broch near the Hall of Rendall are the foundations of the old church of St Thomas, known locally as Tammaskirk. It was excavated in 1931 by J Storer Clouston and his friend Aage Roussell, a Danish archaeologist. They found a church ruin lying true east and west, with both a nave and a chancel. The walls of the chancel are exceptionally thick, and actually form the ground floor of a strong tower, a kind of keep. There are also remains of a thick churchyard wall, which further bears out the idea of a fortified church. Taking similar structures elsewhere into consideration, Clouston arrives at the mid twelfth century as a probable dating for Tammaskirk.

The dating takes us back to the time of Svein Asleifarson again. Around 1150 Svein was one of the most powerful men in Orkney, but at the same time the threat to his personal safety was such that he took his life in his hands if he went anywhere unattended by his men. The fortified church may therefore have been built as his stronghold *pied-à-terre* on the Mainland. Tammaskirk is not mentioned in any records, but then it was privately built on odal land.

The Rendalls remained one of the leading Orkney families and owned the Hall of Rendall until the early seventeenth century. The property was then bought by the Halcro family, and it remained in that family until sometime in the late twentieth century. The beehive-shaped Doocot of Rendall, dating back to 1648, is unique in Orkney. Four circular outside ledges are meant to keep rats away, while holes in the inside masonry have been made to provide nest-holes for the pigeons. The nineteenth-century farm of Breck of Rendall, in the small valley above the Hall, is a very lovely traditional farm. It is built around a courtyard, through which the main road passes.

In the autumn of 1629 an old woman fought for her life in St Magnus Cathedral. She was Jonet Rendall from Rigga in Rendall, and according to the stories about her, she lived in a miserable hovel. The name of Rigga occurs in the Wass Wick area. Jonet Rendall is described in the records as a 'poor vagabond' from the parish of Rendall, and on trial 'for the abominable supperstition and useing of the witchcraftes underwritten'.

There follow some 20 items of alleged witchcraft on her part, where cows and horses have died on neighbouring farms, if she was not given what she asked for. The picture that emerges of superstitions and prejudice is sad and surprising. This is what happened at Skaill in Isbister:

> – in Candlemas evin, fyve yeiris sene, ye cam to Gilbert
> Sandie in Isbister his house and sought ane plack of silver
> in almis fra him for his mearis, that they might be weill
> over the yeir, as ye said David Henrie had done that day,
> quha said to yow that he had naither silver, corne, or meall
> to spair, but baid his wyff geve ye thrie or four stokis of
> kaill, and ye been gane away, the said gilbertis wyff
> followed yow with the kaill; ye wold not tak thame, and
> uponn the second day efter, his best hors, standing on the

floor, became wood, and felled himself and deit, and the
thrid night thaireft thaireft his best mair deit by your witchcraft
and devilrie, qlk ye cannot deny.

So many of the Rendall families were affected by the charges, and most
of them appeared in court, some as witnesses and some as members of
the 'assise' – perhaps some were also present at the execution where she
was to be taken with 'her handis bund behind hir bak, and worried at
ane stoup to the dead, and burnt in ass.' There were so many witch trials
in the early seventeenth century, all over Europe, that it seems almost like
a kind of social cleansing, a way of getting rid of troublesome
individuals. At the same time many of the women obviously exploited the
power that credulity and ignorance gave them.

The number of witchcraft trials did not decrease with the coming of
the reformed church, nor has the church ever publicly deplored them, but
the period after the Reformation was difficult for the Church in Orkney
for many reasons. Parishes became very large, thus Evie and Rendall
seem to have become united sometime in the early sixteenth century. The
Revd Hugh Ross gives a lively description of a minister's work in this
parish in 1795:

> The minister continued, as usual, to officiate alternately in
> these condemned kirks, till the year 1788, when the danger
> became so conspicuous, that he fortunately deserted that of
> Evie, as the walls soon afterwards tumbled down on a
> Sunday, and the materials were set up to auction. The
> minister then travelled every Sunday to Rendall, and
> officiated in that ruinous house, (once with only 17
> hearers), till October 1794, when, having lost his health by
> officiating there, and that house also becoming very
> hazardous, he was obliged, by the injunctions of his
> physician, to desert it; so that, since that period, there has
> been no public worship in this charge, except in the open
> air, in the church-yard.

It seems that many of the parish churches of Orkney were in a miserable
condition at the time, cold and with leaky roofs. Most of the property of
the pre-Reformation Church had been given in feu, often for political
reasons, to people who paid rents if and when it suited them, some property
was diverted to other purposes, but very little reached the Church.
Rendall and Evie were therefore not alone in having ruinous churches.

Gairsay

Gairsay is one of the inner North Isles, close to the Rendall shore and yet strangely remote. Through the centuries its nicely rounded, prominent hill was a familiar landmark, the Wart of Gairsay being mentioned more than once in Mackenzie's Charts of 1750. In saga times the hill was a handy place for keeping a watch-out for enemy ships.

The Norse name of the island was *Gáreksey*, and it seems natural to ask who this Gárek might be, who presumably gave his name to Gairsay. But the saga gives no answer, just as it is silent about Hrolf of Rousay.

Although much of the island is taken up by the hill, which is three to four miles round at the base, there is still much good and fertile land on its western and southern sides. Gairsay is some 250 hectares, and in the old days it was skatted as a 13d land. There is a very good natural harbour in Millburn Bay, protected as it is by the promontory known as the Hen of Gairsay. The isthmus here is low and narrow, so that in Norse times the ships may even have been taken across it, for protection against bad weather or uninvited visitors.

The eastern bay is still known as Russness Bay. The name seems to indicate that Russness – the ness of horses – may have been an old name for the Hen of Gairsay. There is no trace of a farmhouse on the promontory now, and it may never have been cultivated. In a strategic position above the harbour, on the slope just below the hill, lie the remains of the farm of Skelbist. The name derives from the Norse *skála-bólstadr*, which implies an important farm, as *skáli* means a hall. This could therefore be the site of the original settlement farm.

At the south end of the island is the maze of old buildings that was once the farm of Boray. The name derives from the Norse *borg*, for fortification, and the remains of a broch or an even older structure are discernible on the slope above the shore, but the site has not been excavated.

Sweyn Holm has a large colony of grey seals. The Holm of Boray, which covers the entrance to Millburn Bay, is a haunt of breeding birds and seals. It is the scene of a classical love story, involving a seal woman and a young man of the islands. The seals were called selkies in Orkney, and at certain times of the tide they would throw off their skins and dance on the shore with such joyous abandon and in such beauty that it would catch at the heart of anyone watching.

The story tells how Harold of Gairsay was out fishing one summer evening, when he heard the most enchanting music. It came from the small island of Boray, where a grandly dressed group of people were dancing on the beach.

This is the classical opening of the selkie stories. Harold takes the skin of a beautiful girl, he persuades her to marry him, and they enjoy some happy years. But she was restless, and she often asked Harold for the skin. She was baptised as a Christian, but she continued to pine away.

'Tonight is the dancing night; roll me in my seal skin and leave me on the beach. They cannot take me away if I am a Christian.' Harold took her to Boray and left her on the beach there, while he himself sat on the other side of Gairsay, waiting for the sunrise. At dawn he found her on the shore, dead, but with a smile on her face. She had died in peace, and Harold knew they would not be parted forever.

On a prominent site on the south-western shore, the twelfth century chieftain Svein Asleifarson built his legendary banqueting-hall, or drinking-hall, of Langskaill, where he would feast to all hours with his warriors, all 80 of them. The main working farm may still have been at Skelbist. Through some 50 chapters of the *Orkneyinga saga* we can follow the incredible story of his life and times. Eric Linklater wrote Svein's biography, *The Ultimate Viking*, describing him as the last of his kind.

Svein was the second son of Olaf Hrolfsson of Gairsay. His mother Asleif is described in the saga as 'a woman of good birth, great intelligence and strong character'. Just before Christmas on one occasion the whole family retreated to their other estate in Caithness for the celebrations, when a band of men set fire to the house and burned Olaf to death. The oldest brother, Valthjof, was on his way to the Earl's Christmas feast in Orphir in a ten-oared boat, when he drowned with his crew in Stronsay Firth. Thus within the space of a few days Svein was left nominally the person in charge, but we can see from his second name that his mother would have shared some of this responsibility with him.

For more than a generation Svein Asleifarson was a person of eminence in Orkney, aiding one earl to power the one year, only to topple him the next. Impulsive and erratic, he seems to have been swayed by the politics of the moment. Loyalties are constantly changing, yet he is cut to the quick by the betrayal of his long-time friend, the Hebridean chieftain Holdbodi of Tiree, with whom he had shared so many happy harrying forays to the Isle of Man and to some of the other islands in the Irish Sea.

As he grew older, Svein settled into more of a firm routine, and this is how the *Orkneyinga saga* tells us he used to live. 'Winter he would spend at home on Gairsay, where he entertained some eighty men at his own expense. His drinking hall was so big, there was nothing in Orkney to compare with it. In the spring he had more than enough to occupy him, with a great deal of seed to sow which he saw to carefully himself. And when that job was done, he would go off plundering in the Hebrides and in Ireland on what he called his "spring-trip", then back home just after midsummer, where he stayed till the cornfields had been reaped and the grain was safely in. After that he would go off raiding again, and never came back till the first month of winter was ended. This he used to call his "autumn-trip".'

The main purpose of these excursions would have been to secure the supplies necessary to sustain his miniature army. But when earl Harald Maddadarson told him he should cease his raids, Svein agreed, he was now getting on in years, and the next trip would be his last. And so it was to be, as he was killed then in an ambush in the streets of Dublin. Svein Asleifarson was a contemporary of the saga writer, who evidently thought very highly of him, 'people say that apart from those of higher rank than himself, he was the greatest man the western world has ever seen in ancient and modern times'.

After his death his sons built a wall across Svein's large hall, dividing it between them. The year was 1171, and the Viking Age had come to an end – in Orkney also.

But if we are to believe the story so vividly told by Eric Linklater, memories may still survive.

> A school teacher in Gairsay – but there is no school there now – once told me that the ghost of a woman was sometimes to be seen near his hall. She wore a yellow gown, that seemed to hold and reflect a cold light as she walked. Now Sweyn, coming home from raiding in the western seas, brought with him a princess from Man or Ireland, and saffron was the royal colour of Ireland. She may not have liked the rough life in Gairsay, and the noise of eighty men-at-arms. Or when Sweyn went out to Dublin, and his ships came back without him, her grief may have been so bitter that even death could not quieten it.

In the early rentals Gairsay is listed as belonging to the Rendalls of the

Langskaill.

Hall of Rendall, the chief landowners of the parish. In the 1590s the island was the property of William Bannatyne, sometime Sheriff and chamberlain of Orkney and Shetland, who used the designation 'of Gairsay'. He became embroiled in the affairs of Patrick Stewart, and was obliged to raise a large sum of money to settle the Earl's debts. When Bannatyne failed to do so, Earl Patrick forced him to raise money on his own estates, and then, by way of thanking him, had Bannatyne 'chaissit and ejectit' from Orkney.

In 1640 William Craigie of Papdale, who belonged to a prosperous Kirkwall merchant family, bought Gairsay. His son Hugh took an interest in Scottish politics – an interest taken further by the third Craigie laird of Gairsay. Sir William Craigie served as a Member of Parliament for Orkney and Shetland in 1681, and again from 1689-1700, he was tacksman of the earldom, and was knighted by King William III in 1690.

The present mansion house at Langskaill is said to have been erected by William Craigie on the occasion of his marriage to Margaret Honyman, the daughter of Bishop Honyman. The mansion consisted of buildings on the north, east and west sides of a covert. The east building is believed to incorporate the foundation of Svein's drinking-hall, though it has been raised by two storeys. The east and west sides of the square

are joined by a curtain wall, pierced by loopholes for musketry and a finely decorated archway. Outside are the ruins of a chapel. There used to be a bowling green between the house and the sea, and close to the house was a sunken garden which gave protection from the wind. Altogether Langskaill was a mansion house strikingly designed and laid out, making it one of the most interesting laird's seats in seventeenth century Orkney – a period when many ambitious houses were built by wealthy lairds all over the islands.

Sir William Craigie was plagued by misfortune towards the end of his life. His eldest son was killed in the battle of Blenheim in Germany during the Spanish War of Succession 1701-14. And in spite of making three advantageous marriages, Sir William ended up being jailed for owing a debt of £981 to Sir Archibald Steuart of Burray. The bad harvests towards the end of the seventeenth century caused a disastrous slump in trade, and Sir William Craigie became one of its victims.

Around the middle of the nineteenth century there was a flourishing population in Gairsay with 71 people occupying 15 houses. And for a long time there was a school on the island, and the schoolhouse is still there, in the middle of the southern slope, but the children are long gone. After the Second World War Gairsay was left to the sheep.

In 1969 the island was bought by a Cornish family. Their four children attended school on Mainland, quite often by rowing across the Sound themselves. The west part of the old mansion house had by then become derelict, the north part had been demolished, and the east house was a storey shorter. The east house has been thoroughly renovated and restored, as closely to the original style as possible, and is still a very impressive sight. The bowling green in front of the house is now used for hockey, and the sunken garden for vegetables. Part of the land is farmed with beef cattle, but Gairsay is mainly a sheep island, as the crofting laws move in mysterious ways.

Evie

The most striking feature of the parish of Evie is its long, beautiful coast. The promontory of Aikerness hinders the flow of the current in Eynhallow Sound, and a back eddy, in Norse known as *efja*, is formed in the small bay there. This would be left out of the strong tide-race running through Burgar Röst, forming a back current that would make the rowing of a boat in the opposite direction easier.

In the *Orkneyinga Saga* the name Efjusund is used for Eynhallow Sound, but Evie itself is not mentioned. In the *Saga of Fridtjof the Brave*, on the other hand, Evie plays a central part. The saga was written down in Iceland around 1300, but it takes place in prehistoric times. Fridtjof the Brave loves Ingeborg, the daughter of a King of Sogn in western Norway. When the King dies, her brothers will not allow Fridtjof to marry Ingeborg, but tell him to go to Orkney to collect taxes.

Fridtjof sails to Orkney on his ship the *Ellida* in a storm, 'Then the weather cleared, and they saw that they had come to Efjusund, and there they went ashore. His men were very tired, almost worn out, but Fridtjof bravely carried eight men up from the shore'. And there was the earl. 'Angantyr was in Efja when Fridtjof came to the country with his men. It was Angantyr's custom when sitting with his drink, to have a man on guard by the lum of his skáli. He would drink from a horn, and when it was empty, another would be filled.' His man told him:

Six men I see baling
Seven I see rowing
Out on the Ellida
In awful weather.

Angantyr welcomed Fridtjof and his men warmly. They stayed with him over the winter, and he often made them tell him about their voyages. They brought the taxes back to Sogn, only to find that the brothers had not been playing fair; they had burned and ravaged Fridtjof's estate in his absence. But the lovers win through in the end, to perhaps the only 'happy ending' in saga literature. The Swedish writer Esaias Tegnér was so taken by the saga story that in 1825 he rewrote it as a romantic novel in verse. And even in 1913 the story could so thrill the German emperor Wilhelm II that he had a colossal statue of Fridtjof erected on a promontory of the Sognefjord.

Evie is a narrow strip of very fertile land between the sea on the one side and a large, empty hill area, crossed by the highest road in Orkney, on the other. The parish border runs from one hill top to the next, to end up in the west on the highest point of Costa Hill, having cut right through the farm buildings of the farm Crismo in its course, leaving some of them in Birsay and others in Evie. The old hill dyke used to run more or less along the same route, but very little remains of it today. The parish is divided into three main districts: Inner Evie, from Woodwick to the burn of Woo, Outer Evie, from Woo to Burgar, and then Costa in the west.

Costa is the exposed, northernmost part of Mainland. It is a beautiful place for walking, with a view of coastal scenery not usually seen, like the sea stack Standard Rock just off the shore. The cliffs at Costa Head are the highest on Mainland, and should really be seen at sea-level in all their wild grandeur.

At one time Costa Head earned the reputation of being the windiest place in Britain, and was actually mentioned in the *Guinness Book of Records* for this reason. In the hurricane of 1953 a windspeed of as much as 125 mph was registered at Costa Head. It was chosen as the site of an experimental wind generator in a pioneering project just after the Second World War. The experiment was abandoned, partly for technical reasons, but principally because the price of oil became so low that alternative energy seemed irrelevant.

The view from the hill also reveals the frenzied tidal race in Burgar Röst, so named for the row of brochs on the Evie shore, Burgar being derived from the Norse *borgar*, the plural form of *borg*. This is the name usually given by the Norsemen to the Iron-Age defensive structures. And there are a string of them along the shore. From east to west the broch sites are Gurness, Stenso, Grugar, also known as Ryo, Burgar, Peterkirk and Verron. Obviously there was a strong reason for building them that is unknown to us.

The Broch of Burgar is still contained within a large mound, but it is suffering badly from marine erosion. Although it has been dug into several times, the mound has never been properly excavated, and no exact records have been kept, partly perhaps because the owner wanted to keep its secrets to himself.

The broch was first explored as early as 1825, by the local minister's son, who found a skeleton, a comb and a deer's horn. He retained the head, but put the rest of the skeleton back where he had found it. The broch was explored again in 1840 by Mr Gordon, the then owner of

Burgar. It seems clear that some valuable silver relics were found, but what became of them is not known. According to the first writing to tell of the excavation there was a highly ornate silver vessel that could take half a gallon, filled with large amber beads, along with several other smaller silver items. In the telling this grew to eight vessels that could each take two gallons.

When the relics were claimed for the Crown as treasure trove, Mr Gordon changed his tune, and insisted there was only one broken vessel, which he had already given to the Earl of Zetland, as he was so interested in old things. To others he proclaimed indignantly that he had tossed the finds into the Atlantic, as he would 'much rather see them consigned to the depths of the ocean, than be compelled to deliver them up to the Crown officials'.

Today the accepted theory is that the Broch of Burgar treasure was a hoard hidden by a wealthy Pict, sometime in the eighth century, even earlier. The broch had exceptionally thick walls, at 5 m the thickest walls of any broch in Orkney. The treasure was hidden in a cell in the wall; it must have seemed like a safe place.

For a long time the Broch of Burgar was the only one of the Evie brochs that had been surveyed and to some extent explored. One day in the summer of 1929, the poet Robert Rendall was sitting at the Knowe of Gurness, peacefully sketching the view of Eynhallow Sound, when suddenly one of the legs of his stool disappeared into a hole. A narrow and steep set of stairs could be seen going into the mound. The Broch of Gurness had been discovered!

Excavation work went on for nine seasons in the following decade, until the Second World War when everything came to a standstill. This was the golden age of Orkney archaeology, when one outstanding site after another was opened to the public: Skara Brae, the Brough of Birsay and Midhowe Chambered Cairn and Broch in Rousay. At Gurness, a broch tower and the remains of a village are surrounded by ramparts and a defensive ditch. Here as many as 250 people may have lived and worked; it must have been an important settlement in its day, and practically impregnable. The broch site also shows an ingenious use of local stone.

During excavation at Gurness the lower parts of a later building were uncovered on the landward side. It had been built long after the settlement itself was a heap of ruins, and was identified as a Norse house or hall, of a spacious kind. The field where it was found was known locally as Cotastua, the cot beside the stofa, or hall. Another field in the

The Broch of Gurness.

vicinity was known as Lammasgreen. The Orkney historian J Storer Clouston believed that the building might have been a gildhall used for feasts by people of the surrounding islands. Such gild festivals took place on 29 July, the day of St Olaf; people brought their own food and drink and feasted for days.

Aikerness is a large farm, a whole urisland by itself, and was always important. The mansion house of Aikerness was the principal residence of the Stenness estate, and in Walter Traill Dennison's dialect story 'The Heuld-horn Rumpis' we are all guests at a combined dinner and drinking party which was held there in 1730. In the way of Orkney custom the twice-widowed Lady Christiana Crawford kept her own name after marriages, first to William Bellenden of Stenness, and then to James Moodie of Melsetter who was murdered on Broad Street in Kirkwall by Sir James Steuart of Burray in 1725. Her vengeful son Benjamin Moodie became the scourge of the Orkney Jacobites after the '45.

At the Aikerness party the carousing went on after the ladies and the Revd Hugh Mowat had retired for the evening. While the drink flowed freely and most of the men were the worse for it, the Devil arrives to stalk them. In the end they manage to outwit him with the help of a leaf from a psalm book. During all these exciting goings-on downstairs, Lady

Christiana is carrying on her own stalking upstairs. Bringing a heuld-horn, also known as a midnight-horn, filled with 'a mixture of gin and hot ale highly spiced' she made amorous advances to the minister. The Revd Mowat leapt out of the window in his nightshirt, and ran all the way to the manse. The story describes how later she tried to hound him, but it cannot have been too bad, as he stayed on as minister of Evie for another 50 years. This story was told to Walter Traill Dennison by a minister who had it first-hand from the Revd Mowat himself.

The Broch of Peterkirk is so called because the remains of a church, said to be quite a grand one, stand on top of a mound which can be seen to be a broch site, possibly as large as Gurness. The archaeologist Dr Raymond Lamb points out that Orkney has a remarkable number of church sites with dedications to St Peter, associated with major brochs. They seem to be distributed in a planned and deliberate pattern throughout the islands. Eight sites have names referring to a kirk, and the clearest Mainland example of this is Peterkirk in Evie. The network was probably established in the eighth century, as part of the extension of the Pictish Church. There was also an old cemetery at Peterkirk.

The Church was an important factor in Evie also in later times. Around 1500 some 70 per cent of Evie's eight urislands of fertile land was owned by the bishopric. By comparison only some eleven per cent was odal, the rest belonging to the earl. In 1565 all the bishopric land was given in feu to Sir Patrick Bellenden of Aikerness, the owner of the Stenness estate.

The ordinary people rarely appear in the church records of earlier times, but in the Revd James Wallace's *Description of the Isles of Orkney*, from 1693, the women emerge more clearly, and especially one Evie character: 'The Women are Lovely, and of a Beautiful Countenance, and are very Broodie and apt for Generation, one Marjorie Bimbister in the Parish of Evie, was in the year 1683 brought to bed of a Male Child, in the sixtie third year of her Age.'

The prebend of Woodwick, drawing an income from the Woodwick estate, seems to have endowed a local chapel known as Our Lady of Woodwick. Only one chapel is known in Woodwick, and it lay up the Burn of Woodwick, among the moors. It used to be called the Kirk of Norrisdale, or Norrensdale, norrens probably deriving from *norrænn*, meaning Norse or Norwegian. J Storer Clouston points out that the founder of the prebend must have been a large landowner closely connected with Evie. In nearby Wyre the chieftain Kolbein Hruga might be called a Norwegian, and his son, Bishop Bjarni, would be a likely person to endow the church so handsomely. The remains of the church are still visible. There is also a huge Cubbie Roo stone in the upper Woodwick valley, with his finger marks clearly visible!

By 1653 the Woodwick estate was the property of David MacLellan who had become Orkney's greatest private landowner through money-lending and shipping investments. He reputedly had a landed income of just over £1800 a year, and was appointed chamberlain of the earldom lands. In 1727 the estate, which at that time also included North Ronaldsay, was acquired by James Traill at a price of £2222. He was Provost of Kirkwall, and when he died in 1733, left his estate to his nephew, John Traill of Westness in Rousay.

John Traill was one of the lairds who had to go into hiding after the '45 because of his Jacobite sympathies; later, Hanoverian troops destroyed Woodwick House. The Woodwick estate grew, and in the early decades of the nineteenth century it had an annual income of more than £2000. The Traills were lairds of Woodwick up to the middle part of the twentieth century; their lovely home of Woodwick House is now run as a hotel.

The Orkney folklorist Ernest Walker Marwick (1915-77) grew up on the farm of Fursan, not far from Woodwick. Apart from studying for a short while under Edwin Muir at Newbattle Abbey College, he was self-taught. He was interested in everything that involved Orkney history and folklore, and perhaps his scope was wider than that of Dennison. He shows us indeed that dwarfs are remembered in placenames even though they are not part of Orkney lore generally. In the Hill of Dwarmo in Woodwick there is a notable echo, coming from the crags on the side of the hill facing Rousay. Dwarmo derives from the Norse *dverg-mál*, the speech of dwarfs, and reflects the old belief that dwarfs lived in rocky areas, and would echo or answer back whatever was said.

At some point in history a row of six brochs on the shore would impress the newcomer to Evie. In recent decades a row of three elegant, lofty wind-generators on Burgar Hill may have been no less impressive, but were definitely less durable. One of the generators was at one time Europe's largest operating windmill; all three were part of a pioneering project to use wind as a source of energy, and much useful information was learned from them. The new state-of-the-art wind-generators to grace Evie will be slimmer and taller.

The majestic cliffs at Marwick Head and the Kitchener Memorial.

Birsay

The parish of Birsay is steeped in history; from prehistoric times to the Stewart period it plays a central part, and often appears in the *Orkneyinga Saga*. Agriculturally it has always been rich, with the Marwick district usually the first to harvest its crop each year. Local produce made the Orkney writer George Mackay Brown lyrical in his praise, 'Birsay tomatoes – for firmness and lusciousness they have no equal, an exquisite blend of sweetness and tartness'.

Birsay has also long been known for its oats, barley and bere, an ancient form of barley which has been used in Orkney since 5000 BC. Today bere-meal is only produced by the water-powered Boardhouse Mill in the Barony, but bere bannocks were once the standard local bread. Another Orkney word for barley was bigg; a few centuries ago the important archaeological site of Buckquoy was known as Biggaquoy.

The old rentals tended to treat the two main districts of Marwick and Birsay proper as two separate parishes, probably because the system of land ownership differed so strongly. Marwick consisted of odal and earldom property, whereas Birsay belonged almost wholly to the bishopric. Altogether the land in the parish of Birsay represented 13.5 urislands; of this 80.8 per cent was owned by the bishopric, 12.9 per cent was odal property, and 6.3 percent belonged to the earldom.

Today Birsay is the largest of the Orkney parishes, consisting of five main areas: Abune the Hill in the north, Birsay be-North, Birsay be-South and Marwick along the western coast, and The Hillside in the east, as well as the smaller districts of Isbister, Sabiston, Greeny and Beaquoy in the south.

Along the Evie border runs the Loch of Swannay which according to James Wallace in 1693 'will have in some parts a thick scumm of Copper Colour upon it, which makes some think there is some Mine under it'. Today this is a large and good fishing loch. Where a burn runs through a small valley west of the loch, lies the farm of Swannay, which is a large dairy farm, producing cheese. In the early nineteenth century the Swannay estate was acquired by a man called Robert Brotchie, believed to be a Highlander, who evicted the tenants of some 20 crofts in Swannay-side.

Dr Hugh Marwick recounts the story of what happened when Brotchie was erecting a boundary wall around his Swannay estate, and the 'wall was being built beyond his proper boundary and encroaching on the adjacent lands of Fea. The owner of Fea allowed him to go on building for a considerable distance before drawing his attention to the trespass. And it was with no small pleasure that his neighbours – some of whom he had evicted – saw how Mr. Brotchie had to demolish what was already built and re-erect his wall on the proper boundary.'

The district of Abune the Hill is divided by a hilly ridge from the Barony district, and therefore is 'over the hill'. Here are the Knowes of Lin which reputedly were used as a resting place by the procession carrying the body of St Magnus from Egilsay to Birsay, back in the twelfth century. Towards the east and south-east relatively high hills separate Birsay from Evie and Harray, and even today there is a feeling of secludedness and tranquillity in The Hillside and Abune the Hill districts. This part of Birsay is a land of lochs and deep valleys, said to be caused by the West Mainland ice moving towards the north-west in a distant past. The Loch of Boardhouse has wild brown trout, but we are told that they are agile and wary and require an experienced angler; the Loch of Kirbuster is the place for beginners!

The coast is rugged, with only a few breaks in the long line of cliffs.

George Mackay Brown spent some time in his youth recuperating from an illness on a Birsay farm along the cliffs, and these are some of his reflections. 'The north coast of Birsay is indented at two places by immense frightening geos. Yet I forced myself to walk to Longaglebe and Kerraglebe every day...Where is there to be found, anywhere, such courtesy and kindness as in a Birsay farm?...Not in any bar on earth is it possible to buy ale of such quality.' Sadly, the farm is now derelict.

The natural coves of Skipi Geo and Sand Geo both have a long history as landing-places for fishing boats, and both were beautifully restored in the 1980s, after a long period of neglect. We find the large bay of Skipi Geo on the north side of the Birsay village that is also known as The Place; a pathway used to lead there from the Palace. The fishermen mostly lived in the little village of Northside. Close by is the 200 m long narrow gloup known as Longaglebe, a fault in the cliff eroded by the sea into an awesome and very dangerous gorge. The Sand Geo is just a short, lovely walk south of Marwick, not so far from the parish border at Outshore Point, and is practically the only landing-place for small boats on this part of the coast. A cluster of old boathouses are here set steeply into the face of the crag.

To the north, a memorial tower on the majestic cliffs at Marwick Head dominates the horizon. In terrible weather, on the night of 5 June 1916, HMS *Hampshire* hit a mine here and went down with most of the crew, only 12 men managing to climb the precipitous cliffs. On board the cruiser was Lord Kitchener, Secretary of State for War, and known from his picture on government conscription posters everywhere. Kitchener was reputedly on his way to Arkhangelsk to encourage the Russian armies in their war effort. The tower with its plaque was raised by public subscription in 1926.

'Hawks and Falcons have their Nests at Marwick, Birsay and Costahead', writes James Wallace in 1693. There is not much hope of observing these birds today, but the RSPB reserve on Marwick Head is a good locality for seeing the more common seabirds. There is also a smaller reserve on the seaward side of the Brough of Birsay, where puffins breed in rabbit burrows along the top of the cliffs. Wetland birds can be watched in the RSPB hide at The Loons, while on the moorland reserve around Mid Hill there are birds of prey. In the valleys of the inland Birsay hills is a unique rush and fern flora that is normally associated with a woodland habitat.

In the *Orkneyinga Saga* the Norse name for Birsay is *Byrgisheraꝺ*, the district of the *byrgi*, a fortification. The name was used about the parishes of Birsay and Harray, but the byrgi element probably refers to the Brough of Birsay. The Norsemen may have seen the Brough as the most outstanding feature of the area, both for its scenic and its political position. It is a tidal island, with the sea rushing through at high tide. The important question is, of course, at what stage in its history did the hill connecting the Brough with The Point of Buckquoy succumb to the tidal pressure?

The island is green and pastoral, with a lighthouse the only modern intrusion. A most remarkable settlement is situated on the landward slope, with a timespan of some 600 years. Excavations were begun in 1866, and have been going on more or less ever since, but the findings of much of the older work have not been published. A mass of buildings from different epochs can be seen; most of the visible ones being Norse.

A small pre-Norse churchyard, enclosed by a curved wall and containing graves, is still evident. Here in 1935 the famous Birsay symbol stone was found, showing three robed and bareheaded warriors with their weapons. A great amount of Pictish metalwork indicates an early iron smithy, as well as a place of wealth and importance. The Norse settlement seems to belong to two distinct phases, an early farmstead period followed by a later stage that is possibly associated with the earls.

The *Orkneyinga Saga* tells us that when Earl Thorfinn the Mighty came back from his pilgrimage to Rome, sometime around 1050, 'he was finished with piracy and devoted all his time to the government of his people and country and to the making of new laws. He had his permanent residence at Birsay, where he built and dedicated to Christ a fine minster, the seat of the first bishop of Orkney'.

The saga does not specify the exact sites of Christ Church or the palaces of Earl Thorfinn and Bishop William The Old, and in the last few decades there has been much academic discussion surrounding their location. Both the Brough and The Place, the village clustering around the parish church of St Magnus, have their ardent supporters, but traditional memory suggests that Earl Thorfinn's power centre was at The Place.

At Buckquoy, just past the village, a long low mound was threatened by coastal erosion. The archaeologist Anna Ritchie's rescue excavation in the 1970s revealed a site that spanned the gradual transition from Pictish to Norse. Her work was followed with great interest, as until then only

View from the RSPB hide at the Loons.

the excavations at Skaill in Deerness had turned up possible answers to this problem.

How to identify Pictish home and burial sites was long considered a problem by archaeologists. After the Buckquoy excavations, Anna Ritchie defined the question clearly, 'If an archaeological site is found within the geographical area and chronological period of the historical Picts, and cannot be attributed to any known intrusive element such as the Vikings, it is surely not unreasonable to regard it as Pictish.' Her view has since been commonly accepted.

The site revealed a series of houses built on top of each other through the seventh century to the end of the ninth, the late Pictish or early Norse period. The third and last Pictish house was quite elaborate and sophisticated, reflecting a well-to-do society. There was no sign of destruction. After a break of perhaps 50 years, a Norse structure, probably a byre, was built on top of the house, only to be abandoned around 900. A pagan male burial was later made in the ruins, and under the skeleton was placed a deliberately cut halfpenny dating to the mid tenth century.

Saevar Howe, also known as the Knowe of Saverough, is situated on the seashore south of The Place; it was opened and, according to modern

A wooden house above the beach in Birsay.

archaeologists very badly excavated in the 1860s. When in 1997 the site was threatened by quarrying and sea erosion it was excavated again. Beneath a long cist cemetery the remains of three Norse buildings were discovered, which again were superimposed on levels of Pictish dwellings. Perhaps the most interesting object found was a bell, enclosed in a cist by itself. A perforated coin of Burgred dating to 866-8 was discovered in the Norse occupation levels. The Norse phases at Saevar Howe began in the ninth century.

Together the sites of Brough of Birsay, Buckquoy and Saevar Howe indicate that Birsay was intensively settled by Norsemen in the ninth century, and that Norse ascendancy over the native population was established rather quickly.

Birsay may be said to have been the capital of the earldom at one time, and some centuries later the Stewart earls also found Birsay an attractive place. On what may have been the site of Earl Thorfinn's old residence, Earl Robert Stewart built a palace after the plan of Holyrood House in Edinburgh. In fashionable Renaissance style it was constructed around a quadrangle or open court, with a well in the centre. Work began in 1569 and was completed before Earl Robert's death in 1593. After a century it was no longer inhabited, and soon became roofless.

Jo Ben is at his fanciful best in his description of Birsay. 'Birsa is called a Barony where there is a fine palace where once ruled the king of Orkney, but when Julius Caesar ruled the whole world he was charged at Rome with a certain crime of violence, and thereafter Orkney was subject to the Romans, as an inscription on a stone testifies. The name of the king was Gavus.'

The church of St Magnus was built in 1664 as a cruciform church, then rebuilt in 1760 as the parish church which is still in use today. In the southern wall of the church is a stone with *Bellus* engraved upon it, and this has given rise to many different theories, as the name *Mons Bellus* was used in the sixteenth century for the Birsay residence of the Bishop of Orkney.

Sometime in the late nineteenth century a new manse was built up the hill, north-east of the parish church of St Magnus. The old manse was close to the church, on the shore of the village, and to the Revd George Low, who was ordained minister of Birsay and Harray in 1774, it must have seemed a haven. The life of a parish minister would hopefully leave him time for his absorbing interest in nature in all its aspects. He is considered the best Orkney naturalist of his time.

The celebrated traveller and naturalist Thomas Pennant asked George Low to undertake a tour, at his expense, of Orkney and Shetland to obtain information on local customs, natural history and antiquities. To Low the invitation must have seemed a heaven-sent opportunity to follow up his own interests. He set off in early May 1774, and the observations made on his 'tour' are remarkably shrewd and interesting even today. They are set forth in his book *A Tour Thro' Orkney and Schetland*, which was not published until 1879, more than 100 years later.

In the meantime much of his research had been freely used by others, without acknowledgement. When writing about the publication of his work in his last letter, Low asks bitterly, 'But stay, what is to be published? Is it not all published already? One has taken a leg, another an arm, some a toe, some a finger, and Mr Pennant the very Heart's Blood out of it.' His other principal work *Fauna Orcadensis* was published in 1813, but the rest of his work has never been published.

He married Helen Tyrie, the daughter of his colleague, the Revd James Tyrie of Sandwick, just after moving into his Birsay manse. She died within a year, in childbirth. Towards the end of his life his eyesight failed, perhaps because of studying through his microscope in poor light. He died in 1795, aged 49 years.

Many old customs, work habits and lore survived in Birsay. In his report to the *Statistical Account of Orkney, 1795-1798,* his last work, George Low describes how his parishioners make a cloth known as Vadmell on a loom called Upstaganga; he might as well have described the work and words of a Norwegian valley district. On the land between the Lochs of Boardhouse and Hundland is the beautifully situated farm of Kirbuster. Nearby runs the Burn of Kirbuster, the largest and perhaps the only river in Orkney. The farm, which dates from 1723, is now a museum, and was inhabited till the early 1960s; it gives an interesting insight into life on a larger than average farm in Birsay in the not-so-distant past.

When Dr Hugh Marwick worked on *The Place-Names of Birsay,* which was published posthumously in 1970, he was greatly helped by William Sabiston, a farmer at Scrutabeck who was interested in collecting and interpreting the old names. Another Birsay writer was John Spence (1857-1933), a farmer at Evrabist, who found his 'academy on the moor', as he expressed it. Besides being an authority on the local flora, history and customs, he also took an interest in old Orkney words and contributed dialect texts to scholarly magazines.

Another Birsay writer is Robert Rendall (1898-1967) who found his academy by the shore. His marine research on Orkney beaches made him a self-taught conchologist, an authority on shells, publishing *Mollusca Orcadensia* in 1956 and *Orkney Shore* in 1960. He spent some of his happiest moments in his holiday house The Lower P'Lace close to the Birsay beach. For much of his life he was really a Kirkwall businessman as well as one of the leading theologians of the sect known as the Plymouth Brethren. He also published collections of poetry, his last being *The Hidden Land* in 1966. Robert Rendall is perhaps at his best when writing in his own dialect as here, in 'Salt i' the Bluid':

> A'm bydan heem, 'at geed for lang
> Ruggan afore the mast,
> Yet times me thowts they taak a spang
> Aff tae the wild Nor'wast.
>
> On winter nights I whiles can feel
> Me cottage gaan adrift,
> An' wance again I grip the wheel
> Tae the sea-swaal's aisy lift.

Swans in winter on the Loch of Harray.

Harray

Over the ages the parish of Harray has had different names. In early Norse times the united parishes of Birsay and Harray were known as Byrgisherad. In 1490 it appears on its own in the rental as 'the parochin of Burch in the Herray', and in 1492 as 'Burgh Sancti Michaelis'. It appears as 'Parochia de Burgh' in various old documents. The names of Burch and Burgh probably refer to the broch in the tunship of Overbrough that reputedly formed the foundation of the old Church of St Michael's.

The name of Harray derives from the Norse word *heraƌ*, and was used about administrative land units. Although practice varies somewhat from one country to another, the system is still used in Scandinavia. The expression 'in the Herray' in the 1492 rental shows that at the time the name must have referred to a kind of district. It is an interesting question whether this system of land division was ever used all over Orkney. It can be traced in the Outer Hebrides as well. In *Heraidh*, the Gaelic spelling of Harris, the original meaning of the word is conserved.

Harray is known as Orkney's inland parish. Yet such a description is not completely true. Although Harray has no sea coast, its whole west side faces the large, freshwater Loch of Harray. This is connected with the tidal Loch of Stenness, by a gap that is narrow, but still wide enough to have let Viking ships through. The Loch of Harray is not very deep, but then Viking ships were known for their shallow draught.

The writer Eric Linklater spent some years of his life by the Loch of Harray, in his house on 'a heathery knowe, by the northern arm of the lake' and knew the loch in all its moods. He was so fascinated by the Loch of Harray that he opens his autobiography *The Man on my Back* with a description of it. This is how he sees the bird life on the loch:

> It is quick with many birds, with mallard and merganser and the black-headed gull. A tight rabble of coots, rising in sudden alarm, with staccato clapping of their wings will scuttle in a crystal storm from the shelter of a bay. In June comes idly sailing a fleet of swans, and that exquisite warrior, the Arctic tern, hangs like a hawk in the unmoving air. A few pairs of eider-duck prefer its sweet water to the sea, and while a cormorant on a rock holds out heraldic wings to dry, red shanks with indignant whistle patrol the shore.

The Loch of Harray is full of fine brown trout, or at least it used to be. An old story has it that the trout were seized with madness on one occasion and tried to commit mass suicide by getting stranded in the Bay of Howaback at the north end of the loch. People came with carts and shovels to bring them in. Today one has to be an expert angler to catch the trout. It may be that drainage from fields has upset the spawning.

In the south the Burn of Rickla forms the parish boundary with Stenness. At Staney Hill on the slope above the burn stands the Hinatuin stone. Believed by some to have been an alignment for the Ring of Brodgar, it was, in the twelfth century, a meeting place for the procession moving the remains of St Magnus overland from Birsay to Kirkwall. When they arrived at the stone, the Birsay people found the place deserted, in fact the Harray people were so slow in appearing that they were said to be coming like crabs out of the ebb. The word has stuck, and the Harray people have been known as Harray crabs ever since.

But there is another version to the crab story. Harray people are supposed to be ignorant about anything to do with the sea, and have been teased mercilessly about it. The story goes that when a Harray man once ventured into the sea, he was shocked to find a crab holding on to his big toe. 'Let be for let be', he cried, being both naive and fair-minded, and ever since 'I'll let-a-be for let-a-be like the Harrayman with the crab' has been a proverbial Orkney expression. But according to Jo Ben there is an altogether different name for the Harray people, 'Hara is another parish, where they are very idle drones so they are called the Sheipies of Hara.'

From the Burn of Rickla the parish boundary runs along a rather high hill ridge which goes on into the parish of Birsay to the north. The highest point in Harray itself is the Kame of Corrigall at 176 m; it is surrounded by a wild area of hill and heather, with burns and peat bogs, but no roads. The peat in the Harray hill area is of exceptionally high quality, and in the old days people used to come from Sandwick to take it for fuel. For the hillwalker it may perhaps be tough going in places, but grouse can be seen, there may be orchids in the heather, and views from the hillsides are exhilarating.

The writer and naturalist George Low was minister of Birsay and Harray from 1774 until his death in 1795. In his highly readable contribution to the *Statistical Account of Orkney, 1795-1798*, he warns walkers against the dangers of the Harray burns. 'In general, Harray is flat and rather swampy, intersected by a great number of very dangerous burns, which, at most seasons, rush down in perfect torrents from the adjacent hills, and often occasion danger and even death to unwary travellers.' George Low is right in his observations; nature and climate conditions in Harray are among the most difficult in Orkney.

A main road between Sandwick and Evie forms the northern boundary. The land here is open and fertile, and the thriving village of Dounby has grown up at the crossroads as the school and market centre of a large farming area. The Dounby Show is held in August each year, and attracts a large number of visitors. It was at one time an agricultural market where livestock were bought and sold but is now a show where the quality of the animals is judged and trophies awarded. Some of the visitors are genuinely interested in looking at prime cattle, while others come for the fun and games or the social aspect of meeting friends.

The late Orkney writer George Mackay Brown was a frequent visitor to the Dounby event – 'The Dounby Show breaks down barriers. It is a foretaste of harvest and the year's plenitude. All men exist by the fruits of the earth. Here the creatures of the earth – animals, fowls, and folk –

appear at their most splendid and festive. – Beside the huge black bulls at the wall, beside the pens of tinted sheep, and the goats and carolling cockerels and the patient horses, we lingered out the afternoon talking to this friend and that. And I ended, as always, among a throng of friends at the mouth of the beer-tent, relishing malt, that rare ancient earth-fruit.'

Most of the cultivated land is in the central plain along the Loch of Harray. The fertile land is patchy, and is separated by areas of barren heathery ground, known as brecks. This made an early division into tunships quite natural. Thus at one time there were 13 tunships making up four main districts. The tunships of Knarston, Corston, Corrigall, Garth, Mirbister and Overbrough made up a northern district of one and a half urislands, and Noltclett, Howe, Huntscarth and Bimbister together made a one urisland district. The third district consisting of Netherbrough and Russland, made one urisland, and then Grimeston was the fourth district, also consisting of one urisland. Today the tunship names are no longer used, perhaps not even known to the younger generation.

The central part of Harray must have been densely populated in prehistoric times, judging by the small, steep knowes, mounds and tumuli that appear in arable fields everywhere. The best known and most striking of these are the Knowes of Trotty. They lie at the foot of the Redland hills, so presumably the builders of these barrows did not especially want their mounds to dominate the landscape from afar. The mounds are ranged in two rows, and are believed to date from the mid to later second millennium BC.

The largest of the Knowes of Trotty was excavated in 1860 by George Petrie, and proved to be of outstanding richness. A stone-lined cist was found, containing burnt bones, four sun-discs of gold, some pendants and 27 amber beads from a woman's necklace. From one of the Knowes of Trinnawin a fine specimen of a steatite urn was secured, on excavation in 1902.

So far the remains of 11 brochs have been found in Harray. There are three broch sites in the Netherbrough tunship, otherwise they seem to be rather evenly distributed over the cultivated area. The parish church of St Michael at Overbrough is one of the medieval churches that occupy sites associated with the mound of a broch. The Knowe of Burrian has yielded an exceptionally fine symbol stone, with an eagle carved by a

The Knowes of Trotty at the foot of the Redland Hills.

master of the art; it seems closely related to the eagle used in the Northumbrian illustrated gospels as a symbol of St John.

The broch landscape of Harray must have been an amazing sight to the Norsemen. The whole area around the Loch of Harray with the rings of standing stones would have seemed a sacred landscape. It may have been the central area in West Mainland at the time. At any rate the Norsemen seem to have left the area alone, as there are no signs of early Norse settlement. Only one Norse find has been made; in 1886 a burial cist was found in the Knowe of Moan in Russland, containing among other things a ninth-century stirrup.

The distribution of the Norse placename element –staðir, now corrupted into –ston, is rather remarkable in the area around the Loch of Harray. More than half the names of this kind in Orkney are concentrated in this part of the West Mainland. Such names in Harray are Grimeston, Knarston and Corston, and perhaps also Biest and Handest. This placename element is late and such names are never found in early settlement areas. Stadir-names do not contain topographical pointers or pagan beliefs but often have a man's name as the first element; the emphasis is on the individual who believes in his own might and means. The historian J Storer Clouston suggested that these farms all belonged to the second round of settlement, and were given to the warriors of the earls while the centre of the earldom was still in Birsay.

Harray is not mentioned in the *Orkneyinga Saga*, and we hear of no great families or chieftains from the early Norse period. The old house at Winksetter, just below Burrien Hill, may be the oldest standing Norse building in Orkney, although what is left of it will probably not remain standing much longer. The old Winksetter house ruin has very thick walls, and the characteristic sae-bink, a place for putting a pail of water, and a goosenest, in which hens and geese were kept inside for nesting, can still be seen. The first part of the name is believed to derive from Viking, and it is possible that the outlying farm was once a hunting lodge. According to old tradition 'Winksetter was the traditional seat of the youngest son of the King of Norway'.

A grave of 'the Harraymen'.

Through the centuries Harray remained a stronghold of odallers who in spite of often grinding poverty held on to their farms. The farmers have been mostly owners as well as occupiers, there have been few if any tenant farmers, and the idea of 'the hundred lairds of Harray' has long been a part of Orkney lore. The rental of *c.*1500 shows more than 80 per cent of the land as odal property. There has never been a dominant landed family in Harray, but there have been a lot of Fletts, the main surname.

George Low gives us an interesting description of the social fabric of the 'peerie lairds'. 'The people are as well contented as poor people can be expected; can put a new suit of clothes upon their backs now and then, partly of their own making, and partly bought; and can make a feast, at a wedding or a christening, on their own provisions, with a drink of their own ale.'

But Low also tells us that the 'young men of Harray are pretty fond of quarrelling over their ale, but I have never heard of any murders.' There were no licensed ale houses in Harray in the seventeenth century, but still it was perhaps not the wisest thing the authorities ever did to start the collection of excise duties from Orcadians, in the parish of Harray. In about 1670 officers and militia were sent out to enforce payment, but were routed by the Harraymen. Their victory is commemorated in an old ballad known as the 'Harray Rant'.

> So the Harra-men upon them fell,
> Wi' flail and staves and stones;
> Some women wi' the kettle cruick,
> And others wi' the tongs.
> Come drink a health to Harra-men
> Fill cogs and don't be scant,
> Drink barley bree, and whisky tae,
> and sing the 'Harray Rant'.

The Kirkwall men later spoke of Harray as 'a place where devils dwelt.'

There was a good deal of malt brewed in different houses, and as the product was taxable, it was important to find a safe hiding place for it. An ingenious place that was never discovered by the excise men was the 'mattie hole' dug in the moss and heather in the Knowes of Stankieth, two mounds close to the Knowes of Trinnawin.

Food was often scarce towards the end of winter, in the period known as 'the lang reed'. At a time when Orkney was near starvation a group of Harraymen walked to Rendall to collect ebb-maet, or shellfish found on shore at low tide, from the shore. On their way they were caught in a freak blizzard on the forbidding moors between the two parishes. They were buried in the Rendall hill, north-west of Blubbersdale, and today stones set on end mark the site of 'The Harraymen's Graves'. Their story is still told in Harray, and is believed to have happened in one of the disastrous harvest periods of the eighteenth century.

Norse speech lingered in Harray until about the second half of the eighteenth century, longer than in any other part of Orkney. The Revd Barry tells us that so 'late as 1756 or 1757, as a respectable native of this country was travelling from Kirkwall to Birsay, he had occasion to lodge all night in a house in Harra; where, to his surprise, he heard two old men for an hour or more converse together in an unknown tongue; which, on inquiry, he found was the Norse language.'

In the heart of Harray – and West Mainland – is the Corrigall Farm Museum, which was opened in 1980. The work of reconstruction and restoration of an old traditional farm steading was tackled with enthusiasm by a group of youngsters under skilled guidance, and the result has brought the past to life. It was the good life then, in many ways. Here the famous poem 'Grandad had a cruisie lamp', the dread of Orkney school kids having to learn the verses by heart, strikes a chord. The writer was George Corrigall, who farmed at West Ballarat in Netherbrough and was at one time the bard of West Mainland.

> Grandad had a cruisie lamp (he'd never heard o' watt or amp).
> He lighted up an' he thanked the Lord that he had no rows
>   wi' the Hydro Board.
> On brose and tatties, kale and pork he aye kept fit for his
>   daily wark.
> He bought no meat from the butcher van so Grandad was a
>   wealthy man.
>
> Grandad had his annual trip to Harray loch for his annual dip.
> He had no cistern belching steam so he saw no need for a
>   water scheme.
> His wool came straight from the auld grey yowe and he lit his
>   pipe with a heather cowe.
> And the only power plug he knew was the cork from the
>   bottle o' a good home brew.   (Traditional oral poem.)

Another popular Harray writer was Harriet Campbell (1878-1933), who spent much of her later life at her grandfather's old home of Nisthouse in Mirbister. She published two collections of essays, and also painted. In her poem 'Mirbister', (Marwick, E., 1949) she describes her own people,

> There's Harray lairds a hundred, who work the land themsel's;
> They're honest and they're mannerly, for old blood always tells.
> There's guid folk i' the parishes, as there's fishes i' the sea;
> There's Orphir, Holm, and Deerness, but – the Harray Lairds for me!

Yesnaby in full storm.

Sandwick

Historically Sandwick is one of the largest and most fertile of the Orkney parishes. Its Norse name of *Sandvík* – sandy bay – refers to the Bay of Skaill. The white sand of the large Skaill beach is perhaps the most striking physical feature of the area, and to the Norsemen it would have been important for the access it gave to the sea.

The Bay of Skaill is one of the few breaches in the line of cliffs which runs the whole length of the Sandwick coast from Outshore Point to Lyre Geo, which mark the parish borders. The walk southwards along the western wall from the natural arch known as the Hole o' Row is spectacular as well as interesting. Cliffs to a sheer height of 30 m and more are exposed to the full onslaught of the Atlantic, but are still home to all kinds of seabirds. Sea and wind have worn away the weaker parts of the rock wall and caused fantastic formations. The tall stack known as the Castle of Yesnaby consists of hard, thick strata of Stromness flags, and is backed by steep walls.

Still, the most striking rock formation along this coastline is perhaps Ramna Geo – raven-geo – surely the longest geo in Orkney. The name is apt, as it is a haunt of ravens even today. The rock walls are high, steep and inaccessible, so the ravens have truly found a haven of their own.

Only sea-hardy plants can thrive in an environment constantly showered in spray, but sea-pinks make the cliff-edges glow. The purple flowers of the modest *Primula scotica* are found here in summer, as are edible mushrooms.

At Inga Ness, not far north of the parish border between Stromness and Sandwick, a small stretch of the coast is known as Harra Ebb. As the parish of Harray was land-locked, the Sandwick people at this point allowed their neighbours access to the shore to fish and collect ebb-maet, the shellfish found on the shore at low tide. In return they obtained the right to cut peat moss in the Harray hill, as they still do to this day. The Harraymen had to cover a long distance to get to the fishing, even if they first crossed the loch by boat.

It is possible to walk for miles along the cliffs and see few signs of human habitation. Today two of the farms nearest to the coast, Borwick and Forcewell, are empty and ghostlike. It is perhaps not so strange that few families in Sandwick used to own a boat in the olden days, as much of the cultivated land lies at a distance from the sea. Still, both breaches in the western cliff have names indicating they were landing-places for boats: The Noust of Bigging and The Noust of Borwick.

At Yesnaby the snug Noust of Bigging was popular with lobster-fishermen, who built their own wooden huts by the shore, where in the summertime they would bring their families as well. Only a few indeterminate stones in a field nearby remain of what was once a chapel, said to have been dedicated to St Bride. There is also a tradition of a holy well with curative powers, called Crossiekeld. The whole area is picturesque, and is a popular motif for local painters.

It must have been considered important to protect this breach in the wall, and the small peninsula called the Brough of Bigging provides a natural shelter. At some time, probably towards the end of the first millennium BC, it was made into a fort. Compared to the number of brochs, promontory forts are rare in Orkney. The low and narrow isthmus has traces of a rampart on each side, with some distance between. At the narrowest part of the entrance are several stones set on edge; according to tradition these mark the graves of sailors from a Spanish Armada ship.

More striking, as well as uglier, are the remains of the naval gunnery range from the Second World War on top of the Yesnaby cliffs; obviously the area was of strategic importance even some 2000 years later. The military road disturbs the pastoral peace, but it gives dog-owners a welcome chance of exercising their pets along the cliffs. Yesnaby is a popular excursion point, but the area may be dangerous because of the continual erosion, which caused a sizeable cliff fall some time ago.

There are remains of many brochs in Sandwick: Stackrue at Lyking, Burrian in Wasbister, Scarrataing in Tenston, and Clumly on a small ness jutting out in the Loch of Clumly. But the most interesting of them all, both to the archaeologist and to the interested visitor, is the Broch of Borwick, or *Borgarvík* as it was known to the Norsemen.

The broch is situated on a sheer-sided headland, some 30 m high, and it completely dominates the small bay. Perhaps the Broch of Borwick, to a greater extent than any of the other Orkney brochs, leaves us with a feeling of what it must all have been about: territorial protection. From the broch an intruder could be met by a hail of stones. But the broch must also have been a kind of territorial marker. This was never a large broch; today much of the seaward part has fallen away, but traces of the moat that once ran from cliff to cliff are still visible. A cave, known as Hell's Mouth – a corruption of Old Norse *hellir*, a cave – runs underneath the broch.

The Broch of Borwick was first excavated in 1881 by William Watt of Skaill, the owner of the Breckness estate. Its interest to present-day archaeologists seems to be connected with the traces of two phases of occupation. The many irregularly constructed outbuildings that were found between the moat and the broch, along with a secondary wall inside the broch itself, have been interpreted by archaeologists as evidence of reuse at a later date.

Sandwick is on the whole rich in all kinds of antiquities. The Stones of Via, near the Loch of Clumly, may have had some cultic importance. This is indicated by the name, as Via may be derived from the Norse *vé*, a word used about a pagan, holy place. In the area known as The Brecks, just north of the Ring of Brodgar in Stenness, lies the Chambered Cairn of Bookan. It was excavated in 1861 by the English archaeologist James Farrer, while he was also working on Maeshowe. Close by is the little-known Ring of Bookan where large stones lie helter-skelter around a circular, clearly defined trench. The site looked more or less the same when it was examined by Captain Thomas, RN, in 1848. His comment then was, 'Even this deeply entrenched spot has been ravaged by the plough...'

The great blocks of stone used for the three rings between the lochs are believed to have come all the way from Vestra Fiold in the north of Sandwick. Fiold is the Sandwick variant of the Norse *fjall* for mountain. There is an ancient quarry on the hillside, and somehow the stones were dressed and dragged to where they now stand.

Still, the historical sight that outshines everything else in Sandwick, is the Stone-Age village of Skara Brae. When it was in use, according to radiocarbon dating between *c.*2500 BC and *c.*3100 BC, the village may have been sited close to a small freshwater loch and well back from the sea. At some point it was buried in sand during a violent storm, forcing the inhabitants to flee in a hurry. Some prized possessions were left behind, and, as in Pompeii, village life was frozen in time. Unlike the people of Pompeii, however, the inhabitants apparently were all able to escape. For centuries a large sandy dune covered the site, until in 1850 another severe storm blew it away.

During the next ten years William Watt of Skaill carried on some excavation from time to time, aided by other zealous amateurs. Then for many years nothing happened. The writer Eric Linklater describes his childhood memories of the site with delight. 'Nowadays Skaill is chiefly famous for its prehistoric village of Skara Brae, about which archaeologists have different opinions. But I have only one opinion and that is that it was much pleasanter and more entertaining before they excavated it: for there used to be little more than a couple of grassy cup-like hollows, with little tunnels of masonry running down and away from them, and it was the best picnicking place on the island. We simply called it the Picts' Hoose then, and were quite content with such a description. But now it has become a National Monument, with a keeper and three thousand visitors in the season, and one cannot picnic there any longer.'

Then in 1928-29 Dr V Gordon Childe, an internationally acclaimed expert on European prehistory, carried out a classic excavation at Skara Brae. He uncovered one of the most important Neolithic sites in Europe, consisting of several one-room dwellings linked together by a paved alley. The rooms are rectangular, with rounded corners, and have drains emptying into a sewer. The village is built of undressed slabs of stone and is banked around by a high midden of sand, peat ash and refuse, which would have given protection against the wind. The furniture is also stone made. Local materials are ingeniously used for everything, thus games were played with dice of walrus ivory. The rather coarse pottery they used is of a kind known as 'Grooved Ware'. Among the designs found on this pottery, the true spiral is represented on one pot-shard; the only example of its kind found in Britain.

To the visitor the most immediate feeling is perhaps surprise at how comfortable and homelike these rooms, or houses, really are. The stone dressers and the wall-recesses are not all that different from what can be found in Orkney's farm museums. The Orkney poet Robert Rendall expresses what perhaps many people feel:

I one time went to Skarabrae
To view with antiquarian dream
The prehistoric housing scheme.

The large mansion of Skaill House stands above the Stone-Age village, dominating the area. Old documents refer to the sixteenth-century building on the site as the 'Old Hall'. This falls in with the name: Skaill is a version of the Norse word *skáli*. The word was used of the main building on a farm, but sometimes it also referred specially to a hall used for festivities. It occurs as a farm name in many places in Orkney. The central section of the house dates from the first part of the seventeenth century, but the building has been extended several times since. Skaill House was opened to the public in 1997.

Today the 900-acre farm of Skaill is one of the largest in Orkney, but in the sixteenth century it was a modest part of the estate of the Stewart earls. It came under the control of Bishop George Graham in 1615 when the Earldom estate was broken up after the execution of Earl Patrick in Edinburgh. Along with the farm of Breckness near Stromness and numerous smaller holdings in the area, Bishop Graham built up an extensive estate for his son John, who became the first laird of the Breckness estate, as the property has since been called. Skaill House was always its centre, but confusingly it gets the name from the farm of Breckness in Stromness, which also was part of the estate.

Later generations of Grahams did not do so well, and in 1787 William Watt, a successful merchant in Kirkwall and related to the Grahams by marriage, became the sixth laird. His son William, besides being interested in archaeology, was also a progressive farmer who introduced new farming methods. The estate is still in the same family, and the twelfth and present laird is Major Malcolm Macrae, who is also the owner of Binscarth in Firth.

House 1 at the Stone-Age village of Skara Brae.

On Muckle Brae to the north of the bay the so-called Skaill hoard was found in 1858, by a boy out rabbit-hunting. The treasure weighed around 8 kg, which places it among the largest Viking-Age silver hoards found anywhere. It contained silver in standard units, probably meant for trade, as well as magnificent silver jewellery. There were as many as 16 brooches of the famous 'ball-type' style. Altogether the hoard consisted of some hundred items, including coins. Some of the coins were Anglo-Saxon and some were minted in Baghdad between 887 and 945. The treasure may therefore have been buried around the middle of the tenth century, which was an unsettled period in Orkney.

Although many chapel sites are known, there was only one parish church, situated in the north end of the Bay of Skaill, and dedicated to St Peter. Probably this dedication goes back to the first church on the site, as this is the name given to so many of the early Christian churches in Orkney. In the old days people in Sandwick did not work on 3 March, as that was the day on which the church was consecrated, nor on 29 June, as that was St Peter's day. In the churchyard the oldest tombstone is from 1623, erected to the memory of Bishop Graham's daughter. The church is a fine building of its period, and has now been bought by The Scottish Redundant Churches Trust.

The interior of Quoyloo Church, which is the present parish church, explodes in colour. Its vivid colour scheme of sky-blue, red and yellow was inspired by the well-known Orkney artist, Stanley Cursiter. At one time an old road that ran roughly in a direct line from Quoyloo to St Peter's Church, was known as the Messigate, the road to church.

The Sandwick and Stromness parishes were for many years united. The manse lay some distance away from both parish churches, on a slope above the Loch of Skaill. Its old name was Coninsgar, a name suggesting Old Norse *konungs-garðr*, king's farm. Nothing is known of its old history, but it became the home of some colourful ministers. In 1747, James Tyrie was appointed minister of the twin parishes, after having been rejected by Cross and Burness parish in Sanday. He was a former Catholic and rumoured to have been involved in adultery. Regular riots broke out against him. In Sandwick women barred the doors of St Peter's against him and threatened 'bodily harm & violence'.

The schoolmaster from Sandwick was arrested, along with 16 women, eight from each parish. Some of them had to stay in the Tolbooth of Kirkwall for quite a few days. The Presbytery were shocked by the ferocity displayed by the women, 'That lawless, unadvisable and Insatiable mob', and believed that it must have been people of "better judgment than themselves who instigated and influenced them".

Things must have worked out for the Revd Tyrie after all, for he remained minister of the parish till he died in 1778. As he grew older and was suffering from scurvy, he applied for an assistant, as he found it more and more difficult to travel the four miles from the manse to Stromness. A later minister, the Revd William Clouston, found it difficult to administer the sacrament of the Lord's Supper because of this distance; instead the funds for this were given to the Stromness poor.

His son, the Revd Dr Charles Clouston, who was minister of Sandwick for many years, until he died in 1884, was a distinguished meteorologist and naturalist. For many years the manse served as one of the stations of the Scottish Meteorological Society. Dr Clouston collected extensive data on the rainfall, temperatures, atmospheric pressures, and the direction and force of the wind, and used these to work out carefully tabulated statistics for the Society. He also contributed 83 new species to the Orkney flora.

Dr Clouston was one of the founders of the Orkney Natural History Society and Stromness Museum, but in Orkney he is perhaps remembered today as much for buying the Sandwick copy of the *Book of Black Art* and burying it ceremoniously, with the Bible on top, in the manse garden. It has not been heard of again!

In 1529 Jo Ben wrote, 'Sandwick is another parish, very fertile and abundant in rabbits, and most of all the parishes it is completely cultivated.' The parish was very highly taxed in Norse times, probably because much of the land was under cultivation. As late as 1653 the total rent in Sandwick was higher than that of any other single parish. The old rentals distinguish clearly between North and South Sandwick, with the dividing line going from the Bay of Skaill to the Loch of Harray. The taxable value was 8 urislands in North Sandwick, and 9.5 in South Sandwick. Even as late as 1568 exactly half the land of North Sandwick was still odal land, in South Sandwick this share was 41 per cent.

The district of Northdyke may have its name from an old dyke or fence; the farm name Garson on the west shore derives from the Old Norse *garðs-endi*, the end of the fence. This district is believed to have been one of the earliest Norse settlements in the West Mainland. Its position so close to the natural landing-place of Bay of Skaill, makes this a logical assumption. 'Very, very venerable then is this Northdyke district', says the Orkney historian J Storer Clouston. Sir Malise Sperra, one of the claimants to the Earldom in 1379, owned land in Instabillie, a tunship in Northdyke. He did not succeed, and became Norwegian governor in Shetland instead.

The inland districts seem to have been taken over by the Norsemen at a later date, as we find several placenames ending in -ston. These names usually consisted of a man's name and a final element *–staðir*, meaning place or stead. When Iceland was settled in the late ninth century, these names were at the height of fashion. In Orkney they are found mostly in central Sandwick and in Harray, which may indicate that these inland areas were taken over by Norsemen rather late.

The three outstanding odal families in North Sandwick were the Kirknesses of Kirkness, the Linklaters of Linklater and the Hourstons of Hourston. At the farm of Upper Housegarth there have been Linklaters for hundreds of years, but sadly now the land has been sold. In South Sandwick there were the Sinclairs of Tenston, Norns of Voy, and Louttitts of Lyking. The 'manor house' of Linklater appears in some records, as does the 'manor house of Kirkness' in a record from 1696.

Nether Benzieclett, which in the seventeenth century belonged to the

The lovely valley below the hill of Kringlafiold.

Linklater family, was at one time the chief house in the Skaebrae tunship. Its ground plan has one end wider than the other, a peculiarity not unknown in early Icelandic houses. It has been considered the oldest inhabited house in Sandwick, perhaps in Orkney: 'I question if there be any more undoubted and characteristic piece of old Norse Orkney than the house of Nether Benzieclett', says J Storer Clouston. According to tradition a king of Norway once spent a night in the now ruinous old house of Nether Benzieclett. And ever since a man was murdered in the ale-hurry, the chamber where the ale was stored, a ghost would appear there at 1 am every morning.

Much of Orkney folklore is connected with Sandwick. Thus the Fin King, ruler of the Fin Folk who lived in Finfolkaheem at the bottom of the sea, was killed by the men of Sandwick in a sea battle in the Bay of Skaill. Mansie o' Kierfa, now known as Kierfold, was brave enough to get himself a fairy wife on the side; she bore him three daughters and gave him such insights that he acquired the status of a physician. In the old days the young people of Sandwick would go to the top of the hill of Kringlafiold at midsummer, for three mornings running, to watch the sun rising. This is an old tradition found in all the Nordic countries.

The best story is perhaps the one known as 'The Belted Knights of Stove', which seems a wonderful mixture of history and lore. It takes place at the ancient farm of Stove in Quoyloo. Until 1887 this farm was handed down from father to son in the Kirkness family, and along with it the story of how they had been ennobled in the 1530s. A red-haired young man suddenly appeared at the farm, asking for a job. He was taken on as a goose-herd, but did not stay very long. As he was leaving, he asked the farmer to kneel, touched him on the shoulder with his stick and said, 'Rise Sir John Kirkness, you and your descendants shall always after this be known as the Belted Knights of Stove'.

The Kirkness family always believed that the young man was King James V, who was known to go around the country incognito. The overwhelming victory of Orcadians over Caithnessians in the Battle of Summerdale a few years before, may have made him curious about Orkney. The young man was wont to sit on a large stone in the meadow; it was afterwards known as the King's Stone, and had the word 'King' carved into it. It remained in the meadow until the 1860s, when it was used for building; today it is part of the foundation of the barn.

The Kirknesses of Stove derive their surname from the old farm of Kirkness at the northern edge of the Loch of Harray. The farm in its turn is named after an old chapel which stood there. Kirkness is one of the first recorded Orkney surnames. A Sir Thomas of Kirkness appears as a witness, along with five other knights, to a charter by Earl Henry to his brother. Sir Thomas's brother Angus was a canon in St Magnus Cathedral, and his son was John Kirkness who was Lawman of Orkney around 1430. Strangely the Kirkness farm is never mentioned in the old rentals; it may be that as Norse knights the Kirknesses had been granted tax privileges. At some time the family may have moved to Stove in Quoyloo. Perhaps the king appeared at Stove knowing full well who they were, or perhaps the story of the Belted Knights of Stove is just the expression of a confused tribal memory?

Today large, regular fields surround well-kept farm buildings and give the parish a prosperous look. Nearly all farmers own their own farms, although a few are still tenants of the Breckness estate. Amalgamation of farms does not seem to have gone so far as in many other districts, but whereas Sandwick had no fewer than nine schools in the nineteenth century, today there are none, all the school children go to school in Dounby. The old Quoyloo school has today become The Orkney Brewery, with brands such as Dragonhead Orkney Stout, Skullsplitter Ale and Raven Ale.

Stromness

The parish name contains the Norse word *straumr*, a stream or current, and refers to the southern ness that projects into the tideway of Hoy Sound. The town of Stromness has had many different names through the ages; the harbour itself was in Norse times known as *Hafnarvágr*, haven bay. This is the Hamnavoe of today, and it would perhaps be a better name for the town, as it would distinguish it from the parish. But Hamnavoe has acquired a romantic aura and seems reserved for verse and fiction.

The belt of ancient rocks – granites and schists – continues from north Graemsay through Stromness into Sandwick, but appears only in small outcrops of bare, smooth rocks in the fields. In Stromness Hugh Miller (1802-56) discovered the Old Red Sandstone bed of fish fossils where he took his Asterolepis. In his book *Footprints of the Creator* with the subtitle *The Asterolepis of Stromness*, he is ecstatic about the fossils to be found in Orkney, and calls it the 'Land of Fish'. He describes how he sets out from Stromness 'hammer in hand' to look for fossils, and finds the 'petrified nail', a nail-like bone that had formed a part of the asterolepis, a gigantic, extinct fish.

The walk from the Ness area, where Hugh Miller found his fossil, takes us along the old shore road to the kirkyard, which was perhaps once the centre of the parish. Here was Monk's Green, the site of the old parish church of Stromness. The church may have been dedicated to St Peter and been one of the first Pictish churches. There was also a place called Monkerhoose nearby, but any remains of it will have been taken by erosion, as the sea has eaten deeply into this part of the coast.

The coastline is a trap for shipping, and in the past it has seen heroic rescues here of ships like the Hull trawler *Shakespeare* that was wrecked on the Point of Spoil at Breckness. This happened in the morning of 11 December 1907. The lifeboat *The Good Shepherd*, manned by volunteers, was launched after the Breckness farmer had galloped on his horse over the hill to give warning. The situation was desperate by the time the lifeboat arrived, the sea was breaking over the trawler, four men had already drowned and the remaining six men were clinging to the masts. They were saved, and the coxswain later got a medal for an 'exceedingly difficult and dangerous rescue'.

In the nineteenth century there existed still the remains of a large and impressive broch at Breckness, but today most of it has been taken by the sea, along with quite a bit of the very rock on which it stood. The site actually seems fairly sheltered, by the skerry of Braga and an outlying promontory, but evidently not enough to withstand the onslaught of the Atlantic. The broch was placed in a strategic position, with a commanding view of the approaches to the Flow.

In 1633, George Graham, Bishop of Orkney, built himself a house at the Breckness peninsula. His main residence was Graemeshall in Holm, but he founded the large Breckness and Skaill estate, and lived at the Breckness house in the summer. His youngest son, John Graham, first of Breckness, was one of the biggest proprietors of land in Orkney in the early seventeenth century. Breckness is a ruin today, but the distinctive mansion house and its walled garden must once have been an impressive home.

The position of the Breckness house gave unequalled views of a dramatic coast. But the site was exposed to the elements, and part of Stromness lore has it that the Laird of Breckness narrowly missed being swept away by a tidal wave, sometime in the late eighteenth century. He never lived at Breckness after that, or so it is said. A young shepherd boy saw the huge wave coming and warned the men at the millstone quarry at Yesnaby, further along the coast, thus saving them from being swamped by it.

The Black Craig contrasts dramatically with the fertile land and low coastline of Outertown, which it protects from the north wind. 'Hawks and Falcons have their Nests at Black Craig', writes James Wallace in 1693, and no less an authority than George Low tells us he saw sea eagles nesting there as well. At the summit is the Peerie Tower, an old coastguard lookout, where the fishermen used to come to see if any trawlers were poaching in their waters. From there the ground slopes steeply to the cliff edge. Old Stromness lore claimed that there was a fatal accident at the Black Craig every seven years.

A Dundee trading vessel struck the Black Craig during a storm in 1836. Charlie Johnston, the one survivor, managed to scramble to safety in a small cave in the crag face, and there he spent several days before the storm abated and he could climb further up the cliffs. The cave is still known as Charlie's Hole.

The Castle of North Gaulton is a huge mass of rock that rises to a height of some 60 m. It has a narrow base, but widens at the top, and has

Breckness, once an impressive home of Bishop Graham.

for years been a favourite nesting place for the great black-backed gull.

At the top of the hill, near the Loons, there used to be an old mineral well, known as the 'Haly Hole' which was believed to work miracle cures, especially with scurvy, so that people from all over Orkney would make a pilgrimage to it. The hill area continues northwards, past the lovely hills of Miffia and Kringlafiold, 'the round mountain', into the next parish of Sandwick, that is separated from Stromness by the Burn of Sowa. The two parishes were united for a long time. The walk northwards through the hills to the Bay of Skaill is surely one of the most beautiful and interesting nature experiences in Orkney.

Some 60 km to the north-west lie two Orkney outposts, Sule Skerry and Sule Stack, which are both part of the parish of Stromness. They consist of Lewisian gneiss, the oldest rock in Europe. The name Sule derives from the Norse *súla*, for gannet (*Sula bassanus*). Sule Stack rises steeply from the sea and is occupied by a colony of gannets. In the old days a boat would go out annually from the West Mainland to collect young gannets. Sule Skerry, on the other hand, is rather low and flat, and has a vast puffin colony. It is also a breeding ground for seals, and until 1786 seals were killed there annually.

Much lore is connected with Sule Skerry. People would sometimes for

Sule Stack has a colony of about 4000 pairs of gannets.

various reasons join the seals, and the selkie, the seal folk, could also become ordinary, always good-looking, human beings. It was believed that the grey seals were really men and women disguised in seal skin. The stories sometimes imply that the life in the sea is the better choice. An old verse tells a story of such a double identity,

I am a Man upon the land,
I am a Selkie in the sea,
And when I'm far from any strand
My home it is in Sule Skerry.

The sad tale of Helen Waters, whose bridegroom mysteriously disappears before their wedding, is also part of Sule Skerry lore. He has gone with friends to Sule Skerry to shoot seals. There they are all found dead; they must have failed to secure the boat. The young bride dies of the shock, and the wedding becomes a double burial.

In 1978 yet another broch site was uncovered in a hill field at the Bu of Cairston, just east of the town of Stromness. The site had a good view of Scapa Flow in one direction and the Loch of Stenness in the other. Unfortunately the site can no longer be seen, as it was ploughed over for agricultural use after the excavation. A radiocarbon test dated the broch to the earliest part of the Iron Age, sometime in the sixth century BC, thus making it the earliest broch found so far, at least four centuries older than at first expected.

The Bu broch was a fortified roundhouse where a single family lived, within a 5.2 m thick wall. They evidently felt the need for strong protection; but then they lived in turbulent times with internecine warfare. The site is valuable in archaeological terms as it seems to show how the idea of the broch developed from a simpler concept to a more ambitious one, such as the Broch of Gurness, and it supports the idea that the brochs developed in the Northern Isles.

At the farm of Howe, just north of the Bu, there used to be a mound so prominent that it was used as a seamark, known as the Hillock of Howe. A linen smoother of black glass, a characteristic Norse artefact, was once found here. The mound was never properly excavated until work began in earnest in 1979, when it was found to contain a multi-layer site. The site started life as a Neolithic chambered burial tomb, dating back to well before 3000 BC, from roughly the same time as Skara Brae. During excavation the beautifully constructed entrance-passage to the tomb greatly impressed local builders with the quality of its dressed stone!

Some 2000 years later early Iron-Age settlers moved in. They destroyed much of the inside of the tomb to make way for a roundhouse, which was defended by a bank and a ditch. The roundhouse was replaced by a small broch tower, an elegant structure with entrance passages and stairs; it was obviously not solidly built as it collapsed completely at some stage. It was replaced at about the turn of the millennium by a more massive one, with 5.5 m thick walls, and a settlement of six houses was constructed around the tower. At some point the small village was severely damaged by an intense fire. The broch was partially destroyed; it then became a centre of industrial activity, with antler and stone tool working, iron smelting and smithying, as well as pottery making, before finally being abandoned.

A Pictish village grew up, initially in the old house ruins, but the settlement area later grew into the rubble of the broch as well. In the period *c.* AD 500-800 Pictish farmers seem to have led a peaceful existence at Howe, as their farmsteads were completely undefended. The Pictish levels at the Howe site were highly important, as earlier knowledge of simple everyday Pictish life was scant. Howe was only the second Pictish settlement to be found in Orkney, Buckquoy in Birsay being the first. The site also gave fascinating insight into community life through a millennium and a half; unfortunately the site had to be demolished to make such an insight possible.

The Cairston area continued into Norse times as an important district, known from the *Orkneyinga Saga* as *Kjarrekstaðir*. Much of it was bordland, that is the property of the earl, and the Bu of Cairston would have been one of his veizla farms. This is borne out by what happened there on Michaelmas Day in 1152, while Earl Rognvald II was away on his crusade. In his absence another claimant to the earldom had turned up, Erlend III Haraldsson, last in the male line of Turf-Einar, and accepted by the King of Norway as one of the Orkney earls. He was still an immature young man, but had Svein Asleifarson of Gairsay as his friend and protector.

Earl Rognvald had left the young Earl Harald Maddadarson in charge while he was away. One day, while Harald was with his fleet at Cairston, he and his men saw a longship coming towards them and, 'expecting trouble, they ran from their own ships into the fortress that used to stand there.'

'Earl Erlend and Svein raced from their ships, chasing Earl Harald all the way to the fortress, and attacked it all day with iron and fire, but the people there made a stout defence till it grew dark and night separated the two sides. There were a good many wounded in both armies and had the attack lasted longer Harald's men would have had to surrender.' Although local farmers persuaded the fighting earls to reach a temporary truce, this confrontation at the Bu really meant the beginning of the so-called 'war of the three earls' that would end with the death of one of them.

The remains of the stronghold, or *kastali*, can still be seen today. It is described by the historian J Storer Clouston as consisting of 'a courtyard 70 feet square including the surrounding wall, then tolerably high and clay-cemented, but with no proper self-supporting donjon. It had, moreover, no natural advantage of position, standing in a gently sloping field close to the beach, and was altogether a very primitive, early type of castle, ill-suited to withstand for long a determined attack by a strong force.' It would have been especially difficult when this force was led by Svein Asleifarson.

The inner harbour area of Stromness is still known as Hamnavoe. Here, below Cairston ridge, was the inn, run by William and Mareon

Clark in the late sixteenth century, that may have been the first beginning of the village. Later, a merchant called William Gow had his house and

Stromness, summer at dawn.

garden there; the life of his son John became the story material of Sir Walter Scott's novel *The Pirate*, whereas his true history was told by Daniel Defoe. Nothing now remains of these old Cairston houses.

Stromness owes its growth to its unique position and the quality of its harbour. It is so close to the Atlantic and yet completely protected from it by the Wardhill, more commonly known as Brinkie's Brae. A westerly storm leaves Stromness untouched, although people can see from the clouds that something is going on! The south-east wind, on the other hand, hits Stromness badly, when it comes raging up the hill, which has many closes.

The westside village had a modest beginning in the seventeenth century when an area of 'waste ground', now known as Porteous Brae, between Graham Place and Dundas Street, was set in feu for a rent of 24 chickens a year. By the middle of the century this had grown to five houses by the shore, forming the nucleus of the present town. The wars of the period 1688-1815 made the English Channel unsafe, so that most ships chose the north-about route into the Atlantic. Stromness would be their last port of call in Europe, and Stromness merchants were quick to benefit from this. The town flourished.

The eighteenth century was an exciting time for Stromness, in many ways its period of renown. More than 300 vessels called at Stromness each year. Among these were the Greenland whalers and the ships of the Hudson's Bay Company, needing provisions and fresh water before starting on their long voyages to the Davis Straits or the fur-trading posts of the Nor' Wast. The ships of the Hudson's Bay Company also offered work opportunities for Orcadians; they would call in early June and stay for two or three weeks to hire men, so that by the end of the century

Orcadians made up most of the company workforce. Stromness was also a touching point for the ships of many expeditions. Thus in 1780 Captain Cook's ships called there on their way back from the South Seas.

The prosperity of Stromness provoked the ire of Kirkwall. Claiming that their position as a royal burgh gave them certain rights, they tried to tax Stromness out of existence. The people of Stromness put up with this for more than 20

George Mackay Brown on a visit to Rackwick.

years, but in 1742 they took the case to court. Litigation dragged on for many years, and went all the way to the House of Lords, but the Stromness merchants won the freedom to trade. The result was largely due to the tenacity of one man, the Stromness merchant Alexander Graham, who bankrupted himself through his efforts to see the case through the courts, freeing not only Stromness, but all the other small burghs as well, from the power of the royal burghs.

In 1817 the town became a Burgh of Barony. Trade expanded still further with passing ships, and there were as many as 38 ale-houses along the narrow, twisting main street. Login's Inn at South End was the place to go for people who had social pretensions. The herring-boom and the First World War further swelled the number of people visiting the Stromness ale-houses as well as carousing in the street, and in a local referendum the town was voted dry from 1920 until 1947.

Today there is a revival of fishing, and Stromness is the home of the *Orcades Viking*, one of Britain's largest freezer trawlers. Fresh lobster is caught by Stromness boats and exported live all around the world. There is boat building and there is manufacture of food, and the tourists come off the ferry *St Ola* in swarms. Some of them want to visit the Folk Festival in May, or the St Magnus Festival in June, or be in Stromness during the Shopping Week, the annual week of carnival in mid-July, or just to wander around.

Many of the cultural events are connected with the Pier Arts Centre which was founded in 1979, and is housed in three old buildings. The house facing the town street was once the home of the Hudson's Bay Company agent; the two buildings on the pier, gable-ended to the sea, were his business premises. The buildings have been converted into a gallery to house the art collection that was presented to the people of Orkney by Margaret Gardiner, who for many years spent her summers at Swartafield in Rousay, and came to love the islands.

The Pier Arts Centre houses some 70 items of twentieth-century painting and sculpture; the early works of the sculptor Dame Barbara Hepworth (1903-75) and the abstract painter Ben Nicholson (1894-1982) form the main part of the collection. They were both central figures in the St Ives Group of artists, and were Margaret Gardiner's friends. The gallery has become a part of Stromness life, with exhibitions of the works of both local and international artists, but also poetry readings and lectures.

Stromness is a busy place and the Town Council forbade bicycles on the street as early as around 1900, until they were challenged and defeated in the High Court. That is probably why they never even tried forbidding cars in the street, and an exciting time is had by all, drivers, pedestrians and cyclists.

For a long time the Orkney writer George Mackay Brown (1921-96) was a well-known and popular part of life in Stromness, and one of the pedestrians often seen about the streets. He might even be part of the group discussing the events of the day, sitting in the pierhead seats known as 'the local Parliament'. George Mackay Brown was firmly rooted in the land of his local community, and that may be one of the reasons why his appeal reaches so far afield.

George Mackay Brown can give his readers an impressionistic picture of people and events in just a few words. He uses the language and the images of his native islands, but the human feelings and conflicts he describes are universal. In the islands he loved so much, where the monuments of millennia stand side by side, it is natural to share his view – that we are all part of the one weave of history.

And this is how he sees his native town – 'what is Stromness but a tumbling stone wave, a network of closes, a marvel of steps from the seaweed up to the granite of Brinkie's Brae'.

Burray

Burray derives from the Norse *Borgarey*, the island of the broch. The large broch on the hill by the shore must have been a striking sight to the first Norsemen sailing this way, and the name of Borgarey was like a map they could give to friends and family to navigate from. And even today the broch site is one of the principal points of interest in Burray.

Burray is naturally divided into two parts: the fertile eastern side and the hilly western peninsula, rising to 80 m at Ward Hill in the centre. Further west is the small heath-covered island of Hunda, which in the old days, like the west side of Burray, provided peat for fuel. Today Hunda is used mostly for pasture, as is Glims Holm, the island just north of Burray.

Hunda is connected to Burray by a natural reef. Because this could only be crossed at low tide, a causeway was built during the First World War to link the islands by road. In 1936 the old mailboat, the *St Ola*, ran aground on Hunda in thick fog. The ship used to pass through Hoxa Sound on its way to and from Scrabster; its compass was believed to have been affected by a car's electrical system.

In the western bay a natural barrier in the form of a narrow ridge separates the freshwater Echna Loch from the sea. Like Ettan's Pow in Papay, the name Echna Loch refers to the Norse *jotun*, a troll-like creature of great strength. In both places he has built a perfect bridge of shingle and sand. A famous pair of swans, known as 'the Burray Swans', make their home on Echna Loch, and every summer they delight the passing traffic with their cygnets.

The eastern part of Burray had two main settlement areas, originally the Nethertoun and the Overtoun, which today are known as the Northtown and the Southtown. The present east-west road to the Bu is the boundary line between them. Today the south-eastern peninsula of Ness is a bird sanctuary, with a wide range of birds.

There are remains of no fewer than three brochs in a row on the north-eastern shore. The eastern broch must have been some 10 m high when still intact, but even as a tumulus it was very large. It was excavated in the nineteenth century by the keen amateur archaeologists James Farrer and George Petrie, and was unusual in having two guard-chambers outside the bar-holes in the entrance, a feature not found in any other broch.

Little remains of the middle broch. The builders of the third, westward broch at Weddell Point evidently chose a very strategic site, as there is a large Second World War look-out tower built on top of it, along with a cannon site, with twin 6-pounder, rapid-fire guns still in place. This would have been built before the passage was blocked by a barrier later in the war. And further west is Ward Point, a beacon site, which shows that the idea of defence had occurred to the Norsemen too. At Warebanks was a prisoner-of-war camp, with another Italian Chapel, which was taken down in 1945.

The name of Weddell may derive from *vé*, a holy place in pagan times, as old variants of the name are Wedale and Weddale, but another possible origin is the Norse *vaðill*, a wading place. The explorer who in 1822 visited and named the South Orkney Islands and in 1823 the Weddell Sea in the Antarctic, was a Scotsman named James Weddell. Was this the farm that gave his ancestors their name?

Burray is not mentioned in the *Orkneyinga Saga* and very little is known of its early history. In the summer of 1889 some people who were out cutting peat at the north end of the island found a large hoard of Viking silver buried in the bog. A spade struck a wooden bowl which turned out to be full of silver items; mostly they were fragments to be melted down or used for bartering, but there was one complete necklace. The hoard weighed 1.9 kg and could be dated to the time around the end of the first millennium, as it contained three Anglo-Saxon coins. This is the second largest find of Viking silver in Orkney, only the Skaill hoard exceeding it.

The beautiful sand dunes of the crescent-shaped bay along the eastern shore must have seemed exotic and different to early Norse settlers. The whole island seems at some point to have become the property of the king or the earl. In the later rentals the farm of Bu was a half urisland in size, and known to be bordland. In the early days of the earldom it was probably a veizla farm for the earl, and would have been much larger, taking in the Northtown and Southtown also.

In 1494 King James IV of Scotland made a grant of Burray to Bishop Andrew of Orkney, and it was later held as a feu from the bishopric. In 1550 Lady Barbara Stewart, the widow of Sir James Sinclair of Summerdale fame, was granted a tack of the islands of Burray, Flotta and Swona by Bishop Reid. The tack was converted into permanent ownership before it ended.

Burray remained in Stewart hands for a long time. In 1687 Archibald Steuart received a baronetcy for services to the Stewart kings. Sir Archibald Steuart, second Baronet, was Steward-Principal of Orkney and a representative in the Scottish Parliament of 1702-7. The home of the Stewarts of Burray was the old earldom farm of the Bu, an impressive, rather secluded site that even today gives the impression of being a laird's seat. The present three-storey house dates from 1749 and is reputedly the third house to be built on the site. The fine Stewart mansion or middle house no longer stands

The old earldom farm of the Bu.

but decorative stones from it are built into some of the present traditional farm buildings. The Bu is still a large and prosperous farm.

In the first half of the eighteenth century the Bu was the home of one of Orkney's most colourful and troublesome characters, Sir James Steuart, third of Burray, an irascible, baroque character. In 1725 Captain Moodie of Melsetter was shot down in Kirkwall's Broad Street, while quarrelling with Sir James and his younger brother Alexander. According to Orkney gossip young Alexander bore a bitter grudge against the elderly captain who had had him soundly thrashed, under humiliating circumstances. Captain Moodie had a young wife, Lady Christiana Crawford, and found Alexander Steuart visiting her. There had been a feud between Sir James Steuart and Captain Moodie for many years, involving politics and trespassing.

The Steuart brothers and their servant Oliver Irving, who is believed to have fired the fatal shot, fled the country after Captain Moodie's death, and the only one of them ever to return was Sir James, who after five years obtained a pardon.

For some years Sir James concentrated on improving his land and becoming a model laird. He farmed the Bu in what was then a new way, using carts and improved ploughs, and planting turnips, at a time when such innovations were seldom to be found anywhere in Scotland. His estate was large, with 25 tenants in Burray, 84 in the northern part of South Ronaldsay, 19 in Flotta and ten on Swona. He also tried kelp manufacture, leasing his kelp shores in Burray to a Kirkwall merchant and renting the Pentland Skerries for his own kelp production.

But Sir James had not really changed, he was as irascible as ever. He fell out with his old friend and benefactor, the fourteenth Earl of Morton, alleging that he had manipulated the weights and measures used for payment of dues in kind. Known as the Pundlar Process, the conflict dragged on through the Court of Session for 26 years and ended with victory for the earl, but ruin for many of Sir James's supporters. When Morton crossed Burray on foot, without asking permission, it so provoked Sir James that he physically attacked the earl, in what was later known as 'the affray at Graemeshall'. Sir James was almost bankrupted by the consequent legal costs.

Although Sir James always openly supported Jacobite interests, it is doubtful whether he ever gave any active assistance to the Stuart cause. He refused to go into hiding after the Battle of Culloden and was the only laird with Jacobite sympathies to be captured by the young Captain Benjamin Moodie, in his personal vendetta against the man he held responsible for his father's death. He was taken to London, where he was charged with high treason, but he died before the trial. To the chagrin of his enemies Sir James's estate was therefore not forfeited, but passed to a relative who sold it to Sir Lawrence Dundas, from 1766 owner of the Orkney Earldom estate. After some 200 years, the Steuart era in Burray was over.

The estate was leased to Dr Thomas Balfour, who was impressed with what he saw at the Bu and carried out some further changes before moving on to Shapinsay, where he bought the old estate of Sound. Mr Gordon, a visitor to Burray in 1782, tells us something of the nature of these improvements, which were not all equally positive. 'From South Ronaldsay I went to Burra...it is thinly populated, but of an excellent soil. The principal farmer, a Captain Balfour, has carried on improvements with success, but has few imitators; it is hard to drive the Orkney people out of their old ways. There has been an old tower in this island, of the same kind with that in South Ronaldsay. There now remains nothing of the old castle but part of the wall; the stones have been employed in building Captain Balfour's dwelling house, offices and enclosures.'

Burray agriculture flourished as part of the Earldom estate; John Sangster, factor of Lord Dundas, was growing large acreages of turnips and trying to improve the stock of the cattle. Around the middle of the nineteenth century a complete reorganisation of the land began, with the arable land becoming enclosed, and each tenant farmer holding his land in a composite block, so as to be easier to work.

In the nineteenth century Burray was thus largely under the plough and doing well. Burray people were prolific and had many children. In 1811 the population was only 212, by 1881 it had risen to 685. Superstition was still strong in the first half of the nineteenth century. The Revd John Gerard, legendary minister of the united parishes of Burray and South Ronaldsay, had a long way to go from his manse in Papley, so he would wait until there were about a dozen children to be baptised, and then perform one ceremony for all of them. He paid no attention to the local belief that if a girl was baptised in the same water as a boy, she would sport whiskers when she grew up.

Lizzie Strachan, a local midwife who had brought many of the Burray children into the world, protested in church against using the same baptismal water. The Revd Gerard, known for his explosive temper, answered, 'I am a minister of the Kirk of Scotland, come here to administer one of its most solemn ordinances, an' if ye dinna lat me bapteeze this lassie oot o' the same water, I'll bapteeze you, ye auld limmer that ye are.' Then he threw the basin of water in her face and stormed away. He did not go back to Burray for quite a while, but Lizzie Strachan's feelings about him are not known.

Until the nineteenth century only the best land was occupied. The east of Burray has light, lime-rich soils and has been called 'The Garden of Orkney'. The soil of the western part, on the other hand, consisted of thin, stony boulder clay and remained uncultivated for a long time. The

Burray village – once a herring fishing community.

area used to be called 'the black hill of Burray' and contrasted strongly with the eastern half of the island, in terms of both agriculture and settlement. There were traces of copper at Wha Taing, close to the Hunda Reef and attempts were made to work it, without much success. The change came with the beginning of the fishing boom around 1820. The crofts along the coast of West Burray were built by fishermen around the middle of the nineteenth century, at a time when at least half the population of Burray was engaged in fishing.

Burray Village grew up on Water Sound in the nineteenth century, mainly as a herring fishing community. There was at one time a busy fishery station in the village, employing local boats and crews. On the whole there was a growing dependence on the fishing, but by 1880 this new livelihood was already in decline. Orkney was far from the British markets and larger boats were necessary to get the fish to centres like Aberdeen. There was also a change in preferred taste; people wanted fresh rather than cured fish.

The oldest building in Burray Village is the Storehouse with its external stair, built in 1645 to store grain for the Burray estate. There is also the long, rectangular Sands Motel which was at one time used for the packing and curing of herring. The old father-and-son boat building business, known as Duncan's Boatyard, has been owned and operated by the same family for generations.

During the First World War blockships were sunk at the eastern approaches to Scapa Flow, to keep the enemy out. By the time of the Second World War the ships had broken up and were no longer an adequate defence, as the *Royal Oak* disaster proved. A more permanent way of sealing off all access from the east to Scapa Flow had been considered for some time and in March 1940 Winston Churchill, who was then First Lord of the Admiralty, approved of the plans for building the barriers, which were named after him. The labour problem was solved by the arrival of Italian prisoners-of-war.

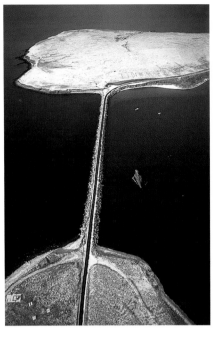

No.3 Churchill Barrier.

The barriers effectively sealed Burray Village off from any contact with shipping from the North Sea area, so that its port function was lost. There are those who think that the blocking of the three natural outlets on the south-east side of Scapa Flow has affected the behaviour of the sea, to the extent of making the tide-level higher. Whales occasionally get trapped in Scapa Flow.

On the positive side, the inter-island road connection makes life in an island easier in many ways, quite simply because the enforced isolation is lost. It also allows Burray to become a dormitory suburb of Kirkwall with many commuting to work in the town. Secondary-school children travel daily to school in Kirkwall. Dairy farming was not feasible until the Churchill Barriers allowed a daily milk collection. The enormous build-up of sand caused by no. 4 Barrier, which links Burray to South Ronaldsay, has created one of Orkney's finest beaches.

On the other hand the connection by the barriers also has a negative side; the number of Burray shops, bakeries and tradesmen has been reduced because of the competition with bigger firms in Kirkwall. But for better or worse, Burray has become a part of Mainland Orkney, except in wild weather, when the sea spray makes any crossing of the Barriers impossible.

South Ronaldsay

The Norse name of the island was *Rögnvaldsey*, the island of a man called Rognvald. Nobody knows who he was, but the bay which is now called St Margaret's Hope was once known as *Rögnvaldsvágr*, and the old farm of Ronsvoe may have been the first Norse settlement farm in the island. When the island of Rinansey in the north came to be called Ronaldsay as well, it became necessary to differentiate between the two, by adding to their names.

South Ronaldsay is large and fertile; between the two world wars it counted more than 2000 inhabitants. The coming of the Churchill Barriers undoubtedly halted the depopulation that might otherwise have occurred, and the overland road has also provided Orkney with an alternative ferry route to the Scottish mainland.

The arable land lies in small valleys between low hills, some of the hill land remaining legally common grazing. After long working of the peat for fuel, it now retains any thickness only in the Blows Moss area in the southern part of the island. The highest point is Ward Hill rising to 118 m, between Sand Wick and Newark Bay, and offering a wide view. The land is popular with the Orkney vole, which has a widespread distribution. 'Hawks and Falcons have their Nests in several places, as in: Halcro, Greenhead and Hocksa', writes James Wallace in 1693.

On the shore at Isbister, in the south-east, is one of the most interesting Stone-Age sites in Orkney. Ronald Simison, the local farmer, was down on the shore one evening in the summer of 1958 looking for some flagstone he might use, when he noticed a wall sticking out of a mound. On checking it, he found an amazing hoard of Neolithic objects hidden there. The wall belonged to a well-preserved stalled tomb, which probably had been part of a larger ceremonial complex.

In spite of initial interest, many years passed without any further development at the site. Mr Simison decided then to take things in hand, and started excavating it himself in the summer of 1976. It turned out to be an extraordinary site. In the tomb were found the skeletons of no fewer than 14 white-tailed eagles, a fish-eating bird that died out in Britain in the nineteenth century. As the eagles seemed to have been placed there complete, they must have been ritually significant to the tomb builders.

The eagles in the tomb had probably enjoyed a lifespan longer than the tomb builders themselves. A study of the remains of some 340 persons found in the tomb, revealed that most of them had died in their twenties. The bodies had been excarnated outside before they were buried, and the bones were all mixed. People's lives had obviously been hard as there were indications of high child mortality, deficiency diseases and widespread arthritis. They constituted a distinct group with long heads and low brows.

The Isbister people used Unston Ware pottery and seem to have grown grain, as wheat and three different kinds of barley were found in the tomb. Radiocarbon dating shows the tomb was used for some 800 years from *c*.3000 BC. The practice of placing eagles along with the disordered human remains continued throughout the period, and we must assume it was an important part of the tomb-builders' culture.

South Ronaldsay also has two striking Iron-Age promontory forts. In the south-west is the Castle of Burwick, which is joined to the mainland by a narrow neck of land. Three rampart lines have been built on the mainland and another on the Castle side; there are also remains of houses. George Low went from Burwick along the western shore, on his tour in 1774. 'Saw on my way to Barth head, a work on an insulated rock called the Castle, but now so much in ruins as to be quite overgrown with grass, and the walls, such as they have been, quite overturned. It has been another of these small strengths so common round the shores of Orkney, but none of which are now so entire as to trace the form, or method of erection.'

The Brough of Windwick in the south-east of the island is a narrow headland projecting from steep cliffs. The fort is defended by two sets of ramparts, between ditches scooped out of the rock. A path runs out between the ramparts. The coast here is beautiful and wild. Seals have their breeding grounds off Hesta Head. On a wild night of wind and sleet in January 1918, the destroyers HMS *Narborough* and HMS *Opal* were returning to base in Scapa Flow, when they ran full tilt into the cliffs near Hesta Head. The one survivor clung to a ledge for 36 hours before he was rescued.

Although South Ronaldsay often figures in the *Orkneyinga Saga*, there is no record of a chieftain actually living there. The saga characters always seem to be passing through the island. The Orkney historian J Storer Clouston suggests that resistance to the Norse bid for power was strongest in South Ronaldsay, which because of its proximity to Scotland

and a fair number of early Scottish incomers, in some ways remained a tension zone. The early rentals show that the south end of the island had the status of being bordland, or earldom land; the veizla farm of Holland was at the south end. Probably this land was seized at an early date by earls who realised its strategic importance.

In South Ronaldsay districts developed from the local topography, and not according to a urisland division. The districts seem to have been largely self-sufficient areas where people looked after their own. Thus until the nineteenth century it was customary at a funeral for every male of the district to attend. The island was skatted as eight urislands around 1500, when the rental shows that as much as 63 per cent of the land was odal property. This was an extraordinarily high percentage, surpassed only by Harray in the West Mainland. But the trend veered towards more land in fewer hands; whereas there were 171 different owners in 1601, two centuries later there were nominally 22, with most of the land belonging to just three families.

In early times the island was divided into two parishes, named after the two parish churches of St Peter's in the north and St Mary's in the south. The little island of Swona and the Pentland Skerries belonged to the parish of St Mary's; both had chapels dedicated to St Peter. Burray became united with South Ronaldsay at an early stage. Apart from the parish churches, there were five chapels in the north parish and four in the south, but most of these have vanished. Many of them were dedicated to early Celtic saints. Even today South Ronaldsay is divided into these distinctive districts: Hoxa, Grimness, Papley, or Eastside, Windwick, Burwick, Barswick, Sandwick, Widewall and Herston.

The north-western peninsula of Hoxa appears early in the *Orkneyinga Saga*, as Thorfinn Skull-Splitter, the son of Turf-Einar and one of the first earls, was buried in a mound there, sometime in the latter half of the tenth century. The saga describes Earl Thorfinn as a strong ruler and warrior, who died in his bed and was laid to rest in a mound at Hoxa, from the Norse *Haugs-eið*, isthmus of the mound. The saga gives no explanation of his nickname, only that people thought him 'a very great man'. Nor does the saga explain why he was buried in South Ronaldsay, which as far as is known, was not central to the earldom. It is possible that the strategic district of Hoxa, with protected harbours on two sides of a low, sandy isthmus where ships could be taken across, would have been seen as the perfect stronghold.

The battery at Hoxa Head, built to guard the entrance into Scapa Flow.

On either side of the Dam of Hoxa lie the farms of Uppertown and Lowertown, which would have formed part of the large, early farm of Hoxa. On the outer edge, on the east side of the bay are the remains of a square enclosure that resembles a Norse *virki*, or fortification, but may be older, and further along the shore we find Lober, which probably derives from *hlað-berg*, a place for loading and unloading ships.

A broch and a low mound, Little Howe, lie on Howe Taing on the west side of the bay. The broch was opened up by George Petrie as early as 1848, at a time when he knew very little about excavations. Afterwards the site was turned into an ornamental garden by the owner. Little Howe was excavated by George Petrie in the 1870s, but he did not find Thorfinn Skull-Splitter's grave.

Strategically situated, close to Hoxa Head, stands the old farm of the Bu, which in Norse times was the private property of the earls, and paid no skat. From there all traffic through the main entrance into the Flow could be watched. Several centuries later, through two world wars, the site was still important. In 1940 the Balfour Battery was built at Hoxa Head to guard Hoxa Boom, which was the wartime name of the main entrance into Scapa Flow.

Another strategic area is St Margaret's Hope with its good harbour, sheltered not only by Burray but also by the tidal skerry The Ruff. Locally it is called just The Hope, a name deriving from the Norse *hóp*, a small bay. The rest of the name refers to an old chapel, long a ruin, that was dedicated to St Margaret.

The name is often, perhaps romantically, connected to the little princess Margrete, The Maid of Norway, who died here in 1290. She was the only child of the Norwegian King Eirik Magnusson, and her mother, who died when she was born, was the daughter of King Alexander III of Scotland. When he died in 1286, Margrete became Queen of Scotland. Her destiny – marriage to Edward, heir to the English throne – was already decided and much was at stake politically. In Norway, King Eirik had to face much criticism for sending his daughter away, and some of it is expressed in this old ballad:

> Gud fyrilati Eiriki kongi,
> God forgive king Eirik,
> hvat hann mundi gera:
> for what he did:
> sendi sitt barn i ókunn lond,
> sending his child to unknown land,
> moykongur at vera.
> to become queen.

Earlier in the same century, at the beginning of August 1263, King Hakon Hakonsson's huge fleet of 120 ships anchored in Rognvaldsvag, as St Margaret's Hope would then have been called. Until the Grand Fleet came in 1914, it was the largest fleet ever to enter Scapa Flow, and it stayed there for almost a fortnight. An eclipse of the sun on the day the fleet arrived must have seemed like a bad omen.

The Hope offered a safe anchorage and was always a gateway to the rest of the island, so that it became central to trade quite early. Even in the eighteenth century a parish-owned sloop made a regular journey between Leith and South Ronaldsay. But the village really grew up around a nineteenth-century fishing station, and it became a centre of some importance. In the 1790s more than 50 fishing boats worked from South Ronaldsay and Burray; by 1840 there were 245 herring boats, as well as 11 larger sloops fishing for cod and ling. A curing station was also established. London firms had smacks there to buy up lobsters from the local fishermen. Most of the working population were involved in the fishing. The Hope kept its position as a port until the Second World War and the construction of the Churchill Barriers.

On the west shore of The Hope is an old three-storey building known as the Storehouse. It is part of the old estate of Smiddybanks, which belonged to Sutherlands and Banks for several hundred years. In front of the Mansion House is a fine old gateway, with the dates 1633-1693 inscribed on it. This was part of the old mansion house, which stood end-on to the sea, but was pulled down in 1832 when the new house was built.

An old tradition is being kept alive in South Ronaldsay with the Boys' Ploughing Match, officially known as The Festival of the Horse, which takes place on the third Saturday of August each year. Nobody knows how old this tradition is, but the first recorded date is 1816. The festival used to be held in the spring, as every year, once the ploughing was over, a competition was held among the men. Children would imitate this as a game, using younger ones as the horses. Today the girls are dressed in the harness and decoration of a Clydesdale horse, the costumes being kept in the family. The competition itself is held at the Sand of Wright, where the boys are allotted a square section, the object being to plough this into straight and even furrows.

In the mid eighteenth century the farm of North Cara belonged to Sir James Steuart of Burray; his tenant John Cromarty married his daughter Barbara. Sir James invested a lot of time and money in improving the farm, and in 1740 he enclosed the Park of Cara, 'containing a square mile of ground', with stone dykes. Probably the farm was larger then than it is today. He also had ambitious plans for erecting a great house there, but when he died in 1746, little more than the ground floor was built. Known as 'the Castle', it has long been a ruin. Some beautifully carved stones were found at the site.

The farm of South Cara on the east side has belonged to the Cromarty family since 1450. They also owned North Cara, but sold that property when they established themselves at South Cara, building a new house there in 1633. Though quite small, the two-storey house was known for having cut freestone round the door and lower windows, a feature that was unique at the time.

The northern district of Grimness got its name from the point of Grim Ness, the most easterly point in South Ronaldsay. The name of Grim may be derived from the Norse adjective *grimmr*, which means dark and

The boys' ploughing match at the Sand of Wright.

uninviting and may describe the ness itself, but *Grímr* was also another name given to the god Odin because he wore a *gríma*, or helmet. The whole coastline of the Grimness district is difficult for shipping, as the sea is shallow and full of underwater skerries.

On 17 March, 1969 the Longhope lifeboat *T B G* was lost with all eight of her crew, a tragedy that reverberated throughout Orkney and far afield. The lifeboat was at the time going to the aid of the freighter *Irene* during a very severe south-easterly gale. The ship eventually grounded on the rocks below Grim Ness, with all the crew surviving.

The area south of Grim Ness is known as Eastside, a rather modern name for the district of Papley, Aikers and Lythes. Papley is an old, venerable site whose name indicates an early religious centre. As in Paplay in Holm there is a parish church by the sea. From the top of the hillside, the land slopes gently down to the sea, creating an enclosed, pastoral world of sea, sky, land and St Peter's Church. George Low was strongly moved by its beauty during his wanderings in South Ronaldsay. 'Enter now upon the most beautiful spot of the island, and indeed preferable to any I have yet seen in Orkney: this is a small vale,

Pool of Cletts and St Peter's Church.

surrounded with declining hills the slope of which is likewise cultivated, encircling the Manse and Church, and producing the most fertile crops both of corn and natural grass, mixed thick with daisies and white clover.'

The most renowned of all the ministers to have lived at the St Peter's Manse and worked for the united parishes of Burray and South Ronaldsay, was the Revd John Gerard (1765-1850). A larger-than-life renaissance character, whose dry humour is remembered and quoted to this day, he often used his native dialect, even in church when he got carried away. He sometimes put his ideas across by expressing them in doggerel verse. He proclaimed the coming of a visiting minister in this way:

'Sound the trumpet, blow the horn,
Walter Weir's to preach the morn.'

The news soon spread around the parish, and people came. And when on one occasion he learned there might be a thief in the church, he announced, 'If the thief does not get up and leave at once, I'll expose him before the whole congregation'. The culprit is said to have complied and made his hurried exit out of the church.

The Revd Gerard was a sincere believer in abstinence and a prominent member of the first temperance society formed in Orkney. He was concerned about the drunkenness that was all too common at the time, and said, 'There are sixteen public-houses in the united parishes, although seven would be sufficient.' He is buried in the cemetery of the church he served so long, and as his tombstone tells us, he died 'in the 85th year of his age, the 45th of his ministry and the 36th of his incumbency'.

A psalter owned and used by the Revd Gerard is in a glass case beside the pulpit in St Peter's Church. The church dates back to 1642, but its interior has been restored to the way it looked in the eighteenth century. It is one of only three Scottish churches with the communion table running the length of the building.

But the history of the site goes even further back. Here stood one of the old Peterkirks, the first Pictish churches, probably from the eighth century. One of the Pictish symbol stones was found here, decorated with a 'rectangle' and a 'crescent and V-rod' on one side, and with a 'mirror-case' and a second 'crescent and V-rod' on the other.

The old parish border crossed the island from just below Stews west to Sandwick. The hill land slopes southwards to Windwick and then rises again, making the farming area around the bay fertile, sheltered land. According to the Orkney scholar Hugh Marwick, the first element of the name Windwick represents the Norse *vin* for pasture, and not wind, as the bay 'cannot be deemed any windier than others'!

In 1787 the young George Stewart of Masseter wanted to embark on a naval career, and joined HMS *Bounty* as a midshipman when the ship called at Stromness. Captain Bligh described him as a young man 'of creditable parents in the Orkneys, at which place, on the return of the *Resolution* from the South Seas in 1780, we received so many civilities, that in consideration of these alone I should gladly have taken him with me. But he had always borne a good character.'

Then the crew mutinied in April 1789. George Stewart does not seem to have taken an active part in this open revolt, but he failed to join Captain Bligh on the overcrowded launch. The mutineers put him ashore in Tahiti. According to tradition he married the daughter of a local chief, and had a child by her. When the frigate HMS *Pandora* called at Tahiti in 1791, Stewart swam out to the ship, but was arrested and brought back as a prisoner. He drowned on his way home when the ill-fated *Pandora* was wrecked on a reef.

Lord Byron was taken with the story of the young midshipman, and made him the hero, known as Torquil, in his narrative poem 'The Island'.

> Who is he? the blue-eyed northern child
> Of isles more known to man, but scarce less wild;
> The fair-hair'd offspring of the Orcades,
> Where roars the Pentland with its whirling seas.

There is interesting cliff scenery between Windwick and Halcro Head, where we find the dramatic Gloup of Halcro. It was visited in the late nineteenth century by John Tudor, who in his famous and much read book on Orkney describes the Gloup as 'by far the weirdest and most gruesome-looking hole of the kind in the group. It looks like an old disused mine shaft grass-grown at the sides, and judging from the cliffs close to, must be about 150 feet deep. The tunnel connecting it with the sea is about one hundred yards long, and it is said, a boat once penetrated through it to the Gloup, but that the roof was so low, that in places, the boatman had to lie down to enable him to shove the boat along.'

In an old folktale the place is called the Gloup of Root. One day a girl was wandering on the seaward side of the chasm; it was untilled but had the marks of ancient rigs. She discovered a fine field of lint here, far finer than any growing in the tunships of South Ronaldsay. She showed her mother and the two of them carried away armfuls of the lint which seemed to belong to nobody.

The mother had never told the name of the girl's father and for that reason mother and daughter were ill-used in the community. The mother made the lint into a lovely dress, and she thought the girl and the dress just fitted each other, they were both so beautiful. And the laird's son must have thought so too, for the story says that the young man came, fell in love with her, and married her. This is the final verse of the song that the old folk used to sing about it:

> I bore him twa sons
> Who travelled afar...
> Yet they never forgot
> Th' rigs twa three,
> Where th' lint grew sae bonnie
> 'Tween the gloup an' th' sea.

The farm of Halcro, on old Holland land, was the modest base of the Halcros, one of the most outstanding Orkney families in the sixteenth and seventeenth centuries. The Icelandic historian Thormod Torfaeus wrote in his seventeenth-century history of Orkney that 'The Laird of Halcro commanded 300 men at the battle of Bannockburn, and fought like a hero. He afterwards returned to Orkney with great honour.' And Torfaeus adds, 'The Orkneymen behaved gallantly in this battle'.

The Ladykirk Stone.

According to Orkney tradition it was the Laird's spirited advice to Robert the Bruce that decided the outcome of the battle, and it seems there may be some truth in this, as apparently Bruce did take refuge either in Norway or Orkney, before invading Scotland from the north, with an outside force, to win the battle at midsummer 1314.

Burwick, from the Norse *Borgarvík*, bay of the broch, is practically the only landing-place on the south coast of the island. Today Burwick is known as the harbour terminal for the summer ferry to John o' Groats. A few years ago the decision was taken by the Orkney Islands Council to have a year-round ferry route from Burwick to Scotland, as an alternative to the Stromness–Scrabster connection. In spite of strong local opposition plans went ahead, and work started on extending the harbour in Burwick. Large granite boulders were brought all the way from Norway. Then a storm ruined the harbour at Gills Bay on the other side of the Pentland Firth, and the plans came to naught.

In the old days, before the days of steam, mail and passengers were transported once a week by rowing boat from Burwick. Another boat left Huna in Caithness, and then both would meet mid-firth and exchange mailbags and passengers. It sounds like a hazardous undertaking, given the ripping tides of the Firth, but it seems there were no accidents recorded. Moving in the same waters, the Aberdeen trawler *Ben Barvas* went aground on Little Skerry in the Pentland Firth on 4 January, 1964. The Longhope lifeboat saved all the crew.

At St Mary's Kirk in Burwick there is a curious block of whinstone with two foot-shaped hollows, which is usually called the Ladykirk Stone, and all kinds of imaginative stories are connected with it. Jo Ben claims that a man called Gallus was in peril when his ship sank, but 'jumping upon the back of a monster, vowed, humbly praying to God, that if he was safely carried to land, in memory thereof he would build a church to the Virgin Mary. His prayer being heard, he was drawn safe to the shore by the support of the monster. The monster was afterwards changed into a stone of its own colour; he himself placed it in that church where it remains as above described.'

In another story the stone has the impressions of St Magnus' feet on it, as he turned a serpent into stone, and then

The trawler Ben Barvas *on Little Skerry.*

used it to hurry across the Pentland Firth, because he wanted to bring the news of the victory at Bannockburn himself! The Revd Brand, writing in 1701, considers such stories 'credible only by these superstitious and silly ones, whom the GOD of this World hath blinded'. Instead he suggests that 'under Popery, the Delinquents stood bare footed suffering Penance' on the stone.

To the west of Barth Head lies the small island of Swona. When Swona was visited by George Low as part of his Tour in 1774, he found nine families living on the island. In the late nineteenth century another traveller described 'the little island of Swona, on which only fourteen families reside. Green sloping uplands, not very high above the sea level, but still lofty enough in some parts to merit the name of hills, met our gaze; and we could see small but comfortable-looking houses and homesteads closely planted together.' (Fergusson, 1884)

The waters around Swona proved fatal for the Finnish ship *Johanna Thorden* when on its maiden voyage in January 1937. While navigating the Pentland Firth it struck the south end of Swona, and of the 38 people on board only eight survived.

The whirlpools known as the Wells of Swona are allegedly dangerous to pass and were often blamed for any shipwrecks that occurred. But the island was ideally situated for line fishing which became the chief source of income. In the sailing ship period, some money was also made from pilotage. The last family on the island left in the 1970s.

It was while lying with their ships in Barswick, east of Swona, that Svein Asleifarson and the unreliable young Earl Erlend realised that the enemies, Earls Rognvald and Harald, had already landed with 13 ships in Widewall Bay. Svein and Erlend manage to escape, but the feud continues. Erlend is killed, and Svein is on the run. Once again he ends up in Barswick, near a cave. 'In the daytime Svein would often sit drinking in some house, but at night he stayed aboard ship, always on guard against his enemies.'

But one morning Svein and his men sighted Earl Rognvald's longship heading straight for the spot where their skiff was beached. They started pelting the Earl's party with stones, but there was no longer the will to fight on either side. As Svein and his men were leaving, the Earl held the shield of peace up to him, and when Svein saw this signal, 'he told his men to row back to the island and said that he wanted nothing more than to be reconciled with Earl Rognvald.' The description of the men's feelings, but also of houses and natural conditions in Barswick, is almost unique in the *Orkneyinga Saga*. The name probably derives from the Norse *barð*, meaning edge or rim, and refers to the dyke of large rolling stones, which is such a characteristic feature of the bay.

Further inland from Barswick is the impressive old school building, known as Tomison's Academy, with its three tall rooms and enormous windows. For more than a century this was the school for the south parish of South Ronaldsay, but since 1968 it has been standing empty.

William Tomison (1739-1829) was one of the many young men who joined the Hudson's Bay Company in Canada. By the end of the eighteenth century as many as 100 young Orcadians were entering the company every year, many of these from South Ronaldsay. Tomison persevered and did well, serving the company for all of 47 years and rising to become chief factor or governor. He expanded the Company's activities into Western Canada, in the teeth of strong competition, to found the city of Edmonton. Tomison's Charity School was built in 1790, close to Tomison's own house. The school was endowed with an annual salary for the teacher, and to this Lord Dundas added a croft of land. Tomison's Academy was built in 1851, with means left for the purpose.

William Tomison preferred to be buried privately in his own garden at Dundas House, just across the road from the Academy. In 1913 a mausoleum was built over his grave, with this inscription, 'To the memory of William Tomison, Dundas House. Born 1739. Died 1829. In appreciation of the munificent bequests he made to his native islands; this stone was erected and the tomb renovated by subscriptions received from fellow islanders and others at home and abroad.'

Widewall Bay is a lovely and sheltered area, and is a popular place for boating and fishing. But even small boats are dependent on the tides, as at ebb tide large parts of the seabed are left dry. Then it is possible to see traces of a submerged forest, probably belonging to a different climatic period altogether. It is therefore likely that the name of Widewall derives from the Norse *viði-vágr*, the bay of wood or forest.

On the eastern shore of the Bay the house of Roeberry stands tall on the hill. It was part of the 300-acre farm of Roeberry, one of the largest farms in the island. It is the home of the old odal family the Grays, which still survives on the distaff side. At Quindry, just south of Roeberry, can still be found traces of nousts and a rubble-built, L-shaped harbour where the Vikings are believed to have wintered their longships.

At Herston, the peninsula on the western side of Widewall bay, there are surprisingly few traces of prehistoric occupation and none from Norse times. Until the 1820s there were no houses where the village now stands, as the land there was still part of the commons. Herston was then divided in half by a stone dyke, running east to west across the land, with the area to the north being common, where sheep and cattle grazed. The village of Herston was built by 1827, as a port for curing herring, 40 years before houses could legally be built on the commons. At one time some 60 boats fished from Herston. Today it is a sheltered, peaceful village, close to magnificent cliff scenery.

Flotta

The island of Flotta lies in the main entrance to Scapa Flow, between Hoy and South Ronaldsay. Perhaps the Norse name of *Flatey*, the flat island, reflects the contrast to its more rocky neighbours. Flotta presents in fact a gently rolling landscape, rising to 58 m at the highest point of the Witter in the middle of the island.

Near Stanger Head, the steep south-eastern point, are the two deep gloups, or clefts, in the cliff called the Big Gloup and the Peerie Gloup. Quite close to them stand the two rock stacks known as the

Wartime relics and modern oil flare.

Cletts. The Flotta story is that the Cletts came out of the Gloups one day!

A fertile, well-cultivated valley runs across the island in the south-east, well protected by a higher moorland in the west and north. George Low walked the heaths of Flotta too, in his 1774 Tour. 'The west side of the island, and that long point called the Rone, as well as the east skirt and round the Panhouse is wholly covered with long heath affording shelter for vast numbers of Moorfowl, and indeed I could scarce walk fifty yards without springing one or more of these birds.' He found even more birds on the Calf of Flotta.

There is no broch in Flotta. Some time in the nineteenth century the cherished Flotta Stone was found. It was in private hands for a while, until it was sold to the National Museum of Antiquities in Edinburgh in 1877. The stone is carved with an interlace-filled cross and is believed to be of quite early origin, perhaps dating back as far as the eighth century. The stone may have been the front panel of an altar, or one of the four sides of a tomb.

In spite of its highly strategic situation, Flotta does not figure in the *Orkneyinga Saga*. But the Wharth, from *varða*, down on the south-western shore, would probably have been used as the site of a warning fire, as was the Witter, from *viti*, a beacon. Near the Witter is a field named Hellywell, with a well of special qualities. The water from Winster's Well, on the shore at Villigar, near Roan Head, was believed to cure diseases, but a certain behaviour was required of visitors. For the water to retain its healing qualities, not a word must be spoken while it was being carried, otherwise all its virtue would be lost. And at one time, Flotta boasted a weather prophet, Mammie Scott, who for a consideration would sell the right wind to the sailor.

Flotta is not mentioned in the early rentals either, probably because it belonged to the bishopric estate, but it was skatted as a half urisland, and was part of the parish of Walls and Flotta. It had its own parish church, in Kirkhope, now Kirk Bay, where there used to be also the remains of an early chapel. The church stood on the lands of the bishopric Bu, a farm that survives as the Bow. The church is still in use every Sunday. There is no resident minister, but the service is conducted by visiting clergy or the church elders.

In 1550 Flotta, along with Burray, Swona, Switha, Glimsholm, Hunda and the Calf of Flotta, was feued out to Lady Barbara Stewart. It remained part of the Steuart of Burray estate until *c.*1770, when it was all bought by Sir Lawrence Dundas, owner of the earldom estate.

The bay on the east side is called Panhope because there was a 'salt pan' on the shore. In the early years of the eighteenth century 50 bolls of salt were produced there annually, one boll being 140 lbs or 63 kilos. The sale of the product was said to bring in as much as 200 Scots pounds a year, but the threat of an excise duty being imposed seems to have ended the salt production after only a few years.

Sir James Steuart of Burray, the notorious Jacobite sympathiser, was inevitably the Flotta laird. He kept and maintained a small house at Panhope, years after the salt pan was no longer in use. He sometimes stayed overnight in Flotta for estate purposes, as he had as many as 19 tenants in the island, but also because he was a keen hunter, and Flotta was a particularly good hunting ground, abounding in eiders and shelduck.

As it turned out, the predatory laird was hunting other game as well. When Christian Ritch in 1744 had to answer in court for her immoral behaviour, she admitted that she was with child to Sir James Steuart of Burray and that it was 'begot in the pan house of Flotta a fortnight before Hallowmass last'. This was not the first time that Sir James had fathered an illegitimate child, but strangely he never had to answer for it in court! He smuggled Christian Ritch out of Orkney, to an unknown destination, and the case was dropped. And when George Low visited Flotta, there was nothing to be seen of the pan house 'but a ruin of the building'.

At the time of Low's visit, the later eighteenth century, kelp burning had reached the island, and Walls and Flotta together had an annual production of some 80 tons a year. After their work was over in the evening, the kelp burners were wont to play the fiddle and dance, something George Low took an exception to. He says that Flotta abounds with 'Snipes, the musick of whose thundering wings pleases a tolerable ear, much better than the wretched fiddles I heard in Flotta, which however seemed to be much relished by the kelp burners, who after their work was over in an evening, fell a hobbling about to their noise, with most inimitable discord'. George Low gives us a lively account of the fishing from Flotta.

> Between Flotta and Switha, and round the latter, there is a
> large fishery of Coal-fish, (to which most of the boats of
> the South isles daily repair and catch vast numbers) which
> begins in May and continues till late in the season, and is
> commonly succeeded and sometimes interrupted by vast
> swarms of the Picked Dog fish which drive every other fish
> from the ground; however the islanders are seldom sorry
> for the loss of the Coal when the Dogs continue with them,
> for they not only afford them victuals but yield vast
> quantities of valuable oil from their livers, all which fully
> makes up for the loss of the other, besides they are caught
> in such surprising numbers, that it is no uncommon thing
> to load their boats twice or thrice a day; however they soon
> go off in pursuit of other fish, which always shift stations
> to avoid this ravenous enemy.'

On the eve of the First World War Flotta had a population of 431 people, living in a peaceful, self-contained world. Mostly they were farmers, crofters, and fishermen, but there were also blacksmiths, carpenters, dressmakers, as well as a doctor, postmaster, minister and teacher. The two world wars and the North-Sea oil boom have transformed the island, making it more of a museum of the past as well as a laboratory for the future.

The fortification of Flotta began during the First World War, turning it into a miniature garrison. Flotta's role was then primarily to guard the main sea entrances to Scapa Flow. A large observation and signalling station was built by the Royal Navy at Stanger Head, the south-eastern point of the island. Leading up to the station is the steep and winding Magnificent Lane, so called because it was built by the men of HMS *Magnificent*. But there must also have been brighter moments for the men, as we can still find on the Golta peninsula the remains of a landing pier which was built to take Navy personnel to the large YMCA building, now a ruin, where among other pastimes they could also enjoy a round of golf.

After the sinking of HMS *Royal Oak* at the beginning of the Second World War, the importance of the southern entrance to the Flow became evident, and Flotta once again became a strategic military base. Existing fortifications got a new lease of life, and new ones were built. In the Second World War the island garrison also had to defend the Flow from air attack. Anti-aircraft guns were placed at strategic points, and barrage balloons covered the island. A cinema that could hold some 1500 people was built close to the Sutherland and Gibraltar piers, which were also wartime constructions.

In the 1970s Flotta was still full of wartime relics, but its rather ageing population of some 80 people were getting used to being on their own again. As it turned out, this post-war period turned out to be the calm before the storm, as in 1973 the Piper oilfield in the North Sea was discovered. The Occidental consortium began looking for a site for an oil terminal, and decided that the Orkney Islands with Scapa Flow would be the best location. Flotta was chosen to be the centre of the oil activities, as on its northern seaboard the deepest and best protected anchorage in the islands was to be found, the only maritime area around without strong currents. In 1914 The Grand Fleet had anchored there.

The site chosen was the old farm of Whanclett, which had to make room for seven huge oil tanks for the storage of oil. The stated goal was to achieve what was called visual integration, by making the terminal blend naturally with the environment. It was also important to protect the social structure in Flotta.

The terminal was originally operated by the Occidental Oil Company, but was taken over by Elf Enterprise. Several oilfields are linked to the Flotta terminal where the oil is stored for loading on to tankers, and large ships come and go from all over the world. Orcadians have become used to the traffic, and it has not done the Orkney economy any harm either. As the scale is small and the traffic is virtually confined to the terminal, the possible adverse impact of oil on Flotta has been less than at one time feared.

The Flotta people have been able to see the humorous side of the oil business as well. The crofter Willick o' Pirlibraes, the imaginary character who features in the dialect stories of David Sinclair of Flotta, does not think much of the oil business or the oil-men, but then in general there are few things to rave about. On the other hand Willick is not averse to any perks the oil business might bring his way.

The Flotta oil flare can be seen from almost all the islands, in Flotta itself it can also be heard. The Orkney writer George Mackay Brown came to see the flare as a symbol of change. 'That huge gas flare at the centre of Scapa Flow, the blazon that illumines Orkney's night sky, might well stand as a sign of the new industrial age. Between the oil wells under the North Sea and the tanks of Flotta stretch, unseen, the vast veins and arteries of the new technology.'

The blockship Inverlain. *The tide is slowly destroying it.*

Graemsay

The green and fertile island of Graemsay guards the western entrance to Scapa Flow, with the hills of Hoy a dramatic backdrop on the one side and the small town of Stromness on the other. The two lighthouses are a warning that island waters are hazardous; both in Hoy Sound and in Burra Sound strong tides race rapidly. The name of Burra derives from *borg*, meaning castle, and in Norse times the now-ruined broch at the north end of Hoy must have been impressive enough to inspire the name. For a long time the rusty bow of an old tanker, the *Inverlain*, has been a landmark in Burra Sound. The stern part can be observed in Inganess Bay, on the north side of Mainland. Mined east of Orkney at the beginning of the Second World War, it became a blockship.

In Norse times the name of the island was *Grímsey*. Perhaps it was the land-take of a man called *Grímr*, but the designation was also one of many that were used for Odin, the Norse god. The later version of Graemsay may have come from confusion with the local surname of Graeme. An old croft near the parish cemetery on the south side of the island is called Veval, and may also refer to pagan times, as *vé* means holy and val probably derives from *vollr*, a field. The island is mentioned twice in passing in the *Orkneyinga Saga*.

Graemsay consists almost entirely of good, arable land, and is also blessed with a good climate. This may be due in part to a rain shadow effect, the damp air in the dominant west-south-west winds being lifted when it passes Hoy. It cools and loses much of its humidity. The dry air is heated when it descends again. As a result Graemsay may have a relatively dry and warm climate compared with the neighbouring islands.

On the north coast, just west of the Bay of Sandside, there is a narrow belt of rougher ground, with outcrops of granites and schists. In Orkney such ancient rocks exist only in Graemsay and in the Stromness area. The island slopes gently eastwards from a height of some 60 m, at West Hill. The lovely Quoys burn drains the only marshy area. The wide beach at Sandside, which consists partly of broken coral, is the only breach in the coastline of low cliffs. Graemsay has no village, but the valley, sloping up from the beach to the old schoolhouse, acts as a centre to the island.

Besides the former parish church at Kirk Geo on the south side, there are also the remains of two old chapels. One of these was sited on the north-west point and was dedicated to St Colm, the other was at Bride's Noust, near Corrigall, and was dedicated to St Bride, one of the early Scottish saints. Originally, Graemsay was considered 'ane pendicle' to Mainland and paid all church dues to the Stromness church, their 'proper paroche Kirk', but from the early sixteenth century it was attached to Hoy. It then became an independent parish with a manse of its own. But today there is neither a manse nor a parish church in use.

The fertile land of Graemsay was used for grain, so there was little grass. Traditionally sheep and cattle were therefore put out to the Hoy moorlands for summer pasture. Similarly Graemsay people depended on getting peats for fuel from outside. There were four large farms or tunships, with a common between them. In the higher, north-west part of the island was the tunship with the arresting name of Oute apoune the Ile, probably derived from the Norse *Úti uppá ey*, 'out upon the isle'. The south-west part was called Corrigill, and in the south-east could be found the largest of the tunships, known as Suthirgarth, from *suðr-garðr*, the south farm. Then there was Sandisend in the north-east – at the end of the sand.

The island was skatted as two urislands; according to the rental of 1500 this was made up of 45 per cent odal land and 55 per cent earldom land. Strangely, much of the odal land belonged to families who did not live in Graemsay. Although more than half of Graemsay belonged to the earldom, Earl Robert Stewart seems to have wanted to own it all. He proceeded to harass the odallers to make them yield the rest of the land. In a complaint made from Orkney to the Scottish Crown in December 1575, we find this item relating to Graemsay: 'Inbringing of Hieland men and broken men in the country of Orkney, whilks were auld enemies and oppressors of the people of before, and causing them to sorn, oppress, and spuilzie [spoil] the country, specially the Isle of Graemsay, and be stopping of countrymen to pursue them and put them af the land, alleging they were his own men and fealls [liege-men].'

The earldom lands as well as most of the old odal land was handed over sometime before 1584 by Earl Robert to his natural son, also believed to be his favourite, who was to become James Stewart of Graemsay. He settled at the old farm of Sandisend, and named it the Bu of Graemsay. He was at daggers drawn with his half-brother Earl Patrick, who at one point had him thrown in jail and his house pulled down.

James Stewart's only daughter, Mary, married Andrew Honyman, Bishop of Orkney (1664-76). Their son Robert kept the designation 'of Graemsay', but by means of a successful marriage, as well as through his own efforts, he added more to the estate property acquired outside the island. His son and grandson extended it further, until by the early nineteenth century the Graemsay estate was second only to the earldom estate, and bringing in some £4000 a year. The Honymans made their home on Mainland at the Hall of Clestrain, overlooking Graemsay across Clestrain Sound, only to have it looted by the pirate John Gow in 1725.

In June 1758, William Honyman, second of Graemsay, was drowned in the Pentland Firth, together with his eldest son and a faithful servant. They were on their way at the time to trade in the Hebrides, perhaps to do some smuggling as well, or so it was said. When three months had passed, his boat was seen, late one evening in the summer-dim, sailing through Clestrain Sound towards its usual anchorage. Then suddenly the boat seemed to dissolve and vanish into thin air. Before leaving the laird had buried a box of valuables by a dyke in the hillside. Since then many people have tried in vain to find this treasure.

In George Low's *A Tour through Orkney and Schetland*, the first lap

The beach at Sandside with Hoy High lighthouse.

of his journey is recorded thus: '1774. *May 4th*. – Left Stromness and visited the Isle of Græmsay.' He found the island 'pretty well inhabited by a very stout raw-boned race of men, which is much owing to their not mixing with others, and marrying mostly among themselves; however this is not now so much the case since they were deprived of the flower of their men by an accident at sea, in a voyage to Suleskerry, whither they had gone in quest of seals.'

The island must have recovered from the loss of its men, as in the nineteenth century Graemsay was densely populated, as were most of the Orkney islands at that time. But since then crofts have merged, and the lighthouses have gone automatic. The resulting fall in population has led to the closure of the school, with Graemsay children being conveyed to Stromness by boat for their schooling. There is an excellent pier, and the Hoy ferry calls regularly on its way to and from Moaness.

The old Bu of Graemsay, once the residence of the Stewarts, is today known as Sandside. It is now the only farm left on the island, all the rest of the land being still held in crofting tenure.

Cliff scenery from the Old Man of Hoy to St John's Head.

Hoy and Walls

The Norse name for Hoy was *Háey*, the high island. The southern part of it is known as Walls, from the Norse *Vágar*, the bays. The *Orkneyinga Saga* calls it *Vágaland*. The island has been divided between two parishes, Hoy and Graemsay, and Walls and Flotta, sometimes sharing one minister. Hoy being a large island, the two parish churches are 14 miles apart, and in the seventeenth century the minister makes a heartfelt complaint, 'of the forsaid 14 mylis ther ar 6 mylis of wilderness quharin ar divers great wateris, neither is ther anie hous be the way'. Although the coming of a modern road has to some extent changed the picture, the minister's words are still largely true; because of distance and diversity Hoy and Walls seem two separate worlds, as effectively divided as if they were two islands.

The hills of Hoy form a bulwark for Orkney towards the south. Almost entirely composed of Upper Old Red Sandstone, they are hard and massive, seeming to cover the whole spectrum of colour between burnt red and orange. The highest point is Ward Hill at 479 m, from afar so dominating in the Orkney landscape that its height was estimated by Jo Ben to be three miles. Along the western coast high barren and awe-inspiring precipices form a wall to the Atlantic; St John's Head at 350 m being one of the highest sea-cliffs in Britain. It was climbed for the first time in 1970, the two climbers sleeping out on the face for three nights.

The Old Man of Hoy, near Rora Head, is at 137 m the tallest sea-stack in Britain. It is composed of a more erosive stone; centuries ago it was part of Hoy. Old prints show The Old Man as an arch, but it lost its spare leg some time ago. It was climbed for the first time in July 1966, by a group consisting of Tom Patey, Chris Bonington and Rusty Baillie, and it took them three days to do so. The climbing was as carefully planned as a military operation. During the ascent they were intensively dive-bombed by a family of great skuas. According to mountaineers the Old Man of Hoy is 'a rotten stack where a hold can come away like an over-ripe apple at any time'.

Some 10 km of superb cliff scenery in yellow or red stretch from the Old Man to The Berry in Walls. A sheer precipice of some 200 m, The Berry is striking both in shape and colour, and is probably the Norse *Rauðabjorg* – the red rock or cliff – where the great sea fight takes place between Earl Rognvald Brusason and Earl Thorfinn the Mighty in *c.* 1045. It is described in detail in the *Orkneyinga Saga*.

The Pentland Firth, where the sea races through at nine knots at flood tide, is an awkward place for a naval battle, and not one the earls would normally have chosen. Over the centuries it has been a dreaded obstacle to be crossed on the way south, and has added to the feeling of separateness in Orkney.

According to a tenth-century legend the dangerous whirlpool of the Swelkie in the Pentland Firth was made by the magical grinding-stone Grotti. It originally belonged to King Frodi of Denmark, but the sea-king Mysing took it from him, along with the slave women Fenja and Menja. They were ordered to grind salt, and so they did, until their ship sank in the Pentland Firth. Since then the sea has been salt, and as it rushes through the eye of the quern, the sea roars and the whirlpool churns. Fenja and Menja were known in later Orkney lore as Grotti Finnie and Grotti Minnie, and were invoked at times to awe naughty children.

The *Historia Norvegiae*, an old Latin text that was found in Scotland in 1849, tells us that the Swelkie is 'the greatest of all whirlpools, which draws in and swallows down in the ebb the strongest ships and vomits and casts up their fragments in the flood'. In 1029 Earl Hakon of Lade, who ruled Norway while King Olaf was in exile in Russia, had been to Britain to see his bride-to-be. It was late into the autumn before he set off on the return trip, and he never made it home. 'Some relate that the vessel was seen north of Caithness in the evening in a heavy storm, and the wind blowing out of the Pentland Firth. They who believe this report say the vessel drove out into the Swelkie; but with certainty people knew only that earl Hakon was missing in the ocean, and nothing belonging to the ship ever came to land.' (*Saga of Olaf the Saint*). The Pentland Firth is considered one of the roughest and most dangerous seas surrounding Britain, and a superb test of seamanship.

Hoy has been called the botanical treasure house of Orkney, mostly because of the rich variety of plants in the small rocky valley of Berriedale, inland from the Old Man. Here grow Orkney's only indigenous trees, and a rich growth of rowans, dwarf birches and alders, smothered by ivy and honeysuckle, gives shelter to the smaller varieties of birds. It is said that nowhere else but in Berriedale can grasshoppers be heard in Orkney.

Many alpine plants can be found a mere 150 m above sea level, as Hoy has an exposed climate. It is also rather wet, with an average of 1500 mm of rain in a year, and while other islands lie in sunshine, Hoy may be hidden in clouds. Biting midges thrive in some of the valleys, as George Mackay Brown found. 'In the most beautiful valley of Rackwick the midges are said to have teeth like sharks. Nowhere in the world breeds them so savage'.

Hoy has no Orkney voles, but romping about the north hills is the blue mountain hare (*Lepus timidus*) which is found only in Hoy, and may be a relative newcomer, replacing an earlier native race which became extinct by hunting. In winter it becomes almost completely white, and is then very conspicuous and vulnerable in the bare landscape. By comparison the brown hare is quite common in Orkney. In the nineteenth century two young hinds and a stag were introduced into Walls by the laird. They thrived and multiplied so much that they were considered a threat to the crops.

A continuous chain of hills stretch the length of the island from Hoy Head to Melsetter. They are rounded but steep-sided and in-between are deep lochs, such as Heldale Water and Hogglins Water in the south. Old angling records of the existence of a rare fish, the Arctic char, as late as

The deep lochs of Heldale Water and Hogglins Water.

the 1950s, led to a search of Heldale Water some years ago. A few stocks of this species might have been left after the last Ice Age when sea levels were falling. No char was found, and it seems unlikely that it has survived in Heldale Water.

The seabird cliffs of Hoy, such as Too of the Head near Rackwick, The Berry in Walls, Aith Head and Bring Head around Aith Hope in the south, and the Kame of Hoy and St John's Head in the north, all house large populations of seabirds, among them the red-throated diver, Arctic skua and great skua, also known as bonxie. As many as 1500 great skuas have been recorded, but this figure will come as no surprise to people who have tried to avoid their divebombing assault on the way up the Ward Hill. The golden eagle and the white-tailed eagle both formerly bred in Hoy.

The parish of Hoy was bordland, the personal property of the Norse earls. It would possibly have been considered an important strategic base as its position would have given a certain control of traffic in the Firth. We learn in the *Orkneyinga Saga* that a man called Jon Wing farmed in the Upland district of Hoy and was one of the first to side with Earl

The beautiful bay of Rackwick.

Rognvald II when he first came to the islands. Probably he was the Earl's representative in Hoy and lived at the Bu, the Earl's veizla farm. The Bu has always been a most important place in Hoy; the present house goes back to the early seventeenth century.

Arable land in Hoy parish is confined to Rackwick and North Hoy, and in the old rentals this was estimated at between two and three urislands. The parish of Walls was mixed odal, earldom and bishopric land. It is more fertile, at least in the district of South Walls, and was skatted as some four and a half urislands.

Hoy was later divided into four small estates. Walls had at first three different landowners, but from the early sixteenth century the incoming Moodie family of Melsetter prospered and gradually came to control most of the whole island. The estate changed hands, but lasted until the general break-up of landed property began in the 1920s. Walls gradually became owner-occupied, while the parish of Hoy remained one estate, largely on crofting tenure.

In 1973 the estate of North Hoy was presented to the Hoy Trust by the owner Malcolm Stewart of Orgil Lodge, 'for the benefit of the nation, and the people of Hoy as a community'. One of the conditions laid down was that none of the land was to be sold. The outcry was therefore quite loud when the news came ten years later that the Old Man of Hoy as well as some 8000 acres of surrounding moorland, or about a third of the estate, was being sold to the Royal Society for the Protection of Birds. Attempts made to try stopping the purchase fell through, and the RSPB therefore became Orkney's largest landowner.

The beautiful bay of Rackwick is perhaps Orkney's most isolated spot. Surrounded by mountains, it was once a working tunship where in 1801, 101 people inhabited 21 houses and shared 87 acres of arable and 44 acres of outrun between them. Almost every household had subsidiary occupations; mostly the men fished and the women spun and knitted. The fishermen of Rackwick were known for their skill at sea, a skill that was vital when the only harbour was the sandy curve of the bay which lay open and unprotected to the Atlantic; the boats always had to be drawn up on the beach and hurriedly launched again between swells.

But the Rackwick men also had a reputation as excellent climbers who would go over the highest rocks to fetch seabirds and eggs, even stray sheep. They were also the strongest and most graceful of country dancers who cheerfully walked through the hills to the other side of Hoy and danced the night through.

Rackwick lay open to more than the sea; according to tradition there were pirate raids over the centuries. In his poem 'Shore tullye' the Orkney writer Robert Rendall describes an attack by pirates and how the Rackwick men drove them away. The incident is traditional and a pirate's grave can still be seen on the hill by anyone who might otherwise doubt the story. This is how the pirate died.

> Him apae the hillside
> Hewed we doun in feud fight –
> Never kam sea-rovers
> Seekan back to Rackwick.

After the Second World War the people left Rackwick and the school was closed in 1954. The crofts have since been used as summer cottages, and the schoolhouse has had a second lease of life as a youth hostel. Two families live there permanently.

The road to North Hoy goes through a glaciated valley between Ward Hill and the Knap of Trowieglen. Here we find the Dwarfie Stane, the only example in northern Europe of a rock tomb. A passage and two small chambers have been hollowed out of the stone, and it is no wonder the Norsemen believed it to be a home for dwarfs and called it *Dvergasteinn*. It was probably cut in the third millennium BC. In the hillside above the tomb are the Dwarfie Hamars, where the echo is famous. Perhaps the story of Hild and the famous everlasting battle on Hoy also took place in this valley?

Hild, the daughter of King Hodne, was captured by King Hedin while her father was away. When he came home and learned what had happened, Hodne pursued them all the way to Orkney. Hedin offered peace, but Hodne drew his sword *Dáinsleif* which had been forged by dwarfs. The fight which is called *Hjaðningavíg*, began and lasted all day. In the night Hild went to the battle site and by magic brought all the fallen warriors back to life, so the fight could go on, as it still does, and will till the end of the world.

The story is very old, it exists in many variants and later sources all agree that it takes place in Hoy. On his Tour in Shetland in 1774, George Low discovered in Foula a variant of the story in the form of a ballad. He wrote this down under the title 'The Earl of Orkney and King of Norway's Daughter: a Ballad.'

The boundary line between the two main districts of Hoy and Walls runs from Scad Head in the east slightly southwards to Sneuk Head in the west. Almost parallel to this is the burn known as the Summer of Hoy, a romantic-sounding name that in the true down-to-earth style of the Norsemen actually means what it is, *suðr-mark-rá*, the southern boundary line of Hoy. Here, in the no-man's land between two parishes, was found the lonely grave of Betty Corrigall, a young girl from Lyness, who some time in the nineteenth century committed suicide because of an unwanted pregnancy. She was buried in the heath on the parish boundary, but her grave was discovered during the Second World War by gunners from the nearby anti-aircraft battery. In 1976 a burial service was held in consecration of her grave.

Along the east coast of Hoy are the two small islands of Rysa Little and Fara. Rysa Little is covered in peat and was never cultivated, but has been used as a hunting ground for the Melsetter estate. Fara, on the other hand, has good farm land which at one time carried eight crofts with the total population averaging some 60 people. There was also a small chapel. The pier was rather exposed to westerly winds and transport was difficult, so the island was left in 1968. In two world wars the people on Fara would have been exposed to worse things than a strong wind and were perhaps closer to world events than they would have liked. On the other hand they would have had a grandstand view of the scuttling of the German fleet by their own crews on 21 June 1919.

The Crockness Martello Tower guarding the entrance to Longhope.

The name of Walls is strictly an invention of the Ordnance Survey, as it is pronounced Waas, and means bays. It is an apt name, as there are five bays and three sounds in the district. It seems always to have been strategically important, as we can learn from the saga stories, and from the landscape still studded with derelict wartime sites from the not-so-distant past.

The scattered hamlet of Lyness was a very important base for the navy and at one time as many as 30,000 men were based there. Most of the activity at Lyness Naval Base concentrated on servicing the warships that came and went, with provisions and fuel. Sometimes the ships left their anchorage in Scapa Flow for engagements that became legendary. It was from here the Grand Fleet sailed, to fight the German High Seas Fleet at the Battle of Jutland on 31 May 1916, in the chief naval engagement of the First World War, and it was to this place they limped back afterwards. The deep-water quay and naval-base buildings at Lyness were not completed until some time after the First World War, but then they came in useful in the next war!

The writer Eric Linklater experienced Lyness in two wars and describes it in this way: 'It never had any visible dignity or attraction for the eye – it was in its heyday something between a mining village, a dockyard, and a Whitehall slum – but for a few years it was dignified by the large endeavour which animated it.' Today the pump house has been turned into a Scapa Flow visitor centre where the history of Lyness through two world wars can be relived.

At the Lyness Naval Cemetery the inscriptions on the graves of two wars remind us of some of the most tragic events of twentieth-century naval history. Here are the names of men who fought off Jutland, went down with the HMS *Hampshire* when it struck a mine off Marwick Head in Birsay on 5 June 1916, or perished on HMS *Vanguard*, blown up off Flotta on 9 July 1917. There are also the names of the men from the first British naval casualty of the Second World War, HMS *Royal Oak*, which was torpedoed in Scapa Flow on 14 October 1939.

The inlet of Longhope is some 5 km long, and cuts Walls almost in two. The word derives from the Norse *hópr*, a narrow, rather protected bay. The bay forms a good natural harbour and in the old days of sailing vessels Longhope was a well-known and popular anchorage. It has also been a notable fishing centre.

Guarding the entrance to Longhope stand two defensive towers, strangely reminiscent of broch structures, which are known as the Martello towers. They date from 1813, the time of the Napoleonic Wars, and are said to have been built to protect Baltic convoys from US naval and private raiders. On the other hand the U.S. declared war on Britain in 1812 for reputedly harassing U.S. ships trading with Napoleon's allies. The rather elegant towers were armed with 24-pounder cannons, but never had to fire at an enemy. Ammunition was stored in the lower storey, with the middle storeys being living quarters for the gunners. The towers were used during the First World War and are still well preserved.

Magnificently sited between Pentland Firth and the well-protected haven of North Bay, lies Melsetter House, which is historically one of the most interesting houses in Orkney. It is also a very fine building. Until the late nineteenth century it was a laird's house for the Moodie family. The house was reputedly at one time a country residence for the bishops of Orkney. The house was twice sacked by Jacobites in 1745 while the owner, Captain Benjamin Moodie, eighth laird of Melsetter, and known for his anti-Jacobite feelings, was away in Edinburgh.

In the eighteenth and early nineteenth centuries the Melsetter estate grew in size and importance under the families of Moodie and Moodie-Heddle. In the late nineteenth century Melsetter was bought by a wealthy

Englishman, Thomas Middlemore. He engaged the distinguished architect William Lethaby to enlarge the Melsetter house in the style made popular by William Morris, with furniture designed by Ford Maddox Brown and Dante Gabriel Rossetti, the well-known pre-Raphaelites. In the early twentieth century almost all the land was sold to tenants. It was requisitioned during both world wars and used by the Admirals. Today it is a category 'A' listed building.

A very narrow isthmus connects North and South Walls. The Ayre is only a few metres across, and South Walls was therefore a tidal island until about a century ago when a narrow causeway was built on the sand. In many ways South Walls is different from the rest of Hoy, perhaps because it is distinctly a farming community and therefore more similar to the rest of Orkney. The Bu of Aith, from the Norse *eið* for isthmus, was always an important farm, the headhouse of a urisland tunship. Strangely the farm does not figure in the *Orkneyinga Saga*, but then the South Isles seem to be mentioned mostly in passing as the scene of incidents, rather than as a settled area where people lived. George Low describes how the peninsula seemed to him in 1774: 'South Waes is much better inhabited than the north side, and very fruitful in Corn, of which in good seasons they dispose a good deal'.

South Walls was considered a strategic place in the *Orkneyinga Saga*, as we find the ever active Svein Asleifarson at one point urging his fellow Viking, the young Earl Erlend, 'to move their fleet over to South Walls where they could lie at anchor close to the Pentland Firth and see the moment anyone put out from Caithness'. It was also thought a good place from which to make an attack.

The inlet that is now known as Kirkhope was in Norse times called *Ásmundarvágr*, Asmund's bay. The name of Osmondwall is still the official name of the head of the bay, but the local form of the name is Owsna. The sagas record that in 995 King Olaf Tryggvason, on his way to Norway, took a break in Orkney. At Osmondwall he ran into Earl Sigurd Hlodvisson the Stout, 'who had three ships and was setting out on a viking expedition.' King Olaf, who had just been baptised himself, forced Earl Sigurd to submit to baptism on pain of death. Sigurd's son Hundi was taken along as hostage, but when news came that he had died, Earl Sigurd reneged on his baptism and returned to his pagan ways.

In 1017 Earl Einar II of Orkney was defeated in battle by Eyvind Urarhorn and the Irish. One year later the roles were switched around.

Eyvind was on his way from Ireland to Norway, when he decided to wait for better weather in Osmondwall. While stormbound there, he was captured and killed by Earl Einar of Orkney who had grown tired of seeing Eyvind playing into enemy hands in Ireland. Earl Einar spared most of Eyvind's men, and in the autumn they went back to Norway and told King Olaf how his godson had been killed. The King did not say much, 'though it was plain he thought Eyvind's death a great loss and took the whole episode as a personal affront'.

Beside the Bay of Osmondwall the foundation of an ancient church, dedicated to St Columba, can still be seen in the churchyard. It was built on a site near the most fertile land; such churches were generally known as St Colm churches. A lovely slab, incised with a cross, was found at St Colm's Kirk in Walls.

On the shore south of Osmondwall lie the remains of the Green Hill of Hestigeo Broch. An unusually large broch, it was part of an amateur excavation project and emptied of its contents in the late nineteenth century. When summarising his views of the finds, one of the amateur archaeologists tried to prove that the brochs would have come with the Phoenicians via a land bridge from Atlantis sometime before the last glaciation! But it is easy to jibe at such theories today, and forget that there was no radiocarbon dating in the nineteenth century.

The shoreline of South Walls is full of caves and natural arches. On top of the inaccessible rock-stack known as 'The Candle of Snelsetter', but called 'The Pillar' locally, are the remains of a chambered-walled structure. There are two chambers, each with rounded corners, within a surrounding wall.

The Longhope Lifeboat Station at Brims in Aith Hope was opened in 1834, and has since then achieved a reputation for the resourcefulness and bravery of its crew. Today it has a 47 ft lifeboat called *Lord Saltoun*. When tragedy struck in 1969, the lifeboat was of the same size but named simply *T G B*, the donor wishing to remain anonymous.

On 17 March 1969 the Lifeboat Station received a distress call from the Liberian cargo ship *Irene*, on its way to a Norwegian port, but in difficulty off the east side of Orkney. The ship was out of control and drifting before a south-easterly Force 9 gale. The lifeboat was launched at 8 pm, in mountainous seas, with waves up to 20 m high. The boat was never heard from again. It was found 16 hours later, upturned, four miles west of Tor Ness in Walls. The crew of the *Irene* was saved; the ship

Melsetter and the narrow isthmus that connects North and South Walls.

grounded hard and fast on the Grim Ness rocks in South Ronaldsay, and is still there.

The loss of the *T B G* lifeboat was the worst tragedy to strike Orkney in the post-war period; it was especially hard for the small village of Brims. The crew of eight men who lost their lives included two fathers each with two sons on board. Dan Kirkpatrick, who was in charge, was regarded as one of the most experienced coxswains in Britain, and held three lifeboat silver medals for gallantry.

The long island of Hoy is a rampart which offers both factual and symbolic protection against the fury of the Pentland Firth. Its dramatic shape also stands in splendid and spectacular contrast to the rest of Orkney. In the words of George Mackay Brown, 'Those noble, lovely shapes haunt Orcadians wherever they go, like immemorial heraldry, and one must believe, in some sense mould our communal life and outlook.'

Bibliography

Anderson, P.D., *Robert Stewart, Earl of Orkney, Lord of Shetland*, John Donald Publishers Ltd, Edinburgh 1982; *Black Patie. The Life and Times of Patrick Stewart Earl of Orkney, Lord of Shetland*, ibid., 1992

Bailey, P., *Orkney*, David & Charles, London 1971

Barry, G., *History of the Orkney Islands*, (1805) Mercat Press, Edinburgh 1975

Batey, C.E., Jesch, J., and Morris, C.D., *The Viking Age in Caithness, Orkney and the North Atlantic*, Edinburgh University Press, 1993

Berry, R.J., and Firth, H.N., *The People of Orkney*, The Orkney Press, Kirkwall 1986

Brown, G.M., *The Two Fiddlers*, Chatto & Windus, London 1974; *An Orkney Tapestry*, ibid, 1978; *Letters from Hamnavoe*, Gordon Wright, Edinburgh 1975; *Under Brinkie's Brae*, Gordon Wright Publishing, Edinburgh 1979; *Rockpools and Daffodils* ibid. 1992

Brøgger, A.W., *Ancient Emigrants*, London 1929

Burgher, L., *Orkney*, Edinburgh 1991

Clouston, J.S., *The Orkney Parishes*, W R Mackintosh, Kirkwall 1927; 'The Battle of Tankerness', POAS, (Proceedings of the Orkney Antiquarian Society) vi, 1927-8;

Atlantic puffins.

A History of Orkney, The Kirkwall Press, Kirkwall, 1932

Coleman, V., and Wheeler, R., *Living on an Island*, The Thule Press, Moray 1980

Crawford, B.E., *Scandinavian Scotland*, Leicester University Press, 1987; (ed.) *Northern Isles Connections. Essays from Orkney & Shetland presented to Per Sveaas Andersen*, The Orkney Press, Kirkwall 1995

Dennison, W.T., *The Orcadian Sketch Book*, W Peace & Son, Kirkwall 1880; *Orkney Folklore and Tradition*, (ed.) E.W. Marwick, 1961; *Orkney Folklore & Sea Legends*, compiled by Tom Muir, The Orkney Press, Kirkwall 1995

Dietrichson, L., and Meyer, J., *Monumenta Orcadica*, Kristiania 1906

Farrell, R.T., (ed.) *The Vikings*, London 1982

Fenton, A., and Pálsson, H., *The Northern and Western Isles in the Viking World*, John Donald

Publishers, Edinburgh 1984

Fereday, R.P., *Orkney Feuds and the '45*, Kirkwall Grammar School, Kirkwall 1980; *The Orkney Balfours 1747-99*, Tempus Reparatum Monographs, Oxford 1990

Firth, J., *Reminiscences of an Orkney Parish*, Orkney Natural History Society, Stromness 1920

Fraser, J., 'The Antiquities of Rendall Parish', POAS, vi, 1927-8

Gelling, P.S., 'The Norse Buildings at Skaill, Deerness, Orkney, and their Immediate Predecessor', in Fenton, A., and Pálsson, H., op.cit., 1984.

Gibson, W.M., *Tales of an Orkney Island*, Kirkwall 1987

Graham-Campbell, J., 'A lost Pictish treasure (and two Viking gold arm-rings) from the Broch of Burgar, Orkney', in Farrell, R.T., op.cit., 1982

Grimond, J., *Memoirs*, William Heineman Ltd, London 1979

Hedges, J.W., *Tomb of the Eagles*, John Murray, London 1984

Henderson, I., *The Picts*, Thames and Hudson, London 1967

Hewison, W.S., *Who Was Who in Orkney*, Bellavista Publications, Orkney 1998

Hewitson, J., *Clinging to the Edge*, Mainstream Publishing, Edinburgh 1996

Holloway, J., *To Fair Isle and Back*, Stronsay Bird Reserve, Orkney 1995

Hossack, B.H., *Kirkwall in the Orkneys*, The Kirkwall Press, Kirkwall 1900

Irvine, W., *The Isle of Shapinsay*, The Kirkwall Press, Kirkwall 1977

Kaland, S., 'Westnessutgravningene på Rousay, Orknøyene', Viking, xxxvii, 1973

KLNM = Kulturhistorisk Lexicon for Nordisk Middelalder, Copenhagen and elsewhere, (22 vols.) 1956-1978

Lamb, R.G., *Iron Age Promontory Forts in the Northern Isles*, BAR British Series 79, Oxford 1980; 'Carolingian Orkney and its Transformation' in Batey, C.E., Jesch, J., and Morris, C.D., op.cit., 1993, 'Papil, Picts & Papar' in Crawford, B.E., op.cit., 1995

Linklater, E., *Orkney and Shetland*, Robert Hale, London 1961

Linklater, M., 'Uranium; a Questionable Commodity', Orkney Heritage, i, 1981

Low, G., *A Tour through the Islands of Orkney and Schetland (1774)*, Melven Press, Inverness 1978

Mackintosh, W.R., *Around the Orkney Peat-fires*, The Kirkwall Press, Kirkwall c. 1899

Marwick, E.W., *The Folklore of Orkney and Shetland*, Batsford 1975; (ed.) *Orkney Poems. An Anthology of Orkney Verse*, The Kirkwall Press, Kirkwall 1949

Marwick, H., 1922/3A, 'Antiquarian Notes on Sanday', POAS , i: 1922/3B, 'The Place-names of North Ronaldsay', POAS, i: 1924/5, 'Antiquarian Notes on papa Westray', POAS, iii: 1926/7, 'Antiquarian Notes on Stronsay', POAS, v: 1947, *The Place-names of Rousay*: Mackintosh, W.R., Kirkwall 1947, *Orkney*: Robert Hale, London 1951, *Orkney*

Farm Names, Kirkwall 1952; *The Place-names of Birsay*, Aberdeen University Press 1970

Miller, R., *Orkney*, Batsford 1976

Mooney, J., *Eynhallow, the Holy Island of the Orkneys*, Mackintosh, W.R., Kirkwall 1923

Muir, C., *Orkney Days*, Edinburgh 1986

Muir, E., *An Autobiography*, The Hogarth Press, London 1954

Napier, F., *Evidence taken by Her Majesty's Commissioners of Inquiry into the Condition of the Crofters and Cottars in the Highlands and Islands of Scotland*, 1884

Pálsson, H., and Edwards, P., *Orkneyinga Saga*, Penguin Classics, London 1981

Picken, S.D.B., *The Soul of an Orkney Parish*, The Kirkwall Press, Kirkwall 1972

Rendall, R., *Orkney Variants & Other Poems*, The Kirkwall Press, Kirkwall 1951

Renfrew, C., (ed.) *The Prehistory of Orkney*, Edinburgh University Press 1985

Ritchie, A., 'Pict and Norseman in northern Scotland', Scottish Archaelogical Forum, Vol VI, 1974; *Exploring Scotland's Heritage. Orkney and Shetland*, Edinburgh 1985; *Viking Scotland*, Batsford, London 1993; *Prehistoric Orkney*, Batsford, London 1995: *Orkney*, The Stationery Office, Edinburgh 1996

Schei, L.K., 'Huseby- og Holland-gårdene på Orknøyene', Historisk Tidsskrift, vol. 77, 1998

Scott, M.A., *Island Saga. The Story of North Ronaldsay*., Reid & Son, Aberdeen 1967

Seip, E., 'Bispegodset på Orknøyene fra ca 1100 til reformasjonen'. MA thesis in History, University of Oslo, 1984, Unpublished

Shapinsay 1985 Folk Studies Project, *The Eviction of the Shapinsay Elders from their Homes*, 1847

Sinclair, D., *Willick o' Pirlibraes*, The Orkney Press Ltd, Stromness 1981

Skea, B.I., *Island Images*, The Orkney Press Ltd, Stromness 1982

Steinnes, A., 'The Huseby System in Orkney, Scottish Historical Review, xxxviii, 1959

Sutherland, D., *Against the Wind. An Orkney Idyll*, Heinemann, London 1968

Thomson, B., *The Bard of Ballarat*, The Kirkwall Press, Kirkwall 1999

Thomson, W.P.L., *The Little General and the Orkney Crofters*, John Donald Publishers Ltd, Edinburgh 1981; *History of Orkney*, The Mercat Press, Edinburgh 1987.

Thuesen, N.P., 'Norrøn bosetning på Orknøyene', MA thesis in History, University of Oslo, 1978. Unpublished.

Tudor, J., *The Orkneys and Shetland; Their Past and Present State*, London 1883

Tulloch, P.A., *A Window on North Ronaldsay*, The Kirkwall Press, Kirkwall 1974

Wainwright, F.T.,(ed.) *The Problem of the Picts*, Edinburgh 1955; (ed.) *The Northern Isles*, Edinburgh 1962

Wickham-Jones, C., *Orkney. A Historical Guide*, Edinburgh 1998

The Earls of Orkney

The Norse line (*c* 890 - 1231)

c 890	descending from Rognvald Eysteinsson, Earl of Møre, Norway
	Sigurd Eysteinsson, the Powerful
	Guthorm Sigurdarson
	Hallad Rognvaldsson returns to Norway
c 933	Turf-Einar Rognvaldsson
950	Arnkel Turf-Einarsson
950	Erlend Turf-Einarsson
c 933 – *c* 963	Thorfinn Turf-Einarsson, the Skull-Splitter
963 – ?	Arnfinn Thorfinnsson
	Havard Thorfinnsson, the Harvest-Happy
c 980	Hlodvir Thorfinnsson
	Ljot Thorfinnsson
	Skuli Thorfinnsson
1014, the Battle of Clontarf	Sigurd II Hlodvisson, the Stout
1014 – 1015	Sumarlidi Sigurdarson
1014 – 1031	Brusi Sigurdarson
1014 – 1020	Einar II Sigurdarson Wry-Mouth
1014 – *c* 1064	Thorfinn II Sigurdarson, the Mighty
c 1035 – *c* 1045	Rognvald Brusason
1064 – 1098	Paul Thorfinnsson
c 1064 – 1098	Erlend II Thorfinnsson
c 1103 – *c* 1123	Hakon Paulsson
c 1105 – 1117	Magnus Erlendsson, the Saint (canonised 1135)
c 1122 – *c* 1127	Harald Hakonsson Smooth-Tongue
c 1122 – *c* 1137	Paul II Hakonsson
1136 – 1158	Rognvald II Kali Kolsson (canonised 1192)
1138 – 1206	Harald II Maddadarson
1151 – 1154	Erlend III Haraldsson
1197 – 1198	Harald III Eiriksson, the Young
1206 – 1214	David Haraldsson
1206 – 1230	Jon Haraldsson

The Angus line (1231 - *c* 1325)

Gilbride, Earl of Angus, married a relative, probably a sister, of Earl Jon I Haraldsson

1231 – 1239	Magnus II, son of Gilbride
1239 – ?	Gilbert
1256	Gilbride II, son of Gilbride
1256 – 1275	Magnus III, son of Gilbride II
1276 – 1284	Magnus IV Magnusson
1284 – *c* 1310	Jon II Magnusson
c 1310 – *c* 1325	Magnus V Jonsson

The Stratherne line (*c* 1336 - 1357)

Isabella, daughter of Earl Magnus V, married Malise, Earl of Stratherne

c 1336 – *c* 1353	Malise, of Stratherne and Orkney

Agneta, daughter of Malise, married Erngisl Suneson

c 1353 – 1357	Erngisl Suneson, Earl of Orkney

The St Clair/Sinclair line (1379 - 1470)

Isabella, daughter of Earl Malise of Stratherne and Orkney, married William St Clair

1379 – *c* 1400	Henry Sinclair, Earl of Orkney
c 1400 – 1420	Henry II Sinclair
1434 – 1470	William Sinclair

Glossary (italic indicates Norse)

ayre - from *aurr*, meaning sandy soil, gravel or from *eyrr*, a shingle bar, a spit of shingle, especially at a river mouth

bailie - a local magistrate

bailie-court - parish court with powers to deal with local administrative matters

bere - a four-rowed barley

bordland - used about untaxed earldom estates; quite literally the land produced food for the *borð*, meaning table

broch - from *borg*, a castle or fortification

brough - used for a hill or a tidal island that might look like a castle, such as The Brough of Deerness

'busses' and **'doggers'** - nicknames for the Dutch herring boats in Orkney waters

commonty - hill land used by adjacent owners in proportion to their holdings

conquest land - land acquired rather than inherited

cottar - a farm labourer paid through the use of a house and some land

croft - a small farm rented from a laird

factor - manager of an estate

feu - a feudal property-holding

geo - from *gjá*, a gully or creek

gloup - a deep chasm in a line of cliffs

hope - from *hópr*, a rather narrow bay

kelp - ashes of burnt seaweed, valued for its alkali/iodine content

kenning - the Norse metaphor

kingsland - refers mostly to the estates which before 1468 belonged to the Norwegian Crown

laird - landowner of a tenanted estate

lawbook - written codification of the laws

lawman - president of the lawting and chief legal officer until 1541, when the office was replaced by that of the Sheriff

lawting - the annual head court under Norse administration

ley - fallow

the north about route - a shipping route much used in times of war when the English Channel was unsafe; it went along the east coast of Britain to Scapa Flow or Fair Isle; ships then headed west

noust - from *naust* - a boat-shed or a boat beaching-place

odal - used of land owned outright, often without title-deeds, inherited among heirs according to odal law

odaller - one who held land by odal right

oyce - tidal basin

pennyland - ancient land denomination

press-gang - a body of sailors, led by an officer, with the power to carry off and force men into service, esp. in the navy

rental - a record of the size and ownership of farms

roithmen - members of head courts, mostly leading landowners

röst - an eddy or a whirlpool

run-rig - a form of land-tenure which involved re-allocating portions of land among the members of a tunship

shag - the cormorant

shun, chun - Orkney forms of tarn, as derived from *tjörn*

skat - land tax from odal property paid to the holder of the earldom rights

sysselman - a royal official

tack - a lease of land or the right to collect revenues

tacksman - lessee, holder of a tack/lease

taing - from *tangi*, a tongue of land or narrow promontory

ting or thing - a local assembly, of a judicial or consultative character

township - from *tún*, cultivated, often fenced off land; in Orkney the word came to mean a community of farmers working close together

udal, see odal

urisland - also eyrisland - district used for taxation purposes, the name derived from an annual tax of one ounce of silver

veizla - hospitality, that those in power had the right to get from their vassals

viti - a beacon

wadset - to mortgage, pawn, pledge lands in security for a debt

Index